VICTORIAN EDUCATION AND THE IDEAL OF WOMANHOOD

VICTORIAN EDUCATION AND THE IDEAL OF WOMANHOOD

Joan N. Burstyn

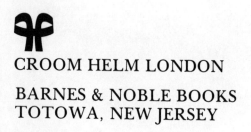

CROOM HELM LONDON

BARNES & NOBLE BOOKS
TOTOWA, NEW JERSEY

© 1980 Joan N. Burstyn
Croom Helm Ltd, 2-10 St John's Road, London SW11
ISBN 0-7099-0139-9

British Library Cataloguing in Publication Data

Burstyn, Joan N
    Victorian education and the ideal of womanhood.
    1. Education of women — Great Britain — History —
    19th century
    I. Title
    376'.941   LC2042

ISBN 0-7099-0139-9

First published in the USA 1980 by
BARNES & NOBLE BOOKS
81 ADAMS DRIVE
TOTOWA, NEW JERSEY, 07512
ISBN 389-20103-2

Printed and bound in Great Britain by
REDWOOD BURN LIMITED
Trowbridge & Esher

Contents

List of Illustrations

Preface

1. Politics of Aspiration: Education for the Middle Classes   11

2. Eduation and the Ideal of Womanhood   30

3. Women and the Economy   48

4. Woman's Intellectual Capacity   70

5. Education and Sex   84

6. Religion and Woman's Education   99

7. The Ideal of Womanhood Confronts Reality   118

8. The Opposition's Influence on
    Higher Education for Women   145

9. Conclusion   167

Select Bibliography   173

Index   181

Illustrations

1. The Ideal Woman *The Duet. A Drawing-room Study* 1872

2. Not All Can Achieve the Ideal. *Chainmakers— Single Bellows Worked at 3d a Day*

3. Work Within Women's Sphere. *Valentine Makers c.1875*

4. A Revolution of Gender Roles. *The Ladies of Creation* 1853

5. A Revolution of Gender Roles. *A Muscular Maiden*

6. A Revolution of Gender Roles. *The Parliamentary Female*

7. A Revolution of Gender Roles. *Robida caricature of 1880*

8. Protecting the Ideal. *Demonstration at Cambridge against the Admission of Women as Students c.1897*

Illustrations courtesy of Radio Times Hulton Picture Library

Preface

This study traverses social history, the history of ideas, the history of education, and women's history. Its conceptual framework could not have been formulated without the work of feminist historians, psychologists, sociologists, and anthropologists. I am indebted to them, and to my colleagues at *Signs: Journal of Women in Culture and Society*, with whom for the last five years I have discussed issues relating to women's lives. In addition, through the Columbia University seminar on women and society, sessions at the American Historical Association, the Berkshire Conference of Women Historians, the History of Education Society, and the History of Science Society I have learned from my colleagues, and refined my ideas. Most recently, I have benefited from a discussion at the Davis Center, Princeton University, where Harold Perkin presented a paper on the professionalisation of British society. His work suggests to me that the struggle over higher education for women is a fine example of the power of professionals to influence society.

For support in the initial research I wish to thank the American Association of University Women who awarded me their Marion Talbot fellowship, and for support in further research and in writing the final manuscript Rutgers University who provided me a year's faculty leave. I should like to acknowledge also the assistance of librarians at the Fawcett Library (in particular the late Vera Douie), the University of London archives, the Institute of Historical Research, Westfield College Library, Girton College Library, the archivist of Lincolnshire who provided me with a copy of an otherwise unobtainable sermon, and of librarians in the United States, particularly those at the Mabel Smith Douglass Library at Rutgers University.

Four scholars who have since died offered me support in the early stages of this project. They were H. Hale Bellot and Alfred Cobban of University College London, A.C.F. Beales of King's College London, and Neville Williams, secretary of the British Academy and previously of the Public Records Office. I recall their encouragement with gratitude. I should also like to thank Sari Biklen, Harold Blakemore,

David Bolam, Patricia Graham, Patricia Haines, John Hurt, Sally Kohlstedt, Harold and Pamela Silver, and David Tyack for their suggestions on this and related topics; Stephen J. Gould, Gerald Grob, and Hilda Smith for reading and commenting on parts of the manuscript; Valerie Sussmann for locating the illustrations; and Arlene Abady for her editorial assistance.

Earlier versions of the material in Chapters five and six were published as articles: 'Education and Sex: The Medical Case against Higher Education for Women in England, 1870-1900', in *Proceedings of the American Philosophical Society*, 117, no. 2 (1973), and 'Religious Arguments against Higher Education for Women in England, 1840-1890', in *Women's Studies*, 1, no. 1 (1972).

Lastly, I should like to thank my husband, Harold, with whom for years I have shared the ideas for this study, and my children, Judith, Gail, and Daniel, who have grown up with them, and who, with Harold, have encouraged me to complete this book.

1 | The Politics of Aspiration: Education for the Middle Class

Their institutions challenged by the social and economic forces of industrialism, the Victorians saw education as a means of both social control and individual betterment. The two themes existed side by side; social control was emphasized in the education of the lower classes, individual betterment in that of the middle classes, but in both cases the second theme was discernible. Thus, the lower classes were taught primarily to know their place, and were given only the rudiments of literacy, but it was possible, through self-improvement or, later in the century, through further schooling for bright lower-class students to improve their position in society. Among the middle classes, though schools came increasingly to emphasise scholarship and competitive examinations, moral behaviour and adherence to group norms were enforced, particularly through the prefect system and team sports.

The variation in emphasis according to class between social control and individual betterment applied particularly to men's education. For most of the century social control was the predominant theme of Victorian education for women of all classes. The thrust towards control was expressed through the ideal of womanhood, which cast woman as an entity and left little room for variations among individuals. The ideal was prescriptive, and spread its tentacles through all the institutions designed for women's education. Hence, women of the middle classes, unlike their brothers, were subject to as rigid a programme of control as their lower-class sisters, although it was different in kind.

The movement for higher education for women was an attempt to break through the prescriptions of the ideal, to provide women of the upper and middle classes with the opportunity for individual betterment. The movement cannot be considered alone; it was part of a broad upheaval caused by the development of industrialism, which affected women's economic well-being, and their aspirations for participation in the political and social life of the country.[1]

This book concentrates on the opposition to higher education for women. It untangles the threads of opponents' arguments in order to

show how serious a threat the movement for higher education was to the ideal of womanhood. At first, the number of women who wanted to attend the universities was small. It may seem indulgent, therefore, to concentrate on those few hundreds, when the history of millions of other women is still unwritten. However, the struggle to obtain higher education had broad implications for all women because Victorian society was hierarchical. The norms for behaviour were set by the ruling classes who came to be identified closely with the upper middle classes. It was they who most eagerly adopted the Victorian ideal of womanhood; and it was they who first discovered its flaws as reality. However, English society in the nineteenth and early twentieth century was like a snake, whose body rippled along the ground following the path taken by its head some time before. While the head stretched across open ground, the body remained deep in the undergrowth. Hence, the Victorian ideal of womanhood was not abandoned by English society, despite the challenge to it from some of those who had turned it into reality. It was modified and, in our own century, was adopted by groups who had not been able to afford it during the nineteenth century.

Only after the Second World War did the ideal become reality for large numbers of women. The current women's movement is in part an extension of the discontent expressed by women of the upper middle classes in the late nineteenth century. At that time the challenge of those who had found the ideal vacuous as reality had to be denied; now, the challenge is so widespread it has to be answered. By looking more closely at the struggle to attain higher education for women we can better understand the meaning of the present shift in relations between men and women.

We shall first examine Victorian middle-class society, and its views on the education of men and women.

The Victorian middle classes

Class in Victorian society was defined through a subtle combination of occupation, income, and values; hence the difficulty historians have in defining the limits of any one class. Definitions of class were linked to the occupations and incomes of males. Females were assigned a class according to the status of their fathers so long as they were unmarried, and of their husbands once they were married. Unmarried women, separated or divorced women and widows were a special problem,

because they retained the status of their fathers or husbands unless they took jobs on their own account, when they acquired a status of their own.

The middle classes were diverse, but they shared certain attributes. They were usually city dwellers, and although some had incomes similar to skilled craftsmen, the latter worked with their hands and therefore were not usually considered middle class. Annual income for the middle classes ranged from less than £100 to more than £1000. These figures varied upwards in the last decades, but from the perspective of our own time, prices and incomes throughout the nineteenth century remained remarkably stable. Historian Patricia Branca has shown that the range from £100 to £300 covered the annual incomes of over two-thirds of the middle classes in 1803, and about 42 per cent of them in 1867. Branca calculated that between those dates the greatest expansion among the middle classes was of those earning under £100 (where the overlap with the lower classes made the extent of the expansion unclear), and of those earning between £100 and £300.[2] However, for our purpose it is important to note also that between 1803 and 1867 the number of families earning over £300 tripled, reaching 150,000 by 1867. If we estimate, conservatively, that families of the upper middle classes averaged at least three children per family, that would make a minimum of 750,000 people in the upper middle classes of 1867. Their influence was significant because their lifestyle became the ideal for all the middle classes.

To these 150,000 families, the expansion of commerce and manufacturing brought unprecedented wealth. Factory owners, merchants, bankers, and shopkeepers expanded their businesses; lawyers, accountants, and doctors added to their practices. Some of these people used their new wealth to buy land outside the cities. Others stayed close to their work but moved to more spacious homes. Most bought additional personal property such as furniture, carpets and draperies, horses and carriages.[3]

However, the number of goods they could buy was limited because society at that time was less attuned than ours to the consumption of luxury goods. Therefore, many used their wealth to purchase services; they employed servants for their homes, and assistants for their businesses. In the latter half of the nineteenth century, as shops expanded into department stores and merchandising became more complex, more people were employed as shop assistants, clerks, and bookkeepers. At the same time, more families moved into larger houses where they employed three or four servants, instead of one or

two. Where there was a housemaid, a cook, and a children's nurse in the home, mothers and children had leisure undreamed of in previous generations.

Branca has pointed out that the majority of the middle classes did not share this affluence. Yet even they, by 1870, were likely to employ one full-time servant who lived in the house. The trend was for wives no longer to keep business accounts, young sons to run errands, young daughters to mend clothes; other people were employed to do such work.

Families found it difficult to adjust to the new circumstances. Wealth rarely enabled men to give up their work; only their families could enjoy the leisure bought by the employment of servants. The change in men's fashions in the first half of the nineteenth century illustrates how completely the masculine work ethic of the middle classes came to dominate British society. At the turn of the century fashionable men had been wearing non-functional attire of bright colours, but by mid-century even men of the aristocracy were wearing black frockcoats and dark cravats, symbols of the sombre work of businessmen. All men had come to be valued for their diligence at work.[4]

Successful businessmen worked long hours. In cities, their place of business was likely to be some distance from home, where wives and children were left all day to their own occupations. Some families had experienced this pattern for generations, but during the nineteenth century it became a new way of life for thousands of families who, in the past, had worked together—father, mother, and children—each performing separate but related tasks, with little time for any members of the family to read, write, or develop their unique talents. By the beginning of the nineteenth century, a growing number of women and children of the upper middle classes had little work to do and much time on their hands.

Their first response was to organise life in the same way as before, with the family, except the father, working together. Older daughters, for instance, were expected to occupy themselves in the same room as their mothers, as they had done in previous generations, although their homes now invariably had several rooms, and as 'ladies' they were less likely to be occupied with the necessities of life, making bread or sewing breeches, than with luxuries such as embroidery or making wax flowers. Sons were more difficult to organize. Some parents followed the example of the aristocracy and hired private tutors for them, but formal schooling arranged separately by each family was too expensive

for most of the middle classes, good tutors were hard to find, and a ratio of one tutor to three or four pupils threatened to exhaust the supply as more families hired them. Quite early in the century, there-fore, it became the custom for sons of the middle classes to be sent to school. They might attend local grammar schools, or, if their parents could afford it, they might be sent to a boys' public school. Until the last half of the century, girls, however, were often educated at home, or attended a private school briefly in order to acquire poise and social graces.

The deference paid to respectability increased among the middle classes from the end of the eighteenth century, and the increase can be linked to the new leisure enjoyed by women of the middle classes. More women began to read books and magazines, which, as a result, began to cater to women's interests and sensibilities. Language and behaviour became less coarse. Exuberant drinking, eating, and swearing among men, popular early in the eighteenth century, was frowned upon by its end. Men and women no longer used the same phrases they had a generation earlier; references to bodily and sexual functions became less direct. A decent married woman was no longer 'with-child', she became pregnant; she was not 'brought-to-bed' but was 'confined'; her husband might 'perspire', but he would never 'sweat'. These euphemisms, extended in number during the nine-teenth century, led eventually to a repression of natural instincts that we associate with Victorian prudery, but their introduction reflected a growing concern for individuals and the quality of their lives.[5]

The increasing refinement of language and behaviour may be linked also with the growth of cities. In the open countryside, people could enjoy a freedom of behaviour intolerable in crowded cities. The closely built houses of the cities and the need to share public transport brought more and more people into close contact with one another; their smell, their noise, their refuse, their excrement, their numbers became public concerns.[6] The Victorians became obsessed with the need to provide public bathhouses, sewage systems, and street lighting. They looked also to a refinement of individual manners as a way to make city life more bearable and to bring self-respect to the city worker, because Victorian cities were viable only so long as all classes were prepared to live together without violence. All people, therefore, were set a standard of refinement — temperance, delicacy of language, prudence, and self-denial (usually phrased in Christian terms) — which the ruling classes believed would enable them to better their own and their families' status.[7]

Increased refinement was illustrated by changes in styles of recreation during the nineteenth century, and by replacement of the militia by an unarmed police force to control the populace. Refinement represented a change in the locus of control for most people; where previous generations had expected to behave with exuberance and spontaneous expression of feeling which might be quelled by outside force, or punished by the law, the nineteenth-century citizen was expected to exert self-control and to internalise the need for restraint. Since respectability could be demonstrated only through behaviour, each person had always to maintain the expected standard.

Education for boys and men

In theory people could become refined and respectable through their own efforts. The lower classes were encouraged to educate themselves, and they founded self-improvement societies for adults.[8] At the same time there was a concern for the education of children. Small 'dame schools' flourished where, for a few pennies a week, children gathered to learn the skills of literacy. Many parents preferred this kind of education, despite its cost, to the formal setting of the new church schools, where moral responsibility was emphasised as much as reading, writing, and calculating.[9]

However, the larger church schools had the advantage of economy of scale, and were supported by middle and upper-class employers who realised that moral responsibility was more easily taught in large schools where parents had little influence, standards were set by professionals, and where the system of instruction enforced conformity. By the time of the 1870 Education Act the larger school had become the norm for educating both boys and girls of the lower classes, and an intricate machinery for preparing teachers, inspecting schools, and administering government aid had been established.[10]

Schools for the lower classes were separate from those of the middle classes, and most children attending them were expected to remain in the social class to which they had been born. In the long run, the schools did much to change the source of initiative for self-improvement from the person who desired it to the teachers in the schools, because class mobility was channelled so that only those few students designated by the school could move on to further vocational education or prepare themselves for teaching.

It was not only the lower classes who strove to improve themselves; the middle classes, also, looked to education as a means for bettering their positions. For men, self-improvement had two components: acquiring the skills for successful practice of a profession or maintenance of a business; and acquiring the attributes of respectability. Lower-middle-class parents were particularly anxious for their sons to learn marketable skills. Many of them thought of education as technical training only, and were prepared to allow their sons to attend school only so long as they were taught something 'useful'. However, most schools of the early nineteenth century did not reflect their ambitions; the school curriculum did not include 'useful' subjects. As a result, parents whose schoolboy sons learned Latin, Greek, and Euclidian mathematics, subjects irrelevant to the counting house or factory, became discontented and agitated to change the curriculum of the schools and universities. By the end of the nineteenth century they had been at least partially successful.[11]

However, there was an ambivalence in the attitude of the middle classes towards the traditional curriculum. Familiarity with Latin and Greek was the hallmark of a gentleman. Merchants and factory owners who aspired to have their power legitimated were eager that *their* sons should have that hallmark bestowed on them. If the curriculum of schools were changed, a distinguishing characteristic of the upper classes would be taken away and the triumph of successful fathers lessened. There were, therefore, people who supported the existing curriculum in boys' schools because of its value in ascribing status, although they had scant respect for the educational value of the classics.

Among professional families there was ambivalence about the curriculum for the same reasons, but those who wished to change it did so because they saw an increased need for professional skills in a changing society. As early as the first decades of the nineteenth century, ambitious men without patronage, particularly apothecaries, surgeons, and attorneys, began to call for a new kind of judgment in making professional and public appointments. They urged that a person's ability be used as the chief criterion, and they suggested formal examinations as the mechanism for assessing ability. Examination results, they believed, would provide a more reliable guide to a person's ability than the recommendation of someone who owed him a personal favour. If success in education were to become the means of obtaining preferment, intelligent people, like themselves, without powerful patrons, would be able to claim a right to positions in

government and the professions.[12]

As a result of mounting pressure the universities of Oxford and Cambridge made their undergraduate courses and examinations more exacting. In 1828 the 'London University' (later University College London) was opened, catering particularly to dissenters; while a second, Anglican college, King's College London, opened three years later. The number of boys' schools grew, and the curricula and administration of existing public schools were reformed. The number of competitive examinations increased, and they were used more and more as criteria for the allocation of jobs. By the 1860s the ambitious son of a tradesman or manufacturer was readily allowed by his family to seek an education. Although the subjects taught at school might not be as applicable to his future work as his parents wished, a boy's success in passing school examinations was recognised as a new way to get ahead in a society that prized upward mobility.

Such an emphasis on schooling could have developed only in a society—like that of England in the nineteenth century—where many families could afford to dispense with the labour of their children. Respect for individual potential was fostered in young men with leisure for learning. The middle classes knew society would reward individual effort, and they came to believe that schools should prepare and examinations select successful individuals.

Separate Spheres

When the Victorian middle classes began to use education as a means of upward mobility they did not expect girls to participate in schooling for the same purpose as boys, because they believed that women acquired their status through men, not through their own efforts. Women's activities varied with the status of the men in their families, not with their own aspirations to become a shopkeeper or a lawyer.

Distinctions of status among the Victorian middle classes could be identified as much by differences in women's activities as by income and property. A family that subsisted without financial contribution from either the children or the women, and without their contributing to the production of saleable goods and services, could definitely be considered middle class. The next step in status was for men to provide sufficient income for the women to stop producing goods even for family consumption, and instead, for the family to employ a cook to prepare meals and a seamstress to make clothes. The one form of

production expected of all married women of the middle classes was childbearing; however, the higher the status of the family, the less a mother had to do with the hourly activities of childcare. Women of lower status were employed for those tasks.

Men and women of the middle classes spoke of working in separate spheres. What was new in this concept was not the segregation of labour by gender, since men and women had traditionally performed different tasks, but the establishment of an ideal that removed women from all productive labour but childbearing, that separated the men and women of a family during their working hours, and that channelled women's energies, and only women's, into arranging for the consumption of goods and services by themselves and their families, and into undertaking services for their families and for those less fortunate than themselves.

The concept of separate spheres provided the middle classes with a rationale for a lifestyle fostered by industrialism. That lifestyle was in turn reinforced by the rationale which restructured women's place in the labour market. Those women who needed work expected to be employed in jobs appropriate to women's sphere; women of the middle classes could not be employed at all if the status of their families were to be maintained. Hence, male employers came to perceive women as an appropriate source of labour only for those jobs within women's sphere, and only for low-level jobs because ones with managerial responsibility were usually filled by members of the middle classes, and women of those classes were not expected to work. While industrial growth brought unprecedented job opportunities to men, social reformers, wishing to raise all women to the ideal of the upper and middle classes, urged a decrease in the numbers of women working.

Separate spheres located women in the home and men in the marketplace, and consequently public and private space became more clearly defined. The physical separation increased men's power in society because women were not expected to speak at formal public meetings, and did not take part in business transactions. Unmarried women of the upper and middle classes were accompanied in public by male escorts or chaperons of older women. While escorts may have protected young women, they served also to deny them free access to the public life of the community. Middle-class women suffered a *relative* loss of freedom and power *vis-à-vis* men during the first half of the nineteenth century, because increased prosperity gave men access to authority in the public sphere, but diminished women's activities

there, and because political reforms in 1832 and 1867 extended the franchise among men but denied it to women, thus increasing the dissonance between the power of men and women of the middle classes. The concept of separate spheres, therefore, served the economic interests of the middle classes, and, at the same time, strengthened the dominance of men in public life.

In private life, it was argued, women had acquired new authority because women had a sphere of their own. Affluence provided some women with a household budget to organise, and at least one or two employees to manage. However, most women had no such authority, and even that of the upper and middle classes, as we shall see in chapter seven, had eroded by the end of the century as other institutions took over household and family functions.

The historian cannot speak of the two spheres as though they were unchanging. Men's sphere changed in character during the century as public tasks were more clearly defined from private, as there evolved a hierarchy of occupations and, within each occupation, a hierarchy of jobs. The process of professionalisation brought with it unforeseen feelings of inadequacy among those who could not climb beyond the lower rungs of an occupational ladder, and unforeseen pressures to achieve among those who climbed higher. One sphere could not change without affecting the other. Although family care and housework often remain pre-industrial in organisation even today, there were attempts to professionalise women's work during the nineteenth century, and thus change the character of women's sphere. Those who worked for this change saw the need for women's skills to parallel those of men. Women had to run their households efficiently, prepare their children to enter school, teach them to live upright, moral lives, organise and run charitable institutions, and for all this they, like men, needed training. Thus the movement to improve women's education in order that they might better prepare themselves for their role as the ideal woman followed closely in time, and paralleled, the movement to improve men's education. It was not a radical movement; it did not challenge the concept of separate spheres, but sought to break the convention that barred women of the middle classes from administrative responsibility within their own sphere.

The separation of men's and women's lives could not be maintained easily, however, in an industrial society. Many women had to work at some time in their lives, and many had jobs in production or distribution that brought them into contact with men. Nevertheless, those

who believed in the desirability of separate spheres were comfortable only when women's work was thought to be temporary, to be undertaken only so long as there was financial need, and when the jobs women did were defined as being different from men's. Thus, where women spilled over into men's public sphere, they were intentionally placed in job categories designed to separate them from men as effectively as though they had remained within women's sphere.

Just as the lower classes were taught self-control, so, towards the end of the century, male escorts and chaperons for middle and upper-class women were abandoned as they were taught to internalise the constraints of refinement. What has been termed the ' "nice girl" construct' served to teach women their place in the public sphere as effectively as external constraints had in the past. 'Nice girls' knew where and how to travel, who to be seen with, how to behave in mixed company, and what jobs to apply for.[13] Schools became increasingly important in teaching girls the details of this construct as women's access to the public sphere increased.[14]

In recent years the Swiss psychologist Jean Piaget has outlined two processes through which new concepts may be accepted by individuals.[15] He suggests that a new concept may be accepted through a process of *assimilation,* in which a person's categories of thought remain the same but are adapted to make room for a new concept. In nineteenth-century England, most of those who came to accept the concept of middle-class women working seem to have done so through a process of assimilation, by which they retained their belief in separate spheres, but came to accept the need for women to professionalise their own sphere, and to tolerate some women working in the male sphere so long as they were assigned separate job categories and were not given positions of leadership.

Assimilation is not the most satisfactory method of accepting new concepts, however. Piaget describes another process, of *accommodation,* by which a person develops a new, broader category of thought in order to incorporate other, apparently contradictory ones. In terms of this process, what was needed was an abandonment of the notion of separate spheres and its replacement by one public-and-private sphere. Such a sphere could be divided horizontally according to tasks, but women as well as men would be eligible for work at every level. With this categorisation, the movement for women's political and legal rights, women's aspirations to enter the professions and skilled occupations, and their struggle for emancipation from prescriptive life as a group into freedom for the individual, all are

comprehensible and acceptable.

In retrospect, we can see that the movement for higher education for women contained both assimilators and accommodators, and that tensions over strategy and goals arose from their different modes of thought. Opponents of the movement, on the other hand, while disparate in many ways, seem to have shared a belief in separate spheres for men and women, and a need to maintain their definition of each sphere inviolate. There were some who saw as the crucial threat of the movement for higher education for women the desire of some advocates to destroy the separation between the lives of men and women. For almost a century, they fought to prevent such a change from occurring.

We shall analyse the various arguments put forward by opponents. Although some arguments had adherents in many decades, and thus quotations may be drawn from the eighteenth to the late nineteenth century to illustrate them, others were specific to one time and to one group of people. From the general literature of the period it is possible to identify what opponents of higher education thought women should be, and how they should be educated, and to trace their ideas on what would happen to society if relations between sexes changed and the separation of spheres were abandoned. Before we examine these ideas, however, we shall look briefly at the condition of education during the nineteenth century for girls and women of the middle classes.

Education for girls and women

Education for girls of the middle classes was unsystematic for most of the century. Until the 1870s those who could afford it employed governesses or sent their daughters to small private schools. Some middle-class girls received only sporadic education, attending school when they were not otherwise engaged. Schooling was considered a way for girls to obtain social rather than intellectual skills, and since private schools were small, parents could readily find one whose pupils came from the same social background as themselves. With support from their parents, girls were taught how to behave as contenders in the marriage market, and as social hostesses; most were given neither systematic intellectual training, nor instruction in the skills of housekeeping and childcare.

The demand for this kind of education most likely came from those who had risen in social position and felt the inadequacy of their own

education to prepare them for their new life. To them, it would seem reasonable that their sons should be trained for their future work, and their daughters taught the forms of polite conduct which they would later pass on to their children, and even to their husbands.

Those families already established in the middle classes had less need for this kind of schooling; both sons and daughters could learn their social skills at home. However, established families, especially professional families, were aware of the numbers of newly rich claiming equal status with themselves, and they wished to protect their own positions. The criticism of girls' education seems to have come from this group who wished to systematise education for girls as they had done for boys.

Their first efforts were to improve the qualifications of governesses. Whether there was a decline in standards among governesses in the 1830s and 1840s, or whether the established middle classes, to advance their own claims to hegemony, were merely demanding greater sophistication from them, is difficult to gauge. Since young boys as well as girls were educated by governesses there can be no doubt that pressure to improve governesses' teaching skills was linked to the greater competence expected of boys entering school. The complaints of employers implied that, since more people were employing govern-esses, women unsuited for such work were being drawn into the market. Employers complained also that they had no way to judge how successful prospective governesses might be.[16]

The Reverend Frederick Denison Maurice, Professor of English at King's College London and a Christian socialist, led a group of concerned citizens in 1843 in founding the Governesses' Benevolent Institution to provide governesses with financial relief during times of unemployment and old age. This move, begun as a way to alleviate economic distress, led to such a deluge of appeals that Maurice and his colleagues decided to extend their plans and found a college in London to improve the standard of education for governesses. Queen's College opened in 1848, and within six months another college for women opened, with a broader aim of educating women who desired further education. Although the two colleges catered to similar groups, their structures were different. Queen's College was Church of England, the Ladies' College, Bedford Square (or Bedford College as it became known) was non-conformist; Queen's College had a governing body made up largely of men; Bedford College was founded by a woman, Mrs. Elisabeth Reid, and women had a major role in managing the college; at Queen's College the preparatory department

came to overshadow the college department, at Bedford College the preparatory department was eventually dropped.[17] However, in the years immediately after their founding both raised the standard of education of hundreds of women in the London area. As a result, the competence of governesses improved, and within ten years there was a new problem of finding other work for applicants who no longer qualified for the job of governess.

Only the upper middle classes, however, could afford governesses or boarding schools. Families with incomes ranging from £100 to £300 annually had to find other ways to educate their children. There were small private schools that accepted day students, and in some places the voluntary church schools were used by members of the lower middle classes to educate their young children.[18] The schools had been intended for children of the lower classes, but the borderline between classes was a fine one, and some middle-class families with low incomes arrogated the advantages to themselves. It is likely, given the attitude of the middle classes towards the relative importance of their children's education, that some families were prepared to send their sons away to school (and hence to spend more money on their education), while they sent their daughters to the local church school. There, the girls might learn the rudiments of literacy. Later, through private lessons or, if the money could be found, at a finishing school, they could learn dancing, music, and other refinements. Joyce Senders Pedersen has shown that small girls' schools taught a variety of ages, and that lower-middle-class families would use as a finishing school for their daughters institutions to which the upper middle class sent only their young girls.[19]

Once the standard of education for governesses had been opened for discussion, it became clear that women teachers in middle-class schools needed to be better prepared also, and that the structure of schooling for girls needed to be changed. From Queen's College and Bedford College came the first women to organise schools for middle-class girls similar to the public schools for boys. The demand for better schools created opportunities for some women to develop new skills in teaching and in running large institutions. It was a heady time. The 1850s saw the establishment of the North London Collegiate School for Girls and of Cheltenham Ladies College, which later became both a school and a teacher-training institution.

In the late fifties, the Universities of Oxford and Cambridge founded the university local examinations, to measure the achievement of schoolboys who would not go on to university but whose

employers wanted to know what they had learned at school. Some people felt the examinations would offer an opportunity to measure women's achievement also, not only for their own satisfaction, but in order to assess the effectiveness of their teachers. At the National Association for the Promotion of Social Science (NAPSS), organised in 1857 with women as well as men participants, women found a platform to express their ideas, share them with one another, and forge links for social action. For the first time, they had the opportunity to function as equals with a group of male professionals and educated amateurs, some of whom supported their ideas for women's education.

Emily Davies gathered support at the NAPSS for a campaign to open the university local examinations to women. By dint of prudent requests, and the backing of influential men, Davies was able to persuade the Cambridge local examination syndicate to allow women to take the examinations on a trial basis, so long as local arrangements could be made to protect the modesty of the young women. This was done, and the results were satisfactory enough to the women students, their supporters, and the university authorities for the arrangement to be continued and, in 1867, made permanent.

Examinations were a breakthrough. They provided women teachers with the impetus to improve their teaching skills. How could they acquire new knowledge? They decided to organise lectures for themselves which would provide both discussion on teaching techniques and additional information on school subjects. In the north of England there was so much activity that local ladies' educational associations combined to form the North of England Council for Promoting the Higher Education of Women which coordinated the lectures in several cities. Women were among the most avid consumers of education in the period, and it was their enthusiasm that helped popularise the university extension programmes. Lecture series were often followed by a brief examination, and those attending received a statement showing they had reached the standard expected of them.[20]

While these lectures were improving the education of women teachers, a group of women led by Maria Grey in London was preparing to establish a number of girls' schools across the country that would share the same standard of organisation and proficiency. The schools would systematise girls' education, and offer the same academic subjects as did boys' schools. Girls would be expected to enrol for the full course of study, and prepare for the university local

examinations or London matriculation, and be bound by regulations concerning attendance, school behaviour, and homework.[21] To this end, in 1872, the group established the Girls' Public Day School Company (later known as the Girls' Public Day School Trust (GPDST)), a proprietary company under whose auspices by 1900 a total of thirty-six schools had been established, serving approximately seven thousand students.[22]

In the schools of the GPDST the local examinations of Oxford and Cambridge and the matriculation examination of the University of London provided goals for excellence. Some young women attending these schools looked beyond them to a higher education. In 1869 Emily Davies had begun the experiment of establishing a women's college at Hitchin, (later to move to Girton near Cambridge,) where women undertook the same college courses as men and were expected to complete them in the same amount of time. This experiment was of great consequence in proving to men that women were indeed capable of undertaking the same higher education, but, as we shall see in subsequent chapters, the experiment aroused bitter opposition.

Some opposed the Girton College experiment out of hand. Others merely opposed that form of higher education, believing that women's education should never be the same as men's, and that it should never be undertaken for the same reasons. They wanted to improve the standard of girls' education and felt that teachers needed a background of higher education; however, they did not want to force women to work as hard as men. People with these views shortly opened halls of residence for women taking the lecture courses provided by the university extension programmes; at Cambridge, in 1871, Newnham college was opened, and in Oxford, in 1879, Lady Margaret Hall and Somerville college. None of these women's colleges (nor Girton college) was officially attached to the universities; they were tolerated as unofficial appendages. When women tried to formalize their ties to the ancient universities they were rebuffed with unrestrained vehemence.[23]

At the University of London, where residence was not required in order to take the degree examinations, women found less opposition to their aspirations. There, in 1878, women were admitted to all degrees of the university, and in 1882 to governance of the university through admission as graduates to the university convocation. The difference between passing examinations for a degree at the University of London and completing a course of study at a women's college in Oxford and Cambridge was that the University of London degree

provided some of the qualifications needed for working as a professional or as a member of those skilled occupations which, during the nineteenth century, claimed professional standing, while an unofficial certificate from a women's college did not.

Many of those who accepted the need for women to obtain some form of higher education still believed in separate spheres for men and women. This can be deduced from the fact that they were not prepared to allow women to graduate from the ancient universities, and thus to participate in university governance there—governance was not women's work—and from their reluctance to open to women any of the professions. Their reasoning seems to have been that the two spheres were, and should remain, distinct, but that women, within their own sphere, should be trained to competence. Women's organisations and institutions were as complex in structure as men's, and those running them had to have similiar skills. Thus, by the end of the century, people behaved as though there were two spheres in vertical alignment, each containing a horizontal stratification of jobs within it. Given the popularity of this vision, we should not be surprised that few women graduates (or those who had completed a course of study in Oxford or Cambridge) during the nineteenth century ventured into work in the male sphere.

It was not this vision of complementary, separate spheres, however, that opponents of higher education for women had feared since the beginning of the movement, but a change in perception that would lead to the destruction of separate spheres, and ultimately to a revolution in relations between the sexes. By publicising their interpretation of what that destruction would mean, opponents of higher education played a major part in arresting any change in perception among the majority of the middle classes.

In the chapters that follow we shall trace the opponents' arguments, see how they changed as the movement for higher education for women developed from a plan to a reality, and, lastly, we shall consider the impact that opponents had on the development of colleges for women. Although opponents joined together on specific issues, such as voting against motions to admit women to various universities, they did not, as their adversaries, form permanent groups. Their opinions have been pieced together from books, popular magazines, sermons, letters, and religious, anthropological, and medical journals. Certain arguments, such as those based on Biblical interpretation, remained strikingly similar in writings a century apart; others, such as those based on scientific data, varied

education to women, when testifying before the Schools' Inquiry Commission was asked whether the problem of motivation of young women was entirely educational. She replied that it was not. Girls had to feel there were goals beyond school for which they could aim: jobs requiring technical skills and professions requiring higher education. As long as women were denied further goals, Davies claimed, their education would lack meaning.[2]

The opponents of higher education were aware of the desires expressed by Davies and her followers for women to develop occupational goals. Opponents realized that once educational opportunities were opened to women, they would train for men's jobs. If women acquired the same qualifications as men, the social structure that denied women entry to many jobs would appear anomalous. However, as long as women had a different education from men, fitting them for their different calling in life, no anomalies existed. Opponents insisted that women's goals were not the same as men's, and no pretence should be made that they were.

According to opponents, the model for boys' and girls' education was to be found among the upper middle classes, where brothers and sisters were educated together in the nursery schoolroom only until the boys were old enough to go to a boys' school. There, and later at university, they learned to compete with others of their sex. Girls were trained to modesty and retirement at home, or attended girls' schools. Though women were thought to need a superior education to develop their feminine qualities, they did not need the higher education provided for men at the universities.

Opponents felt higher education would lead women to have unrealistic goals. First, they would think that professional opportunities were open to them when, in fact, none existed. In 1869 Sarah Ellis, the proprietor of a school for young women and author of several books on the ideal role of women in society, claimed that educated women could not find employment, 'not from inaptness or unwillingness in themselves, but from there being actually no work for them to do.'[3] This issue will be discussed later in relation to assumptions about the structure of the economy. Secondly, women would want to enter the professions, and high-status skilled occupations, but would rarely complete their training because they would leave to get married. As Anthony Trollope remarked:

> It is very well for a young man to bind himself for four years, and to think of marrying four years after that apprenticeship is over. But

over time or were unique to a specific period. What remained constant was the thesis that opponents were defending, that higher education would destroy the ideal of womanhood as they understood it.

We turn first to examine the ideal that opponents were defending, their opinions on how women should be educated to attain it, and the ways that higher education conflicted with the ideal.

Notes

1.   See Barbara Kanner, 'The Women of England in a Century of Social Change, 1815-1914; a Select Bibliography, part I' in Martha Vicinus (ed.), *Suffer and be Still: Women in the Victorian Age* (Bloomington, 1972), and 'The Women of England in a Century of Social Change, 1815-1914: A Select Bibliography, part II', in Martha Vicinus (ed.), *A Widening Sphere: Changing Roles of Victorian Women* (Bloomington, 1977).

2.   Patricia Branca, *Silent Sisterhood: Middle Class Women in the Victorian Home* (Pittsburgh, 1975), pp. 40-5.

3.   These paragraphs refer to the long-term rise in the standard of living among these families. As significant for some of them were the cyclic recessions of trade, and it may be that further research will link the demand for higher education for women more closely to the short-term cycles of the economy. For opinions on the economy between 1790 and 1850 see, E. J. Hobsbawm, *Labouring Men* (New York, 1967), chapter 5.

4.   See Mario Praz, 'The Victorian Mood: A Reappraisal', in G.Métraux and F. Crouzet (eds.), *The Nineteenth-Century World* (New York, 1963), pp. 19-42.

5.   See Maurice Quinlan, *Victorian Prelude: A History of English Manners 1700-1830* (New York, 1941), pp. 58-67.

6.   See Richard L. Schoenwald, 'Town Guano and "Social Statics" ', *Victorian Studies* 11 (1968), pp. 691-710; G. Kitson Clark, *The Making of Victorian England* (London, 1965), pp. 95-107, 126-9; Lewis Mumford, *The City in History* (Harmondsworth, 1966), chapter 15; Steven Marcus, *The Other Victorians* (New York, 1966), p. 99; H. J. Dyos, *Urbanity and Suburbanity* (Leicester, 1973).

7.   See Peter T. Cominos, 'Late-Victorian Sexual Respectability and the Social System', *International Review of Social History* 8 (1963) pp. 18-48, and 216-50; Lilian L. Shiman, 'The Band of Hope Movement: Respectable Recreation for Working-Class Children', *Victorian Studies* 17, no. 1 (1973), pp. 49-74.

8.   See J. F. C. Harrison, *Learning and Living 1790-1960* (Toronto, 1961), chapter 2.

9.   See D. P. Leinster-MacKay, 'Dame Schools: A Need for Review', *British Journal of Educational Studies* 24, no. 1 (1976), pp. 33-48; A. F. B. Roberts, 'A New View of the Infant School Movement', *British Journal of Education Studies* 20, no. 2 (1972), pp. 154-64; Phillip McCann (ed.), *Popular Education and Socialization in the Nineteenth Century* (London, 1977).

10.   See John Hurt, *Education in Evolution: Church, State, Society and Popular Education 1800-1870* (London, 1971).

11.   See J. W. Adamson, *English Education 1789-1902* (Cambridge, 1964), chapters 11, 14 and 15.

12.   See R. J. Montgomery, *Examinations* (London, 1965), pp. 16-31; Geoffrey Millerson, *The Qualifying Associations: A Study in Professionalization* (London, 1964), and for a more general discussion of the professional middle classes, Harold Perkin, *The Origins of Modern English Society, 1780-1880* (London, 1969), pp. 252-70.

13.   See Greer Litton Fox, '"Nice Girl": Social Control of Women Through a Value

Construct', *Signs: Journal of Women in Culture and Society* 2, no. 4 (1977), pp. 805-17.

14. See Joan N. Burstyn, 'The Two Faces of Moral Reform in Women's Education in Victorian England', *Transactions of the Conference Group for Social and Administrative History* 6 (1976), pp. 4-19; Joyce Senders Pedersen, 'The Reform of Women's Secondary and Higher Education: Institutional Change and Social Values in Mid and Late Victorian England', *History of Education Quarterly* 19, no. 1 (1979), pp. 61-91.

15. See B. Inhelder and J. Piaget, *The Growth of Logical Thinking from Childhood to Adolescence* (New York, 1973).

16. Patricia Thomson, *The Victorian Heroine, a Changing Ideal 1837-1873* (London, 1956), chapter 2; Josephine Kamm, *Hope Deferred* (London, 1965), chapter 12; and M. Jeanne Peterson, 'The Victorian Governess: Status Incongruence in Family and Society', in Vicinus (ed.), *Suffer and be Still*, pp. 3-19 all discuss the plight of Victorian governesses.

17. See Elaine Kaye, *A History of Queen's College, London, 1848-1972* (London, 1972); M. J. Tuke, *A History of Bedford College for Women, 1849-1937* (London, 1939).

18. See G. Melly, MP, *The Children of Liverpool and the Rural Schemes for National Education* (1869) cited in Eric Midwinter, *Nineteenth Century Education* (New York, 1970), document 8, pp. 85-7.

19. See Pedersen, 'The Reform of Women's Secondary and Higher Education', p. 65.

20. Edwin Welch, *The Peripatetic University: Cambridge Local Lectures, 1873-1973* (Cambridge, 1973), chapters 3 and 4.

21. See Edward W. Ellsworth, *Liberators of the Female Mind: The Shirreff Sisters, Educational Reform, and the Women's Movement* (Westport, Conn., 1979), chapter 7.

22. Josephine Kamm, *Indicative Past: A Hundred Years of the Girls' Public Day School Trust* (London, 1971), p. 63.

23. See Rita McWilliams-Tullberg, *Women at Cambridge: A Men's University— Though of a Mixed Type* (London, 1975), chapters 6 and 8; A. M. A. H. Rogers, *Degrees by Degrees* (Oxford, 1938).

2 | *Education and the Ideal of Womanhood*

Technological advances changed women's social and economic roles in nineteenth-century England, and polarised the life experiences of working and non-working women. In cities, where families could no longer provide subsistence for themselves, wages became the sole means of support for most families. Among the lower classes, women, like men, spent most of their day earning money for the family's subsistence. They worked either at home on materials supplied by their employers or in workshop, mill, or factory. By mid-century many women of the lower classes left home each day to earn money. Women of the middle classes, on the other hand, remained at home and became consumers only. The pressures on middle-class women *not* to work developed because their families came to measure success by the amount of leisure afforded women members of the family. Leisured women were symbols of the economic success of their male relatives. Not all men of the middle classes could afford such symbols, but since the definition of a lady, (and hence a member of the upper or middle classes) came to depend upon her isolation from the workforce, men often dissembled in order to preserve their family's status.

Leisured life for the middle classes differed, however, from the life of the aristocracy, on which it was modelled. In aristocratic families, where neither husband nor wife was obliged to work, there was a rough equivalence of privileges and obligations between the sexes, although their lives were structured differently. This equivalence was lost in the new way of life among the middle class, with its presumption of male production and female consumption of financial resources. Women spent their time organising the household, overseeing the care of their children, shopping for necessities and luxuries, practising philanthropy, and nurturing friendships, while their male relatives left home each day to earn money for these activities. This way of life became the ideal for the whole of society.

According to the ideal, home became a place where only women — mistresses of the household, servants, and daughters — spent their lives. Except when they were very young, boys and men spent their time away from home, at school or at work. For them school, or

office, or mill was the centre of their activity; they began to look at home as a retreat — a peaceful haven to return to after work.[1] This was a new concept. The homes of earlier generations were no retreats; they incorporated businesses; they were integral parts of people's working lives. Wives as well as husbands shared the frustrations of work and the rewards it brought. But, with the economic changes of industrialisation, a new family structure gradually emerged for the middle classes wherein wives became onlookers and sympathisers. A new ideal of womanhood began to gain hold.

Once women were divorced from work by their physical confinement and by their lack of training, it was but a step to believe they were both weaker and purer than men. Men were prepared to be chivalrous to women when they had no rights of their own and no remedies against men's mistreatment. Men, it was argued, had to protect women because of their essential physical weakness. And yet women had the strength of a pure conscience. Unlike men, they did not have to compromise their ideals each day by turning them into reality. Women did not have to bargain, to weigh profit and loss against better working conditions or shorter hours. They were able to preserve the traditional virtues of society in face of the iron will of industrialism. From this notion of women's purity developed the idea that women were men's superior consciences. If a husband were tempted to place his profit above all else, his wife would dissuade him, or at least assuage his guilt by works of charity.

By the middle of the nineteenth century many people felt that women should take the lead in regenerating industrial society, in bringing it back to moral purity. 'Let us make use of the engine God has placed in our hands', urged the *Quarterly Review*. 'Pour into the corrupted stream the pure, healthy disinfectant of English womanhood.'[2] Extraordinary as this metaphor may appear, it expressed a longing for stable values, felt by men and women alike, which drew strength from fear of the tensions in Victorian society and from nostalgia for the supposed simplicity of life in former generations. Though conservative, looking backwards to the re-establishment of pre-industrial moral standards, this longing offered women a new role as the standard-bearers of morality. Each sex was to have its distinct sphere of influence: woman's superior morality was to match man's superior reasoning and business ability. Woman's mission was not to be confused with man's. A woman could not count on the rewards afforded a man: woman's work was the work of the spirit; her reward was spiritual, not financial. These themes were expressed in a more

sophisticated version fifty years later by Frederic Harrison. Harrison and his fellow Positivists, followers of Auguste Comte and his design to reorganise life 'by faith in our common humanity', worked to emancipate all women, not just those of the upper classes, from the need to work:

> Our true ideal of the emancipation of Woman is to enlarge in all things the spiritual, moral, affective influence of Woman; to withdraw her more and more from the exhaustion, the contamination, the vulgarity of mill-work and professional work; to make her more and more the free, cherished mistress of the home, more and more the intellectual, moral, and spiritual genius of man's life.[3]

By the cultivation of characteristics particularly feminine — self-denial, forbearance, fidelity — women were to teach the whole world how to live in virtue. They were to do this not by writing books about moral values, nor by preaching about them in public, 'but by manifesting them hour by hour in each home by the magic of the voice, look, word, and all the incommunicable graces of woman's tenderness.'[4]

The ideal woman was to be responsible for organising the household, bringing up the children, and providing tranquility to which men returned as to a haven of peace from the turbulent world outside.

> *Home* is clearly Woman's intended place; and the duties which belong to Home are Woman's peculiar province. . . And it is in the sweet sanctities of domestic life, — in home duties, — in whatever belongs to and makes the happiness of *Home,* that Woman is taught by the SPIRIT to find scope for her activity, — to recognize her sphere of most appropriate service.[5]

Women should remain at home all day, quietly participating in the routine of the house while their menfolk were away facing the hardships of the world. The organisation of the household should be entirely arranged by the mistress of the house. Although husbands made the major financial decisions, they should not be burdened with details of household affairs. Women had to protect men from such details because the world outside the home presented them with difficulties enough to try their tempers. Women were men's solace when they returned home, giving them the security they could not find among their business associates. This crucial role for women was

spelled out by Hester Chapone in her *Letter to a New Married Lady,* a book which enjoyed popularity for one hundred years after its publication in 1777. According to Mrs. Chapone, a husband was bound to be irritated at times by things that happened at work, 'but when he returns to his own house, let him there find everything serene and peaceful, and let your cheerful complacency restore his good humour, and quiet every uneasy passion.'[6] A woman's temper might have been tried by the household problems she faced during the day, but she should not expect to share her burdens with her husband. With forbearance and submission she should refrain from mentioning them to him.

The ideal woman was protected from such evils as dishonesty, cheating, and profligacy since she did not have to take part in worldly transactions. Men would admire her purity, although they could never aspire to it. As John Burgon, an Oxford divinity professor, preached in 1884: 'Woman's strength lies in her essential weakness. . . . Removed from the stifling atmosphere in which perforce the battle of life has to be fought out by the rougher sex, — she is, what she was intended to be, — the one great solace of Man's life, his chiefest earthly joy.'[7]

Morally pure and a guardian of the home, the ideal woman was expected to be clever as well. However, cleverness in women could not be measured as it was in men, since women were not expected to train their intellects. A clever woman relied on intuition to guide her in the social arts. She was a manipulator of men, but her influence was indirect and benign. These characteristics were extolled by the *Saturday Review* in its obituary tribute to Lady Morley in December 1857: 'The power of a clever woman,' such as Lady Morley had been, 'is probably greater upon the men with whom she comes in contact than all the books they ever read, or all the speeches they ever hear. The social arts are of all others the most difficult to acquire, and certainly not the least refining to those who are capable of their discipline.'[8] Cleverness in women, therefore, was measured by social success. Women achieved influence over men indirectly, by listening to them, agreeing with them, passing on to them the opinions of other men or occasionally, but with discretion, offering an opinion of their own. Women's power lay in discretion; they would gain nothing by trying to influence politics or commerce directly.

The ideal of virtuous woman reigning supreme in the home, endowing it with peace and security, running the household with skill and efficiency, and rarely venturing into the world beyond, remained for a long while to inspire Victorian England. Constance Maynard, an

early student at Girton College and first Principal of Westfield College, London, suggested why the ideal was so cherished:

> From 1840 to 1860 the Early Victorian tastes, fashions, opinion, and modes of thought, were all in full bloom. The reign of the four Georges was over, with their drunkenness and their laxity, and a wholly new generation surrounded the young Queen. . . Loyalty had been on a dying bed for at least forty years, but it now regained new life: evil was hastily thrust into dark corners, the key of silence was turned on all the regions of vice, and domesticity and a happy home life were honoured as it had never been possible to honour them before. . . Innocence was made an idol of among women of the upper classes. . . The simple and blooming girl with her smile, and her curls, and her rosy cheeks was the ideal. She stands before me even now with her white muslin dress, blue sash, white stockings, and pretty little thin cross sandalled shoes, always sheltered, always content with her own little domain.[9]

Victorian society felt able to afford such extreme naiveté in young women of the upper and middle classes. They did not need to work — unlike women of the lower classes who did — and therefore they could lead lives of sheltered domesticity. The press encouraged them to do so. Women's magazines in the years after 1825 abandoned discussion of political affairs and filled their columns with moral tales, poetry, and advice on etiquette. The growing extravagance of women's clothes was matched by an increase in space devoted to fashion news.[10] Both men and women began to behave according to a code of social respectability that entailed repression in language and actions. Only through ignorance (referred to as innocence), it was believed, could women truly be preserved from the dangers of vice, for to have knowledge that something existed was to savour its quality, as Adam and Eve had learned in the garden of Eden. Men could not hope to escape a life of worldliness but women in England could rise above such contamination.

Despite the zeal of the upper and middle classes to spread their ideal of leisured womanhood to the lower classes, a large number of women in Victorian England continued to earn their own living, and, by the 1860s, some middle-class families began to question the ideal as it applied to their daughters. An increasing number of women in mid-Victorian Britain had to remain unmarried as the surplus of women over men grew ever larger. From 1851 to 1871 among those aged 15

and over the excess of women over men increased by 42 per cent.[11] Though the population as a whole was increasing, the number of women was increasing faster than the number of men. More boys than girls died young; more men than women emigrated to the colonies; many young men found careers in the army, the navy, or the colonies which kept them away from England for a number of years, perhaps for life.

At the same time the standard of living for the middle classes was rising, and it became customary for young men to postpone marriage until they had accumulated sufficient capital or were earning sufficient income to provide homes for their wives equivalent to the parental homes they were leaving. Children were expected to begin married life at the standard which their parents had reached after about twenty years of marriage. A change in the age of marriage helped increase the numbers of single women, as did the feeling of some men that they were unable to afford marriage at all.[12]

Perhaps as significant was the unwillingness of middle-class parents to see their daughters marry below them in the social scale. Families wanted to better their positions, and while it was possible, perhaps, for a son to marry below himself and thereby raise his wife up to the level of his family, this possibility was not open to a daughter. Indeed one of the dilemmas faced by an unmarried woman was that either the need to support herself by working or a 'bad' marriage would lower her status.

Middle-class families were dismayed to think their own daughters might never find husbands. Professional men, especially, found it difficult to provide life incomes for several daughters, and since working entailed loss of status for the girl, as well as opprobrium for her father, everything had to be done to ensure that a suitable marriage was made. Despite the best efforts of well-intentioned parents, however, many women remained single. As a result, by the last decades of the nineteenth century, some parents were willing for their daughters to find a paid occupation until they married, to relieve their fathers or brothers from the financial burden of their support. On no account, however, would most parents countenance the kind of education or occupation that endangered their daughters' nubility. The ideal demanded that all women receive the same kind of education, and those who, for economic reasons, could not reach the ideal saw no reason why they should be educated any differently from their more fortunate sisters.

Education for the Ideal Woman

Faced with an increase in leisure and the need to behave with elegance in order to make the best possible marriage, many young women in the early nineteenth century sought an education in accomplishments not household skills. They learned to dance, to play the piano, and they mastered the fine details of drawing-room etiquette. However, those who espoused the ideal described earlier in this chapter sought to replace this emphasis on the skills needed before marriage with emphasis on skills that women needed throughout their lives. They strove, therefore, for an education that would develop women's spiritual nature, teach them how to run a house and how to bring up their children. For guidance they turned to a body of didactic litera-ture written from about 1770 onwards for those entrusted with the upbringing of 'young ladies'. Many such books of the early decades of the nineteenth century were written in reply to the audacious advocates of women's rights: to Mary Wollstonecraft's call for self-reliant women, they replied that the mothers and grandmothers of the present generation had found fulfillment in serving as helpmeets to their husbands. They outlined a training for modest, efficient, and contented wives. These books were reprinted often; those written by clergymen began as sermons, but found a far wider audience in printed form. The picture of women they fashioned was so perfect that change could not be contemplated. To the cries that a changing world demanded new responses from women came the reply that woman's life was pre-ordained; she had only to live up to the highest ideals of the past to accomplish her mission. Thus the 'new' role for women was described as a revival of the role people believed upper-class women had played a few decades earlier, with the addition of a new moral responsibility.

The ideal woman was trained to accept the limitations of woman's sphere. In one book, a mother wrote to her daughter returning from a year at school: 'You are returning *home*. It is a comprehensive word, my dear Laura: upon your right estimation of its value greatly depends your future happiness. It is chiefly *there* that the lustre of the female character is discernible; because *home* is its proper sphere.'[13] To make sure the ideal woman was content to cultivate domestic virtues, she had to be taught to accept physical boundaries to her activities, and her bodily movements had to be constrained by the conventions of ladylike behaviour. A girl's brothers might often take expeditions, she seldom did; they might climb trees, run and wrestle, she was not

allowed to do so. Her back had to be straightened, her waist drawn in, and her mind trained for the awesome responsibility of becoming a wife and mother.[14]

With such a pattern of constraint an accepted part of a woman's education, it is not surprising that censorship of a woman's reading was also recommended. Male writers were eager to give advice on how this should be done. Dr. John Gregory, in *A Father's Legacy to His Daughters,* while claiming he did not wish to influence their taste, urged his daughters to 'Shun, as you would do the most fatal poison, all that species of reading and conversation which warms the imagination, which engages and softens the heart, and raises the taste above the level of common life.'[15] Parents, uncertain they would live to see their children reach maturity, seem to have appreciated Dr. Gregory's book which reflected their own solicitude for their daughters. Dr. Gregory feared that too wide an access to books would make a woman discontented. He was concerned, also, that reading might interfere with the development of natural womanhood. 'I want to know what Nature has made you,' he wrote, 'and to perfect you on her plan.'[16] Nature granted to every woman the power of intuition, and one aim of those charged with educating the ideal woman in the nineteenth century was to foster woman's natural intuitive judgment. Learning, it was claimed, was necessary for men, the less well-endowed sex, for whom reasoning had to take the place of intuition, but women did not need it:

> Women in general are probably best as they are—in possession of that intuitive right judgment which is safe at first thought, though with the stronger half of the intelligent creation "second thoughts are best."[17]

Learning interfered with the functioning of intuition because it trained women to reason. A learned woman, therefore, lost the very essence of her femininity. As marriage was woman's vocation, a girl's training had to enhance not diminish her femininity. No father wanted to be accused of educating his daughter so as to make her unsuited to marriage and motherhood; better to ignore the possibility of her remaining unmarried and in need of supporting herself than to run the risk that her very education would make her an old maid. A woman, therefore, was to receive only sufficient learning to perform her work well, and was to read no books that interfered with the free play of her intuition. Her purity had to remain unimpaired by her

education, also, and thus any book that might inform her of 'unlady-like' facts had to be kept from her.

The ideal woman's vocation of marriage and the management of a home required training. However, secrecy was part of the mystique of femininity, and it was no business of men to understand the details of women's duties. Household subjects were traditionally taught by mothers; only with moral and religious subjects was the assistance of men—the clergy—necessary. Therefore, only women and clergymen wrote in detail about the education of women; other men had to be content with generalisations. Men had no idea how much time it took to learn cookery or catering. Their only response to women's reports, by the early nineteenth century, that traditional household skills were being neglected was a general uneasiness; detailed recommendations were beyond their ken. Men feared that contemporary teaching with its emphasis on French, music, and art was responsible for the neglect of truly feminine subjects. Matters would surely become worse if women were encouraged to study mathematics and Latin. What was needed was a revitalisation of the traditional feminine subjects. As the magazine *Punch* pointed out 'the model daughter' was a woman with detailed knowledge of how to run a household:

> She looks attentively after the holes in her father's gloves. She is a clever adept in preparing gruel, white-wine whey, tapioca, chicken broth, beef-tea, and the thousand little household delicacies of a sick room. . . She does not invent excuses for not reading to her father of an evening, nor does she skip any of the speeches. . . She knows nothing of crotchets, or 'Woman's Mission'. She studies housekeeping, is perfect in the common rules of arithmetic. . . She checks the weekly bills, and does not blush if seen in a butcher's shop on a Saturday.[18]

Although there were a few proprietary schools run by women capable of teaching domestic virtues, mothers were the best teachers. By watching and copying what was done at home, daughters would receive the best training. However, standards of household management changed during the nineteenth century as many families acquired greater affluence, and some daughters could not receive guidance from their mothers on how to manage their affairs. They turned for advice to books on household management such as Mrs. Beeton's *The Book of Household Management* (1861), which was widely acclaimed because it dealt with the intricacies of household

management and care of the sick as well as recipes for meals. Middle-class wives found invaluable Mrs. Beeton's advice on managing cooks, housemaids, and nannies, since wives in affluent families had to learn there was a hierarchy among their servants as intricate as the hierarchy among employers, and each servant was zealous of her position and her power. For the less affluent Mrs. Eliza Warren wrote *How I Managed My House on Two Hundred Pounds a Year* (1864), and there were several other popular manuals.[19]

As well as in household management, the ideal woman had to be given a thorough grounding in moral principles, to enable her to carry out her mission as moral preceptor to her family. Early in the nineteenth century it was accepted that moral principles could not be taught in schools. There could be no courses in that subject as in Latin or mathematics. Boys and girls depended on their mothers to teach them the moral principles upon which to build their lives. For a boy, who had to face the world outside the home, such teaching was crucial:

> Happily for [the mother], she is not called upon to disentangle the knotty questions of the political economist. But she is called upon to prepare her child as well as she can for that great battle against temptation which he will have to carry on throughout his after life.[20]

Although girls did not have to be educated to face such hazards as boys, they needed to be taught moral principles in order to give their lives a deeper meaning, and to teach them what they, in their turn, had to pass on to their children. For the task of moral preceptor a mother did not need to be a scholar, she had but to learn the 'science of life' which, according to Sarah Ellis, author and proprietor of a school for girls, had several aspects: social duty, the law of kindness, and another that comprehended 'that true estimate of the worth of things visible and invisible. . . And this the mother can teach to her children as no one else can, having first learned it truly herself.'[21]

Over the years people's attitudes changed towards the teaching of moral principles in schools. Formal schooling became more highly valued than before; boys' schools introduced new subjects and remodelled their discipline largely under pressure from middle-class parents. Under the leadership of Thomas Arnold at Rugby, boys' public schools assumed more responsibility for the moral development of their charges.[22] Parents began then to criticise the frivolity and

fatuousness of their daughters. Despite the best efforts of writers to encourage parents to take upon themselves the proper education of their daughters, most refused, or were not competent to do so. Girls often received only desultory intellectual training from tutors or governesses, or else they attended school fitfully; their moral training was ignored. Girls' schools in the first half of the century had poorly educated teachers, and students who saw no need to attend regularly or to enrol for a period of several years. Changes in boys' schools, however, persuaded parents there might be some virtue in allowing girls to study the same subjects as their brothers. With a basic knowledge of the liberal arts women might prove to be better companions to their husbands, better housekeepers, and better parents:

> So long as they receive the peculiarly whimsical education which is at present thought good enough for all practical purposes, and are confined. . . to the weakest kinds of make-believe activity, we cannot expect them to hold very sound notions about the whole duty of wives.[23]

By 1870, therefore, education for the ideal woman came to include the development of a woman's intellect as far as her femininity would allow. Here I take issue with Walter E. Houghton who speaks, in *The Victorian Frame of Mind* of 'three conceptions of woman current in the Victorian period' — the submissive wife whose character and life were completely distinct from her husband's, the 'new woman' demanding equal rights with man, and those in the middle who wanted to remove legal disabilities 'and give "more breadth of culture"; but higher education is unwise, the vote is dubious, and professional careers are dangerous. For after all woman is not man; she has her own nature and function in life, not inferior to his but entirely different.'[24] Historically, the position of those 'in the middle' was merely a later adaptation of the first Houghton described, not a separate conception of woman. It *allowed* woman new rights, but did not envisage her exercising them in the world at large. It claimed a woman's nature and function were not inferior to man's, and yet man's function was to control the world outside the home, and to be head of his family in the home. Hence, a wife had to be submissive, not because of her husband's selfish egotism, but because of the laws of nature and society. A woman's education had to prepare her for her duty as a wife. When it became clear that the education offered to

women was undermining their dutifulness, calls for a more 'rational education' found ready acceptance. It was hoped that systematic learning and the discipline of school-life would provide women, also, with the moral fibre they needed to sustain society. There was a new acceptance, by mid-century, that moral principles could and should be taught in school. (Elementary schools for the lower classes taught moral principles through religious instruction.[25] Such instruction was not thought appropriate for children of the middle classes, who were expected to receive their religious training from their families.)

The change in attitude towards women's education accounted for some apparent inconsistencies in the arguments used by supporters of the feminine ideal. The *Saturday Review,* having in July 1864 condemned the suggestion that women should enter University local examinations,* declared the following month:

A girl will be none the less feminine because she has some serious interests in life, none the less graceful because her tastes have a wider range than mere schoolroom accomplishments, none the less attractive because she sympathizes, and to some extent shares, in pursuits of a graver kind.[26]

Those who supported the ideal had no intention of encouraging, or even of allowing, women to enter the universities. Women's domestic duties precluded their contributing to the advance of knowledge. Household organisation, moral and physical training of children, and the companionship they were expected to give their husbands took up so much time that, unlike men, women could never devote themselves to study.

The Ideal versus Higher Education

Those supporting the Victorian ideal of women claimed that universities provided a vocational education inappropriate for woman's role. While most people believed no woman was capable of sustained study in the first place, there was also a general belief that study itself would leave a woman discontented and ill-prepared for marriage and motherhood. Not only was it feared that higher education would encourage women to desert domesticity, but it would make marriage

*See Chapter 8 for a discussion of women and the university local examinations.

seem undesirable. The assimilation of girls' education to boys' would lead women to adopt men's attitudes towards sex, which would in turn lead to changes in marriage relationships. This prospect was alarming. Middle-class men insisted on chastity for their wives and daughters; they believed the very knowledge of sexual immorality was harmful to them. The study of literature at the university would introduce women to such knowledge, lead them to become promiscuous, and therefore threaten the institution of marriage.

There was also a fear that the marriages of educated women would prove unstable. It was believed that those educated women fortunate enough to marry were bound to be argumentative wives. They would join in discussions of public affairs and disturb the household by challenging the opinions of their husbands and sons. No matter how well women might reason (indeed, the better their reasoning the worse the result), the possibility of domestic discord could be looked upon only with horror. In vain was it suggested that anxiety on this score might be misplaced, that, though educated women might acquire independence of thought, the probability of arguments with their husbands on everyday matters would be diminished — uneducated women invariably taunted men by tears or emotional outcries until they gave way; it might be hoped that a woman educated in rational discussion would not resort to such strategies.[27] However, many men felt it would be a disgrace to be bested in argument by a woman; they were appalled at the thought of gentle, retiring women so far unsexing themselves as to participate in such masculine affairs.

Higher education, it was claimed, would not only affect adversely the lives of women once married; it would blight the hopes of single women looking for husbands. Learned women, or 'bluestockings' as they had come to be known from a group who held literary conversations in place of evenings playing cards, were anathema to men. There was no point in endangering a woman's chances of marriage by educating her so highly that she was sure to become an old maid. Did anyone believe

> that *Pater Familias* would be a happier man in his mind if he were mated with a 'being' who, instead of mending his clothes and getting his dinner cooked, had a taste for a literary career upon the subject of political economy?. . . There is a strong, an ineradicable male instinct, that a learned, or even an over-accomplished young woman is one of the most intolerable monsters in creation.[28]

Clearly it was the 'ineradicable male instinct' that had led Dr. Gregory

to warn his daughters to conceal any learning they might have, and that, almost a century later, prompted a reviewer in the *Quarterly Review* to claim that 'sensible men' rarely took wives 'from the ranks of those ladies who have courted the appellation of "blues" '.[29]

Men's instincts with regard to learned women were thought to be right, for there was also medical evidence that education made women sterile, so that there was a danger of 'the sex being unsexed.'[30] This was not a reproductive danger only; the whole fabric of Christian society was likely to be destroyed. God had created woman from man and for man, and in return he treated her 'with unceasing care and solicitude,' but this idyll would come to an end once she set out to become man's rival: 'Henceforth you have in a manner unsexed yourselves, and must needs put up with the bitter consequences. You have acquired Man's faults. You have lost your own feminine graces.'[31] Women would lose their power over men once they were educated. There would be an end to chivalry and to all the virtues of womanhood.

Since it was believed that women were inferior to men both in mental ability and in bodily strength, they would enhance their nubility by being simple and compliant, retiring and subservient. In contrast, an adventurous spirit, rebelliousness, and a love of competition were signs of masculinity. Even supporters of higher education for women had reservations about the wisdom of girls entering into competition with boys. Thomas Dyke Acland wrote to Emily Davies, when she was leading the movement to open the university local examinations to women, that he felt women needed a degree of privacy for their proper development. 'I confess, therefore, that I feel a shrinking disposition to throw the girls of England into public competition with the boys.'[32] Those who did not support higher education for women spoke out even more strongly against competition between the sexes:

> For boys and men the stimulus of emulation is wholesome and desirable; but as it is quite out of place among girls, whose sphere is the home circle and whose grace a sweet retiringness, it is surely enough if their schooldays be spent in acquiring such modicums of knowledge as can be easily digested. . . Elder women of thought and tact will discourage the unfeminineness of rivalries and competitions among meek-eyed maidens, and deem the fervid emulation of honours and classes more suited to the 'palaestra' than the 'gynaeceum'.[33]

Men were accustomed to competing and measuring their ability

against one another. Since women's intellectual ability was believed to be less than men's, it was argued that women should not compete with men on examinations; the women were bound to do less well. It was unchivalrous to tease women by pretending that men's and women's abilities were comparable. Some people, although certain that women would be outstripped in any intellectual competition with men, buttressed their certainty by suggesting that intellectual competition would endanger women's health. Others felt a woman had to be warned against achieving academic success for social reasons: 'Supposing she obtains them, honours — Will none of you have the generosity or the candour to tell her what a very disagreeable creature, in Man's account she will infallibly become?'[34]

The focus of these arguments was the danger of changing the relations between the sexes. The *Saturday Review,* discussing John Stuart Mill's *The Subjection of Women* in rather more temperate tones than it usually allowed to the subject, concluded that, although women should be allowed to develop their intelligence and lead lives of interest, there were profound differences between men and women and 'the relation between the sexes is one with which it is exceedingly dangerous to play tricks without much consideration and a careful feeling of the way.'[35] According to this argument, the patterns of relationship between the sexes were settled: nuances of social behaviour might change, but men had discussions with women only on social occasions. The 'business' of life was conducted among men, and women entered it only far enough to understand the financial limits within which household affairs had to be carried on. Although Mill pleaded that men no longer (as in the eighteenth century) took their recreation alone, that there was a growing need for manly women and womanly men if they were to interact in serious discussions, not many people found it congenial to discuss serious matters in mixed company.[36] Eliza Lynn Linton, a journalist who later wrote disparagingly of 'the girl of the period,' in 1868 wrote to T. H. Huxley:

> We meet you [men] in 'society' with crowds of friends about and in an atmosphere of finery and artificiality. Suppose I, or any woman — let her be as fascinating as possible — were to bombard you with scientific talk — would you not rather go off to the stupidest little girl who had not a thought above her pretty frock, than begin a discussion on the Origin of Species?[37]

At a time when modernisation was affecting men's lives even more

dramatically than it was affecting women's, and when the constraints of refinement were curtailing activities previously enjoyed by men, there were those 'who felt that, for their own social comfort, the relations between the sexes must not be tampered with. Women's demands were seen as yet another encroachment upon the proper definitions of masculinity and femininity.

The danger of changing relations between the sexes had to be guarded against through the careful supervision of women's education. Since women's purity needed to be preserved, supporters of the ideal felt strongly the dangers of allowing women access to the same education as men even at the secondary level. Women might be enough like men to succumb to the temptations described in the literature they read. Greek and Latin literature would introduce women to a knowledge of sexual licentiousness and thereby ruin their purity; yet, if women were to prepare for entry to the universities, they would have to study both subjects.[38]

Sometimes these fears were discussed openly; more often women were praised for whatever was in keeping with the ideal of womanhood, thus dissuading them from wanting to participate in the affairs of the world. However, as the pressure from those who wanted women to have the same education as men increased, supporters of the status quo became more outspoken about the dangers of change.

The demand for higher education challenged the ideal of womanhood, and opposition to the demand brought together people whose attitudes to the other social and intellectual issues of the day were far apart. Both conservatives and reformers — to use terms descriptive of the debates on evolution, religion, and labour — found themselves defending an ideal of womanhood based on what appeared to be the existing relations between the sexes. Fundamentalist Christians preached the subordination of woman and her inferiority to man, a notion which was anathema to believers in the religion of humanity like Frederic Harrison. Yet both fundamentalists and humanists[39] could unite in their opposition to the higher education of women.

Opponents used three primary kinds of arguments to support their opinions, those based on the economic ramifications of higher education for women, on the evidence from comparative anatomy and physiology, and those, the most conservative, based on Biblical authority and social convention. All the arguments attempted to prove that differences between the sexes were either innate or that, if they were environmental in origin, their continuance was essential to a civilised society and therefore they were as binding as innate

differences. To tamper with Nature's plan for humankind was to court disaster. We now turn to the economic arguments used to oppose higher education for women, concentrating on the question of goal differences for men and women based on their different roles in life.

Notes

1.   The theme of home as a retreat was expounded by several Victorian writers, most notably John Ruskin in *Sesame and Lilies* (London, 1865), pp. 148-9. For other exponents see Walter E. Houghton, *The Victorian Frame of Mind, 1830-1870* (New Haven, 1957), pp. 341-8, and for an insight into the evolution of this theme, see Raymond Williams, *The Long Revolution* (New York, 1966), p. 95.

2.   'Female Education', *Quarterly Review*, 126 (1869) p. 478. This extensive article reviewed five works including the *Report, Minutes of Evidence etc. of the Schools Inquiry Commission*, 1868.

3.   Frederic Harrison, *Realities and Ideals* (New York, 1908), p. 100. Harrison laid great stress on the educational opportunities that would open to women by their emancipation from work as proposed by the Positivists. (*Ibid.*, pp. 98-9).

4.   *Ibid.*, p. 70.

5.   John W. Burgon, *To Educate Young Women Like Young Men, — A Thing Inexpedient and Immodest. A Sermon* (Oxford, 1884), p. 17.

6.   (London, 1828), pp. 108-9. This work, first published in 1777, was reprinted as late as 1868.

7.   Burgon, *Sermon*, pp. 29-30.

8.   'Lady Morley', *Saturday Review* 4 (1857), p. 557.

9.   Constance L. Maynard, 'Autobiography' (1915), pp. 331-3 (MS Westfield College, London).

10.   For details of changes in women's magazines, see Cynthia L. White, *Women's Magazines 1693-1968* (London, 1970), pp. 38-43.

11.   See J. A. and Olive Banks, *Feminism and Family Planning* (London, 1964), p. 28, footnote.

12.   *Ibid.*, Chapter 3.

13.   Mrs. [Ann] Taylor and Jane Taylor, *Correspondence Between a Mother and her Daughter at School* (London, 1817), p. 140. Although this work does not appear to have been reprinted after 1821, its sentiments are similar to Ann Taylor's *Maternal Solicitude for a Daughter's Best Interests* which was reprinted as late as 1855.

14.   Details of the physical constraints of Victorian women are well outlined in June A. Kennard, 'Women, Sport & Society in Victorian England' (Unpublished Ed.D. Dissertation, University of North Carolina, Greensboro, 1974), Chapter 3.

15.   (London, 1828), pp. 86-7. This work first appeared in 1774 and was reprinted as late as 1877, often together with one of Mrs. Hester Chapone's works.

16.   *Ibid.*, p. 44.

17.   [James Davies], 'Review of 1. *Principles of Education* by the author of "Amy Herbert," 2 vols., (1865) and 2. *Woman's Mission*, 10th edn, (1842) from a male point of view', *Quarterly Review*, 119 (1866) p. 50.

18.   'The Model Daughter', *Punch* 14 (1848), p. 230.

19.   Patricia Branca, *Silent Sisterhood: Middle Class Women in the Victorian Home* (Pittsburgh, 1975), Chapter 1 examines Victorian household manuals.

20.   Sarah S. Ellis, *Education of the Heart: Woman's Best Work* (London, 1869), p. 157.

21.   *Ibid.,* pp. 224-5.

22.   For a succinct account of these changes see S. J. Curtis, *History of Education in Great Britain* (London, 1963), pp. 143-54.

23.   'Husbands', *Saturday Review* 18 (1864), p. 416.

24.   Walter E. Houghton, *The Victorian Frame of Mind*, pp. 348-9.

25.   Phillip McCann, ed., *Popular Education and Socialization in the Nineteenth Century* (London, 1977) describes moral instruction in the elementary schools.

26.   'Women's Friendships', *Saturday Review* 18 (1864), pp. 176-7. The opposition to the university local examinations was expressed in an article entitled: 'Feminine Wranglers', *Ibid.* pp. 111-12.

27.   See Emily Pfeiffer, *Woman and Work. An Essay Treating on the Relations to Health and Physical Development, of the Higher Education of Girls, and the Intellectual or More Systematized Effort of Women* (London, 1888), pp. 17-20.

28.   'Feminine Wranglers', *Saturday Review* 18 (1864) p. 112.

29.   [James Davies], 'Review of *Principles of Education* and *Women's Mission'*, *Quarterly Review* 119 (1866) p. 510.

30.   The medical evidence is discussed in detail in Chapter 5.

31.   Burgon, *Sermon*, p. 30.

32.   Thomas Dyke Acland to Emily Davies (ca. 1863), quoted by Barbara Stephen *Emily Davies and Girton College* (London, 1927), p. 85.

33.   [James Davies], 'Review of *Principles of Education* and *Women's Mission'*, *Quarterly Review* 119 (1866), pp. 502, 509.

34.   Burgon, *Sermon*, p.20.

35.   'Review of J. S. Mill, *The Subjection of Women'*, *Saturday Review* 27 (1869) p. 813. This sentiment was expressed also by the author of 'Female Education' in the *Quarterly Review* 126 (1869) p. 448-79.

36.   See John Stuart Mill in *Hansard* 187 (May 20th, 1867), p. 823.

37.   Letter of November 11th, 1868, Huxley Papers, Imperial College London.

38.   James Davies, a Classical scholar, felt, however, that: 'Nothing in the Latin language is more dangerous than the ordinary type of French novels, teeming, as they do, with a subtler, because less manifest, poison.' (*Quarterly Review* 119 [1866], pp. 502-3.)

39.   I use 'humanist' here in its modern sense. Harrison called himself a Positivist, which has changed its meaning since Harrison's day, when it meant a follower of Auguste Comte.

3 | *Women and the Economy*

Women's role had been carefully defined, and the more the definition was challenged by the proponents of higher education, the more vigorously it was defended. Those who opposed higher education for women believed it would endanger the social and economic structure of the country. They extrapolated from suggested reforms to a total destruction of the ideal of womanhood. They believed the public should be told how radical the reformers' ideas for women really were: one change would lead to another until there was a revolution of relations between the sexes.

This chapter examines the opponents' arguments on the economic effects of higher education for women. They were arguments raised in the general literature; embedded within them were assumptions about women's ultimate goals, the purpose of higher education, and the structure of the economy. We will explore the arguments by examining these assumptions.

Women's Ultimate Goals

A major contention of the opponents to higher education for women was that the sexes had different goals in life and should, therefore, be educated differently. According to this view, education was functional. Women's work was in the home, men's in the world; each sex needed to be educated to perform its role effectively. Because men appreciated supportive wives, women's education could be broadened to include, (as well as skills of literacy, housekeeping, and child care,) an understanding of culture and the tasks men performed. However, women did not need extensive knowledge of these areas: 'A man ought to know any language or science he learns thoroughly,' claimed John Ruskin, 'while a woman ought to know the same language, or science, only so far as may enable her to sympathise in her husband's pleasure, and in those of his best friends.'[1]

Discussion about women's education was usually linked to women's ultimate goals. Emily Davies, a leader in the drive to open higher

such a prospectus will not do for a girl. While the sun shines the hay must be made, and her sun shines earlier in the day than that of him who is to be her husband.[4]

Since women wished to marry, it was clear that their professional ambitions would be shortlived. Married women were not expected to work if their husbands could support them; hence, even if women completed training for an occupation, they would leave their employment as soon as they had the opportunity to marry. Their years of training would then go to waste. Economically, therefore, women professionals were an unsound investment. Men found the competition among themselves for skilled jobs intense; women should be discouraged from the unrealistic goal of competing also.

Behind these arguments was an assumption that mésalliances would more easily be formed if women attended universities and entered the professions. Education was perceived by some groups in society as a mechanism for upward mobility; a clever woman, from a tradesman's family, might use the opportunity to go to university or enter a profession to make a better marriage than would otherwise have been possible for her. Opponents found the thought of this personally discomforting. They were unwilling to allow it to happen because they believed the stability of society depended upon a well-defined class structure.

Although by the mid-nineteenth century there was an imbalance in the numbers of men and women in society, so that a number of women were likely to remain unmarried all their lives, the opponents felt that the working of society should not be changed for the sake of a few people. Those few were unfortunate, but society as a whole had to be considered, and the way of life of the majority respected.

Higher education and entry into the professions was no solution to single women's problems, argued the opponents. The proponents' belief that a changing society called for a change in the position of women was fallacious. Such a change could lead only to the destruction of the family, and thus of society. If too many women were remaining unmarried, marriage had to be made more attractive to men. In the opinion of some opponents, marriage had become a hurdle from which too many men shied away. Obstacle races were interesting only when the hurdles were not impossibly high and the stakes were worth winning. In marriage, however, parents of the middle classes demanded too high financial standards from prospective sons-in-law, while daughters, trained often in a multitude

of frivolous accomplishments rather than in moral and domestic duties, proved expensive and unsatisfactory wives. A change in expectations would lead to more marriages and avert the danger of unbalancing relations between the sexes. Thus, if marriage were kept in its rightful position, women would not wish to enter the professions.

> Married life is a woman's profession; and to this life her training — that of dependence — is modelled. Of course by not getting a husband, or by losing him, she may find that she is without resources. All that can be said of her is, she has failed in business, and no social reform can prevent such failures.[5]

Since women were not expected to become skilled workers or professionals, what point was there in educating them as though they were? Education was expensive, and resources in any family were limited. There had to be priorities. Men were expected to work throughout their active lives; the better their job, the higher their salary. Higher education for a boy was a sound investment as well as a social asset. Girls had different goals and should be educated accordingly. Governesses, if families could afford them, or otherwise private girls' schools, would give girls all the education they needed. A woman's chances of attracting a husband were unlikely to be enhanced by her going to a university or becoming a 'blue-stocking'. Nor were a woman's chances of finding employment improved by attending university, since any work suitable for a woman did not need a university education as a qualification.

Higher education, it was argued, would make women begin to agitate more forcibly for the opening of new fields of work to them. That would be disastrous. The best ways to ensure against such agitation were to maintain the difference between the education of boys and girls, to keep women from becoming qualified in any profession, and to make women's life at home as attractive as possible.

The Purpose of Higher Education

Throughout the nineteenth century, issues in the dispute over higher education for women were confused because there was no consensus on the purpose of higher education. Patricia A. Graham has suggested that in the United States the lack of consensus over educational goals between 1875 and 1925 served well those groups, including women,

who were trying to establish a place for themselves in society. Women were able to be educated through a 'heterogeneous array of acceptable and praiseworthy institutions.'[6] In England there was less heterogeneity in higher education, but lack of consensus over its purpose was advantageous to proponents of higher education for women. The motivations for going to university, and for allowing one's daughter to go, could be as varied as people's opinions. Certainly, opponents found, as a result of the confusion, that they needed a barrage of arguments to defend their position.

Many people expected education, particularly higher education, to be occupational training. Some who held this view believed women as well as men had a right to become doctors, lawyers or ministers if they chose, and therefore supported women's demands for higher education. Others who held the same view, that university education was occupational training, disagreed. They felt there was no reason for women to go to universities because women had no place in those occupations for which a university education was the preparation. The disagreement was carried further when the occupations of creative artist, author or composer were discussed. Those who supported women's right to choose occupations for themselves often claimed that women lacked only the opportunity, not the capacity, to produce great creative works. Some opponents, on the other hand, claimed that no amount of opportunity would suffice; women, by their nature, lacked the capacity for creativity.

A smaller number of people thought of higher education as primarily the transmission of a general cultural heritage. They looked to the universities to provide a liberal education. Whether these people supported or opposed higher education for women depended upon whether they believed or did not believe that women could benefit from advanced study of cultural achievements.[7] (Some people believed women *could* benefit from higher education but claimed they *should* not, either because God had decreed the subordination of women or because physiologically and socially it was undesirable for them to do so. These arguments will be discussed in Chapters 5 and 6.)

Confusion over the purpose of education affected the whole development of public education in England.[8] Discussions were strongly influenced by the idea that each class had to be educated for its role in society. There was fear of 'over educating' the lower classes. At the same time, a woman's role as wife and mother was perceived to transcend class, and to represent the true vocation of all women. What need a shopkeeper know to be successful in his trade? What need a

woman know to be successful as a wife and mother? These questions were often equated, and the answers seemed straightforward: boys and girls needed different kinds of education because their vocations were different. 'The knowledge which will pay in the business and pursuits a lad is likely to enter, is fully appreciated by the parents, but the only business in life which they contemplate for their daughters is marriage, and they ask for an education which will fit her for this end.'[9] Maria Grey, one of the most outspoken advocates of reform in women's education, deplored the narrow focus on vocational education. She believed that once people were taught to distinguish between vocational and general education, there would be an end to all discussion about what education would be good for a shopkeeper or a labourer, a man or a woman. 'The technical education may be different for all these, but the education of reason, and conscience, and will, and affections, must be the same for all.'[10]

Despite Grey's confidence that people could be taught to differentiate between general and vocational education, many appear to have found the distinction hard to make. The contradictions in people's thought were illustrated in the *Saturday Review* which, in 1877, agreed with Robert Lowe, vice-president of the Committee of Council, when he insisted 'on the characteristic of a general instead of a special or professional training, as essential to the true idea of University education',[11] but, later in the same year, claimed: 'In its earlier stages education is general, in its final stage it is, or ought to be, a preparation for the calling in life; and to send men and women to the same Universities is to pronounce that their calling in life is the same.'[12] Like most Victorians, the *Saturday Review* considered the movement for higher education for women as a challenge to the professions to accept women members, and thus reinforced the view that the primary purpose of higher education was occupational training.

Structure of the Economy

A pessimistic framework for discussion of women's economic roles in society was provided by Robert Malthus, David Ricardo and James Mill. This pessimism was eased, but not eradicated, later in the century in the work of John Stuart Mill. Although the general literature did not often raise issues of economic theory, authors expected that the assumptions discussed below were shared by their readers.

Although the consumer market in England had expanded rapidly in the early decades of the nineteenth century, most people at that time expected that expansion to level off. Few expected economic growth to continue forever through increased buying-power among consumers, new technology, or the opening of new markets. Production, people believed, could not increase significantly. It depended upon two sources: capital and labour; hence, the returns from production had to be shared between those two sources in the form of profits and wages. If wages were too high, capitalists would be deprived of their profits; if profits were too high, labourers would starve. In his *Principles of Political Economy and Taxation* (1817), David Ricardo expounded a law of economics which kept wages, over the long run, at subsistence level. There was an inevitable tendency, he wrote, for any benefits from temporary increases in wages to be offset by an influx of new workers attracted by the higher wages, and increased rents which led to higher food prices as well as more expensive housing. Any benefits from prosperity were bound to transferred rapidly from workers and employers to landlords. The campaign to repeal the Corn Laws was an attempt to mitigate this tendency.

Nassau Senior, better known as a social reformer than economist, claimed, in his *Letters on the Factory Act* (1837), that the amount of profit to be gained from manufacturing was linked to the length of the work day: the first hours of production covered costs of machine maintenance, raw materials, and wages; only the last hour of production covered return on capital in the form of profits. Though the theory was criticised, many employers clung to it, fearful that a slight reduction in the work day would lead to an immediate drop in profits. John Stuart Mill mitigated the pessimism of these theories, but he confirmed their basic outline. He believed in the possibility of population control, however; and he expected increased accumulation of capital (and thus increased production) as new techniques improved working conditions, and as more people adopted the middle-class habit of deferring gratification, and thus saving.

Discussions over higher education for women have to be examined within the framework of this economic thought. The numbers of those who considered themselves to be middle class increased throughout the century. With this increase came the need to expand those occupations thought appropriate in status for the middle classes.[13] Higher education for women, it was believed, would increase the number of applicants for high-status jobs. Those who argued against higher education for women applied the laws of economics to all classes, and

often cited the plight of women in the labouring classes to illustrate their points about what might happen if women of the middle and upper classes entered the labour market.

As described earlier, the ideal of the middle classes was that men should work while women supervised the home. The middle-class wife found her model in the aristocracy, but her husband was usually prevented by the need to earn the family living from sharing her interests except vicariously. In the upper classes, husband and wife could both indulge their whims in dress and toilette, gossip and patronage, accomplishment and social ability. For many of the middle classes, however, the price of woman's leisure was man's exclusive devotion to work. Only in the middle classes did men and women come to lead entirely separate lives, for even labouring men and women shared the common experience of work.[14] Technological and industrial changes in nineteenth-century England polarised the middle and lower classes greatly. These changes brought the middle classes affluence and status they had never known. Standards in every area changed, reflecting the new power of the middle classes.

However, the changes of affluence were not reflected in the lives of women of the labouring classes who worked long hours in factories and sweat shops. More than two million women had some kind of employ-ment in 1851, about one-third of all women in the United Kingdom. Most were industrial workers or domestic servants.[15] Thousands of women had been drawn into the vortex of factory work. Although textile factories were not the predominant form of women's employ-ment during the nineteenth century, as Louise A. Tilly and Joan W. Scott have pointed out, they became symbols of working conditions in the new industrial society.[16] Social reformers from the middle and upper classes, who feared that discontent or even revolution would result from working women neglecting their families, were prepared to take legislative action to ameliorate the conditions of the labouring classes. These conditions, in the light of middle-class conceptions, were appalling: women worked while men remained idle, children ran wild in the streets until they were old enough to work, (even those nominally enrolled in schools attended in desultory fashion), religion had no part in the lives of many families, and women indulged all the vices of men.

Nothing would tend more to elevate the moral condition of the manufacturing population, than the restoration of woman to her proper social rank; nothing would exercise greater influence upon

the form and growth of her off-spring, than her devotion to those womanly occupations which would render her a denizen of home. No great step can be made till she is snatched from unremitting toil, and made what Nature meant she should be — the centre of a system of social delights.[17]

With its overtones of security and stability, home life was cherished among the middle classes as never before, but for vast numbers of the community, it seemed to contemporary reformers, home life was being destroyed by the demands of factory labour. In the labouring classes, girls were trained only to work; wives and mothers often worked outside the home for twelve hours a day.

Because of a new convention of propriety, crime and vice were rarely discussed in middle-class homes, yet growing cities were bedevilled by criminals and many girls found prostitution an escape from the spectre of starvation. Such happenings were horrifying to Victorian respectable opinion. They were comprehensible only as individual failures. The factory worker had failed to provide for his family as he should. The criminal and the prostitute had not tried hard enough to follow the ideals society set them; at best, they were misguided individuals who, given an opportunity, could be saved from their lives of vice. People were loath to believe that the structure of society was responsible for the evils they saw and that a collective response was needed to alleviate them. Established institutions had worked successfully in the past. Poverty and crime had always existed; private charity and the law had succeeded in preventing their spread. If there was more poverty and crime than before, the fault was believed by many to lie with individuals, not with the institutions of society. The nineteenth-century ideal dictated a return to the old, healthy, righteous way of life, which men were forsaking in their eagerness to find fortunes in towns. Women, likewise, were motivated by greed insofar as they were discontented with their work in the home. Their heads were turned with new fashions of life, and they were neglecting their true vocation. More emphasis had to be given to teaching proper behaviour and to inculcating the ideals of society. Previous generations had expounded the natural duties of women; they had only to perform them to achieve fulfillment.

While women in the middle and upper classes were devoting more time to homes and families, women of the labouring classes alone were forced to neglect them. Thus, reformers thought, if the hours of work were cut down, women in the factories would not have to neglect

entirely their homes and families, and young girls their domestic training. Industry must have its freedom, but this much interference was considered justifiable. Evening courses in domestic subjects were also encouraged so that girls who had spent all their adolescent lives in the factory would know how to run a home properly when they married. After the passing of the first Acts regulating factory hours, the number of women attending these courses increased.[18]

Reformers also worked to remove women from factories and mines completely, so that men would be able to resume work by filling jobs vacated by women. Men would be paid better wages, families would be properly cared for, and the 'natural order of society' would no longer be violated. The early factories, with their reliance on female and child labour, had threatened to undermine that order. Hence, the loud insistence on the sanctity of home for women and of work for men arose as much from fear of the consequences of change, of which Victorians had actual experience, as from the strength of their belief in the ideals themselves. According to social reformers, the factory owners threatened social, economic, and political stability:

> You are poisoning the very sources of order and happiness and virtue; you are tearing up root and branch, all the relations of families to each other; you are annulling, as it were, the institution of domestic life, decreed by Providence himself, the wisest and kindest of earthly ordinances, the mainstay of social peace and virtue, and therein of national security.[19]

In the struggle to remove women, especially married women, from factories, the life middle-class women spent at home was held up as an example for the labouring classes to emulate. Devotees of the middle-class ideal for women wished to extend it to the whole of society. They encouraged women of the middle classes to become aware of the need to set an example to the labouring classes by remaining in the home, and by undertaking charity work. Example could change society; working women had to be shown how important it was for society that they should follow the example of middle and upper-class women.

In this view of society, economic welfare demanded that, as soon as possible, women be replaced by men in all work outside the home. Although it was believed that wages could increase only at the expense of profits, factory owners were felt to be enjoying unfair advantage by employing women at wages below subsistence level. It was only fair that men, who were known to have families to support, should be the

wage earners. This belief found expression also in the view that the development of a civilisation could be measured by the status of women within it: 'Man, in European communities, has deliberately adopted the view that, as much as possible, women should be relieved from the necessity of self-support. The measure of civilization is the maximum at which this end is attained in any given community or nation. Women labourers are a proof of a barbarous and imperfect civilization.'[20]

The attitudes expressed above were applied to families of the middle classes as well as to labourers' families. Those who opposed higher education for women in the years after 1850 believed that higher education would encourage women to press for entry into the professions and skilled occupations. Their presence there could lead only to employers driving down salaries, men being ousted from jobs, and women neglecting their homes, husbands and children. Opponents of higher education wanted to prevent further disintegration of society, which they felt was being caused by the break up of the family. Society's health demanded that women find their fulfillment in the home, not behind a doctor's desk or a draper's counter.

Competition

Reforms to alleviate the plight of women factory workers were backed by working men as well as by middle-class reformers, but for less altruistic reasons: they wanted to reduce the number of women working in the hope that men would be employed in their place. For too long, skilled men had been forced out of work, while unskilled women and children took their places at new jobs in the factories, employed in bad conditions for very low wages. It was argued that employers would not better working conditions as long as a supply of cheap labour was available. There was no reason to employ men when women were willing to do the same work for lower wages.[21] The interests of working men and middle-class reformers coincided on this issue.

For the middle classes, the idea of women working outside the home was particularly distasteful because it entailed women taking jobs away from men, and women competing with men in the world of business. It was feared that the demands made on behalf of some women of the middle classes who failed in their 'duty' to marry and tried to find jobs to support themselves financially, would unbalance

the economy of the country. Thus, for the sake of a few women, men would be expected to accept competition for jobs which were the life-blood of countless families.

It would be just as reasonable to demand that every boy should be taught two or three professions because he may fail in one, as it is to argue that all our social habits should be changed because one woman in fifty—or whatever the statistics are—is a spinster or widow without resources.[22]

By the 1850s the number of gentlewomen who needed to earn their own living had risen to several hundred thousand. Most were eking out meagre existences as needlewomen, governesses or companions.[23] The plight of these women had already attracted attention, and after 1850 attempts were made to find new fields of work for women of the middle classes. However, demands that they should be better educated, perhaps even at a university, and encouraged to train for well-paid jobs, even those that demanded professional training, were opposed by men who feared the effect of such changes on the British economy.

Those who opposed higher education for women found the challenge of competition from women profoundly disturbing. They did not wish to contemplate its effects, and yet the danger of it occurring came closer to realisation as the years passed. In 1856, Jessie Meriton White had the audacity to petition the University of London for permission to enrol for a medical degree. She was refused, but in the 1860s her example was followed by Elizabeth Garrett who later applied also to the Universities of Edinburgh and St. Andrews. Garrett's persistence led, eventually, to her receiving medical training, and being licensed to practise medicine by the Society of Apothecaries.[24] These actions reinforced the belief that a university education would be only a first step towards women entering the professions. So strong was the distaste of some people to the idea of women becoming professionals that even when colleges for women began to be founded few parents wanted to allow their daughters to go there. One father tried to stop his daughter by offering her a new pony instead.[25] She did not accept the offer, but later, as Principal of Westfield College, London, she still found parents unable to comprehend the value of higher education for their daughters. 'But, tell me, what is the *use*? If you could be a clergyman, now!—or a lawyer, or if it was for training missionaries it would be different. But that great effort, all that expense, all that absence from home, and

whatever is *gained* by it?' parents asked.[26]

Opposition to middle-class women entering professions and skilled occupations had many of the same roots as opposition to women working in factories. The number of jobs available was thought to be fixed, and subject to very little fluctuation. Women could gain employment only at the expense of men. Each woman in the labour market cut off the source of livelihood for one man who was, or would be in the future, responsible for the support of his family.[27] For the sake of employing a few single women, then, at a higher standard than had been possible in the past, the well-being of countless families was to be jeopardised.

This argument was reinforced by evidence that because of pressure on employment men already were leaving the country in thousands to seek employment in the colonies.[28] How could single women expect to find jobs if men who were already entitled to them could not? Worse still, if women did succeed in ousting men from jobs the effect would be more disastrous than unemployment, because more men would be driven from England to the colonies. Already some women were unable to find husbands because so many men were emigrating. If women took jobs away from men, more men would be forced to go abroad to find work, which would leave a new crop of spinsters to support themselves. 'The very act of thrusting men out of employment would be the way to send them in greater numbers to the colonies, or to distant quarters of the world, thus creating a still greater disproportion in our female population at home.'[29]

It was feared, also, that the wage structure would suffer if more women worked. As Emily Pfeiffer commented in the 1880s, it was this fear that generated the deepest opposition to women:

> It must be allowed that the real tug of war, the utmost bitterness of invective, begins only with the cheapening of the market. As might be predicted, this inimical feeling is deepest, if more restrained in expression, in those higher intellectual spheres where there is most to lose or gain; but every calling upon which the pressure of bitter need has forced an entrance to women has found irate and powerful defenders.[30]

Women, it was argued, were under a misapprehension if they thought that they could increase their wages by entering new fields of work. If women entered the labour market in large numbers there would be a huge surplus of workers and, as a result, wages would fall. Those who

agitated for new jobs to be opened to women forgot 'that profitable employment is a fixed quantity which will cease to be profitable if divided up among 75% of additional labourers.'[31]

The suggestion, made by Barbara Leigh Smith who was working to open new occupations to women, that 10,000 women should be apprenticed to watchmakers, another 10,000 trained as teachers, and another 10,000 trained as accountants was thought ridiculous, because if there were that number of watchmakers' apprentices wages would be depressed below those of governesses.[32] As far as teaching was concerned, one reason why governesses were paid so little was that there were so many women ostensibly qualified for the job. How could more women be absorbed into the teaching profession?[33] Even women themselves were baffled by the dilemma of how they were to find employment. As Charlotte Brontë wrote to a friend:

It is true enough that the present market for female labour is quite overstocked, but where or how could another be opened? Many say that the professions now filled only by men should be open to women also; but are not their present occupants and candidates more than numerous enough to answer every demand? Is there any room for female lawyers, female doctors, female engravers, for more female artists, more authoresses? One can see where the evil lies, but who can point out the remedy?[34]

Women were prepared to work for lower wages than men because they seldom had families to support. Whenever women entered a trade or profession, wages were bound to be adversely affected. The man was much mistaken who argued:

'Wherever we have a pound of work to be done, and a hundred-weight of women anxious to do it, the balance can only be adjusted by opening fresh fields of labour, by which we draw off and employ the excess. In this mighty maze of London there are scores of occupations that could be immediately thrown open to female skill but for the obstinate prejudice of both masters and men.'[35]

The author was a watchmaker, concerned at the success of Swiss manufacturers in claiming the market for their products, and he knew as well as anyone else that they were able to do this by producing cheap watches with female labour! If women were used in watchmaking, or in any other skilled trade in England, they also would be paid less than

men for the same job, and many men would be thrown out of work. Neither the masters, who doubted the skill of women for the job, nor the men, who saw their livelihoods threatened, were as obstinately prejudiced as the writer claimed; they were merely following common sense.

Since wages went down as soon as women were employed in a trade, men would find their positions jeopardised whenever women competed with them. It might be that lower wages were 'the act of man, not of God, and can therefore be altered',[36] but no employer would raise wages when women were available who would work for less than men. Women were a reasonable source of labour so long as they were cheap, for then even their lack of skill could be compensated for without a loss of profit. When women began to demand equal pay for equal work they would find that employers would cease to employ them, for men were more efficient and reliable.[37]

Overall, the competition of women in the labour market was thought to be grossly unfair. With the blessing of employers who saw it as a way to reduce wages and increase profits, women had usurped the place of men in factories; there was no doubt, in the minds of those who wished to maintain the status quo, that, if allowed, women would usurp the place of men in skilled trades and professions. Salaries would drop in any occupation women were permitted to enter. The mere presence of women would cause loss of status for an occupation. This could prove disastrous because many occupations had only recently attained their full professional stature; their regulations had been newly drafted to discourage amateurs from claiming membership. Women, with their dilettante interests and their lack of formal training, could hardly expect their applications to be considered seriously. If, as the proponents of women's ambitions were suggesting, women were allowed to train and qualify for the professions, a number of intelligent young men, who otherwise would qualify for such jobs, would be thwarted in their ambitions. Higher education, whether at a university or outside it, aimed to prepare young men for their future work; women's work was different from men's, and women needed a different preparation. Even if there were a few women capable of becoming lawyers, doctors, or clergymen, they should not be encouraged to do so. Aside from the fact that their interest in a profession would be shortlived, vanishing when they married, they would find no clients, patients or parishioners. Who would want to rely on a female attorney, a female doctor, or a female clergyman? 'We are afraid the clerical line is closed to the ladies. We do not see

where the congregation would come from. Men would scarcely like to be taught theology by women.'[38]

If women became more reasonable in their demands, perhaps men might become less eager to leave the country for the colonies. If fewer women worked, there would be more work in England for men to do. According to the people who opposed them, those who advocated the extension of women's education and women's occupations were making the wrong analysis of the way to treat existing difficulties. The way to do that was not to try to induce more women to work, but to *reduce* the numbers of women working, and to legislate better conditions for those women who were compelled to work.

The sight of men struggling to maintain jobs against the 'unfair' competition of women, whose wages were lower, and whose demands on the employers were fewer, was hateful to the nineteenth-century defenders of the ideal of womanhood. Industrial towns seemed full of men who had no work to do, who idled away their lives while their womenfolk worked. This was no picture to present to society as the model for the future. Professional men had to struggle in their careers; they knew the trauma of competing for jobs with their male friends. That they should compete also with women was inconceivable. Women were respected precisely because they were not men's rivals. The labour market could not expand to absorb an influx of women into the professions. One could imagine the misery that would arise from the replacement of men by women; fathers and sons would be without work, with no means of earning a livelihood. This was no solution to the problems facing women. They had to return to their proper sphere of life, the home, and leave the business and professional world to men.

These attitudes towards competition between the sexes, embedded as they were in theories of the economy, explain the Victorian belief in the need for men and women to function in separate spheres. Separated, men and women would not compete, and thus mutual respect would flourish. If some women had to work, they should take jobs expressly designed for women; they should not step outside their sphere and apply for jobs designed for men.

Implications of Class

Middle-class beliefs in the purity of women, the need for their protection and the rightful division of labour between the sexes were

challenged by the pattern of life of the labouring classes. The middle classes, therefore, exerted their influence to change the mores of the labouring classes to match their own. Their interpretation of the ideal of womanhood called for all women to refrain from work, where that was financially possible. If, while they were single, women had to support themselves, they would surely withdraw from the labour market once married. The ideal, however, was for women, especially those of the upper and middle classes, to shun employment. To people supporting this ideal, it was incongruous for those whom society considered ladies to think of working at all, whether as watchmakers, attorneys, or clergymen. How could they earn money and still remain ladies?

> As society is at present constituted, a lady may do almost anything from motives of charity or zeal. . . But so soon as a woman begins to receive money. . . so soon as she makes money by her own efforts. ˙. she is transformed into a tradeswoman, and she must find her place in society as such.[39]

There were many jobs that might be done by way of charity, and as the century wore on these increased to include prison visiting, Sunday School teaching, workhouse inspection, and the reclamation of prostitutes.[40] Women were not expected to accept remuneration for such work, because men of the middle classes took financial provision for their female relatives as a duty. Their success in fulfilling this duty was a sign of their success in life. As one rebellious Victorian daughter commented in retrospect: 'Papa, as a true Victorian gentleman, felt it was rather a slur on him that a lady of the family should go out to work; ladies should live on an adequate income supplied by father, husband or son.'[41]

No one doubted that the various classes in society had different functions to perform. For the performance of these functions they needed different kinds of education. Few people of the middle classes saw any incongruity in advocating the teaching of domestic subjects to daughters of the poor, while encouraging the exclusion of domestic subjects in favour of French, German or music for their own daughters. The lives of the two groups as adults would be so different that they needed different kinds of education. The wife of a labourer was not expected to perform the same duties as the wife of a factory owner.

Yet, some people seemed to be suggesting that the pattern of life of

the labouring classes should be copied by the rest of society: 'We all know that factory-girls make the worst wives; and if the ideal of the advocates of women's work were carried out, all classes of society would but repeat, under modifications, the type of a factory wife.'[42] Those advocating that more women should work outside the home seemed unaware of the hardship this would cause to others. Advocates were encouraging women in the higher ranks of society to work, when by doing so they would be depriving the needy of their livelihood. It was unfair of any woman with private means to take work from those women who had no other way to support themselves. 'A lady, to be such, must be a mere lady, and nothing else. She must not work for profit, or engage in any occupation that money can command, lest she invade the rights of the working classes, who live by their labour.'[43]

According to these arguments, women who needed work were able to find it; the census figures showed just how many women were employed. Why was it necessary to open other jobs to them? It was hinted that no 'respectable' woman need fear that she would ever have to work, since her male relatives would provide for her. However, some middle-class women were being persuaded that it was in some way ignoble to accept money earned by a male relative. The movement encouraging women to work, prompted by such writings as those in the *Englishwoman's Journal*, had far wider aims than its promoters claimed.[44] It threatened to create a disastrous independence of spirit in young women. The movement was not only concerned with relieving the distress of women who had to work: 'It has a much wider tendency, or at any rate a wider desire. The idea is that women will ennoble themselves by making themselves independent, by working for their own bread instead of eating bread earned by men.'[45] Such an attitude was considered not only dangerous socially, but economically nonsensical, since large numbers of women thrown into the labour market would glut it. The demands for higher education for women were obvious attempts to prepare women to enter the skilled occupations. Already professional bodies were faced with men who failed to qualify and therefore had to accept positions less lucrative and socially less well regarded by society. If women were to enter the competition, the number of men unable to enter the occupations they wanted would increase.

If the ideal of womanhood could be made a reality for all women, they would be protected from the anxieties of business life. They would cherish and comfort the children while their husbands would take on themselves entirely their allotted burden of providing finan-

cially for the family. When the ideal seemed so close to realisation it was unbelievable that women should be dissatisfied. Yet, some claimed that they were:

> Humanity and chivalry have succeeded after a long struggle in teaching the man to work for the woman; and now the woman rebels against such teaching, — not because she likes the work, but because she desires the influence which attends it. But. . . I wrong the woman. . . it is not she who desires it, but her philanthropical philosophical friends who desire it for her.[46]

It was believed that the misery of the labouring classes was caused by women neglecting their rightful jobs and usurping those of men. Reformers struggled to make it possible for labouring women to return to the home. However, while the mill wife was returning to her proper sphere, advocates of women's right to earn a living were arguing that the pattern of life followed by the labouring classes should be adopted by members of the middle classes. That argument had to be countered:

> How is the house to be managed, and the children cared for, if the wife is to be encouraged in the notion that it is her business to earn either her separate income, or to contribute to the common stock? Is that type of domestic life which the factory wife exhibits to be the rule in the English middle class society?[47]

Here, indeed, was a curious inversion of the way the world should work. Men, whose upbringing should have taught them better, were advocating, on behalf of women, a change that would destroy the work of generations and bring the society they knew toppling about their ears. Just as the ideal society came in sight, it was being undermined by malcontents. In Victorian England, more women than ever before had been relieved of the burden of work. Theirs was a life of comparative ease and contentment. Naturally they had periods of distress: no family could exist without them, and since women were human they had to expect their share of hardships. But how preferable were their troubles to those of men! Women were troubled to know what to do with their time, but men worked so hard that they had no time for their own pursuits. Women complained that they had little knowledge of the world, but men had too much. Women of the middle classes had to learn to appreciate their preferred position in the

British economy and within the family structure; factory women had
to be taught to desire the middle-class ideal for women. This was the
way to prevent a breakdown of society and preserve the purity and
innocence of womankind.

In Chapter 7 we discuss the economic realities of nineteenth-
century England, and show how the middle-class ideal of womanhood
proved unworkable. However, in this chapter the interpretation of
economic events by defenders of the ideal has been described. As more
middle-class women found it necessary to work while they were single,
the opponents of higher education for women and defenders of the
ideal of womanhood truly feared for the economic stability of the
country; they resented the growing loss of male labour and secure
professional status. The arguments just presented manifest this
increasing concern. We now turn to the case against higher education
for women based on beliefs concerning women's intellectual capacity.

Notes

1.   John Ruskin, *Sesame and Lilies* (London, 1865), p. 161.

2.   Parliamentary Papers. *Schools Inquiry Commission. Minutes of Evidence.*
(1867-68,) 28, part 4, p. 239

3.   Sarah Ellis, *Education of the Heart* (London, 1869), p. 15.

4.   Anthony Trollope, *North America* (London, 1862), Vol. 1, p. 403.

5.   'Queen Bees or Working Bees?', *Saturday Review* 8 (1859) p. 576.

6.   Patricia A. Graham, 'Expansion and Exclusion: A History of Women in
American Higher Education', *Signs: Journal of Women in Culture and Society* 3, no. 4
(Summer 1978) pp. 759-73.

7.   W. B. Hodgson, *The Education of Girls; and the Employment of Women of the
Upper Classes Educationally Considered* (London, 1869), pp. 3-5.

8.   Raymond Williams, *The Long Revolution* (New York, 1966), pp. 140-4.

9.   Joshua G. Fitch as quoted by Maria Grey, *On the Education of Women*
(London, 1871), p. 19.

10.   Grey, *Education of Women*, pp. 24-5.

11.   'Mr. Lowe on Universities', *Saturday Review* 43 (1877), pp. 135-6.

12.   'Women at the Universities', *Saturday Review* 43 (1877, pp. 660-1.

13.   F. Musgrove, 'Middle-Class Education and Employment in the Nineteenth
Century', *Economic History Review*, 2nd series, 12 (1959-60), pp. 99-111; Geoffrey
Millerson, *The Qualifying Associations: A Study in Professionalization* (London, 1964).

14.   [John Duguid Milne], *Industrial and Social Position of Women, in the Middle
and Lower Ranks* (London, 1857), pp. 19-29.

15.   [Milne], *Position of Women*, pp. 168-223. The total numbers of men and
women employed in Great Britain from 1835 to 1850 are given by Wanda F. Neff,
Victorian Working Women (London, 1929), p. 26.

16.   Louise A. Tilly and Joan W. Scott, *Women, Work and Family* (New York,
1978), p. 64.

17.   Peter Gaskell, *Manufacturing Population of England* (London, 1833), pp.
166-7.

18.   Neff, *Victorian Working Women*, pp. 64-76, surveys the effects of legislation on the lives of women textile workers.

19.   Lord Ashley, *House of Commons Debates* 73 (1844), col. 1100.

20.   'Queen Bees or Working Bees?', *Saturday Review* 8 p. 576.

21.   Neff, *Victorian Working Women*, Chapter 2; Lord Ashley, *House of Commons Debates* 73 (1844), cols. 1095-9. In the 1830s a cotton mill near Manchester paid average weekly wages of 18s. 6d. for men, 10s. 2d. for women, and 5s. for girls; only 19% of the employees were grown men. (J. P. Kay-Shuttleworth, *Four Periods of Public Education* [London, 1862], p. 131.)

22.   'Queen Bees or Working Bees?', *Saturday Review* 8 p. 576.

23.   [Milne], *Position of Women*, pp. 128-34, 174, 182. The 1851 census lists:
Teachers, Authors, Artists....................64,336
Annuitants 121,220
The latter figure would have included retired governesses and companions. The total number of women engaged in the needle trades was 388,302. This figure grouped together a multitude of jobs including slop-workers, some of the most degraded workers in the community. However, there were some women of genteel background who earned their livelihood as dressmakers and milliners: 'It is not women of the most indigent class alone who become dressmakers and milliners. . . the class from which they are drawn verges closely on what is called the educated one, dressmaking being a species of skilled labour, requiring some little capital of time and money to start with.' ("The Dressmaker's Life," *Englishwoman's Journal* 1 (1858) p. 319.)

24.   Most of the correspondence relating to Jessie Meriton White's attempt to gain admission to the University of London was published as an appendix to Barbara Leigh Smith, *Women and Work* (London, 1857). Details of Elizabeth Garrett's attempts are in Jo Manton, *Elizabeth Garrett Anderson* (London, 1965).

25.   C. B. Firth, *Constance Louisa Maynard* (London, 1949), pp. 102-3.

26.   Constance L. Maynard, 'Autobiography' (MS, Westfield College, London, 1915), p. 337.

27.   Frederic Harrison, quoted in a letter from Josephine Butler to Harrison, 9 May, 1868, Josephine Butler Collection, Fawcett Library, London.

28.   J. A. Banks and Olive Banks, *Feminism and Family Planning* (Liverpool, 1964), pp. 28-9.

29.   Sarah Ellis, *Education of the Heart* (London, 1869), p. 15.

30.   Emily Pfeiffer, *Women and Work* (London, 1888), p. 35.

31.   'The Englishwoman's Journal', *Saturday Review* 5 (1858), p. 369.

32.   Leigh Smith, *Women and Work*, pp. 16-17. Leigh Smith's argument is criticized in: 'Industrial Occupations of Women', *Saturday Review* 4 (1857), p. 63.

33.   'Industrial Occupations of Women', *Saturday Review* 4 p. 64.

34.   Charlotte Brontë to William S. Williams, 12 May 1848, as quoted by Clement Shorter, *The Brontës and Their Circle* (London, 1914), p. 352.

35.   John Bennett, 16 April 1858, letter published in the *Standard*, 19 April 1858, as quoted in 'Watchwork versus Slopwork', *Englishwoman's Journal* 1 (1858) p. 282.

36.   Josephine Butler to Frederic Harrison, 9 May 1868, letter in Josephine Butler Collection, Fawcett Library, London.

37.   In 1833, at a mill in Scotland, men spinners harassed the women who had replaced them at lower wages until the management raised the women's wages to equal men's. The men apparently expected to be rehired once wages were equalised, but in this case the management spited them and kept the women on at men's wages. (See Parliamentary Papers, 20, (1833), pp. 84-5.)

38.   'Industrial Occupations of Women', *Saturday Review* 4, pp. 63-4.

39.   Ellis, *Education of the Heart*, p. 14.

40.   Patricia Thomson, *The Victorian Heroine, a Changing Ideal. 1837-1875.* (London, 1956), Chapter 1, details the charitable work carried out by women.

41.   Margaret Murray, *My First Hundred Years* (London, 1963), p. 79.

42. 'Englishwoman's Journal', *Saturday Review* 5, p. 370.

43. Margaretta Grey, Diary for 1853, as quoted by Josephine Butler, *Memoir of John Grey of Dilston* (Edinburgh, 1869), p. 326n. Sophia Jex-Blake's father begged her not to accept a salary when she became a tutor of mathematics at Queen's College, because if she did so she 'would be considered mean and illiberal. . . accepting wages that belong to a class beneath you in social rank.' (Margaret G. Todd, *Life of Sophia Jex-Blake* [London, 1918], p. 68.)

44. 'On the Adoption of Professional Life by Women', *Englishwoman's Journal* 2 (1858), pp. 1-10. Other relevant articles appear in Volume 1 (1858) of this periodical.

45. Trollope, *North America*, Vol. 1., p. 405.

46. *Ibid.*

47. 'Caius and Caia', *Saturday Review* 4 (1857), p. 56.

4 | *Woman's Intellectual Capacity*

Differences between the intellectual characteristics of men and women were constantly discussed during the nineteenth century. Women seemed insightful and sensitive, but without the ability to concentrate or weigh evidence in making judgements. Men seemed to be more ponderous, measured, and careful; they could sustain arguments and develop new ideas. Whether these attributes were inherent or acquired became hotly debated as demands by women for higher education grew.

At first, writers described but did not try to explain the reasons for the intellectual characteristics of men and women. They assumed that readers shared their social experiences and therefore accepted the differences between the sexes. However, some people did not believe that all women shared the same intellectual characteristics, any more than all men did, and they attributed many differences between the sexes to women's lack of education and the narrowness of their lives. They challenged the inevitability of women's intellectual subordination to men. Once they did so, they met opposition from those who claimed that the intellectual differences between the sexes were innate, and that they applied to each man and each woman as a member of a discrete scientific class. According to this argument, those who differed from the characteristics of their sex had to be considered as aberrations from the norm, not prototypes for social change. The lines of the debate were drawn, and the literature began to abound with arguments on the causes for the intellectual differences between the sexes. Each side used scientific evidence to support its position on a social issue—whether women should be entitled to higher education.

We turn first to nineteenth-century descriptions of the intellectual characteristics of men and women.

Intellectual Characteristics

Men and women had different thought processes, it was argued.

Women had greater intuitive power than men, hence, while men reached their conclusions by careful analysis, women flew to theirs and would only reluctantly consider how they had reached them. According to *The Lancet*, women's intellect was deductive in character, men's inductive. The two types of intellect were constructed for different purposes. To employ the two sexes in the same jobs would be to use delicate instruments designed for rapid action to perform tasks that needed cumbrous machines of great power.[1]

Men, who were strong and powerful, were capable of long, earnest thought; women were not. Lack of depth, which flightiness of thought implied, made women naturally inferior to men. Their inferiority had implications for social policy which were pointed out early in the century, before the movement for women's suffrage had gathered momentum: Women did not have the physical or moral resources needed for statesmanship; their very nature forbade their interfering in politics.[2]

These sentiments were expressed by women writers as well as men. Elizabeth Barrett confided the following to Robert Browning:

> There *is* a natural inferiority of mind in women — of the intellect
> . . . not by any means of the moral nature — and that the history of
> Art and of genius testifies to this fact openly. . . I believe women
> . . . all of us in a mass. . . to have minds of quicker movement, but
> less power and depth. . . and that we are under your feet, because
> we can't stand upon our own.[3]

Few people in the first decades of the nineteenth century challenged this analysis. Even supporters of improved education for women seldom questioned what could so easily be verified by observation; they felt that women should be encouraged to study more subjects, but that no amount of study would make it possible for women to compete seriously with men. As late as 1873 Sir Stafford Northcote, while speaking in support of the founding of the Girls' Public Day School Company, commented that the two sexes had different types of intellectual skills: women were quick to catch a point, adept at picking out details, and applied themselves with grace to whatever they did. On the other hand, they were undoubtedly inferior to men in their stamina for study and their power of reasoning.[4]

Despite Elizabeth Barrett's claim that women's inferiority of mind

was 'not by any means of the moral nature' some authors were sure that all women, like Eve, had a tendency to err. This defect could be remedied only by an education designed to spell out for women their path of duty, lest they fall prey to the temptations towards which their nature led them.[5] Women's inability to disentangle their passions from their reasoning, their emotions from their judgment, was a source of constant anxiety to men it was claimed. Only with outside help from religion and from men who cared for them could women develop self-control. 'They do not calculate consequences, and they are reckless when they once give way; hence they are to be kept straight only through their affections, the religious sentiment, and a well-educated moral sense.'[6]

Given their 'natural tendency' to lack self-control, women could fulfill the moral duties defined for them by the ideal of womanhood only after an education designed specially for them. They had to spend more time than men developing moral sentiments, not only for themselves but that they might fulfill their duty of dispensing moral values to the next generation. 'There is no question that affection, and the moral qualities generally, form the best part of a woman's character. To stint these for the sake of her intellectual development, which will never be worth the sacrifice, is to create a monster, and a foolish one.'[7]

Women's powers of intuition were thought to be superior to men's, although this was of dubious value since intuition was no substitute for rational thought when it came to decision-making. However, since women's intuition could at times help men, and certainly added to women's charm, it had to be preserved from the encroachment of reasoning. Women's superiority to men in intuition was used by at least one woman to justify her inferiority in status. Women's minds, she claimed, supplied like poets' with 'the higher reason' of intuition, could sweep towards truth without hindrance.[8] Though women might appear to defer to men in matters of authority, the power remained theirs.

> They who are most truly women are naturally most conscious of this power; and such are, for the most part, like wise courtiers, content to hide the appearance of power behind its reality, and make little outcry for more privileges for their sex. Such women deal with men much as they do with spoiled children, and let them have their way, while all the time securing their own.[9]

This argument, used to rationalise women's subordination to men,

called for no change in the behaviours of men and women, only a change in their attitudes towards the significance of those behaviours. Yet even that change posed a threat to male dominance. Few men could subscribe to a picture of women's covert superiority; most men saw no reason to do so.

Women's superior intuition seemed to have no effect on their creativity. Men, not women, were the great creative artists of history. The world, it was claimed, had produced no female counterparts to Shakespeare, Mozart, or Raphael, although women writers were an accepted phenomenon in society, and most middle-class women were taught music and painting. Since it appeared that the opportunity for developing women's creativity was not lacking, the ability must be. Obviously there was a link, though it was not clear what it was, between the intellectual capacities of men and creativity. 'Imagination, memory, and quickness of perception are different things from power of sustained thought, judgement, and creativeness.'[10] The first group were the attributes of women and the latter of men. Women were thought to be unable to comprehend, let alone share, the creative powers of men. There was no point, there-fore, in making girls spend time on studying subjects boys did; girls' genius lay elsewhere, and they should be trained to perform their own duties with excellence.

This argument had two corollaries in relation to higher education for women. First, as education was costly and resources had to be carefully allocated, only those with the highest potential should receive extensive education. Since women had less potential than men, scarce resources should not be diverted to their education. Second, the higher one went up the educational ladder the less value was there in educating women since they were not capable of great creative work.

> The reasoning powers are more perfect in [man] than in [woman]. The creative powers belong almost exclusively to him. It has been justly said, that no woman ever succeeded in drawing the characters of men, because it was impossible for her ever completely to know or to realize the tempest of passions which sway the souls of an Othello or a Faust.[11]

Women's lack of creativity made it impossible for them, in any field, to do more than follow in men's footsteps. Their minds were not original, it was claimed; they were no more fitted to expound new scientific theories than men were to unravel the intricacies of

needlework. That needlework had its own forms of creativity did not occur to those who raised these arguments. Women, they argued, had the characteristics of faithful followers who paid meticulous attention to details. 'But they have not the grasp of intellect and the vigour and the boldness which make the great discoverer of the unknown.'[12]

Nevertheless, it had to be conceded that women excelled men in sensitivity, and sensitivity might be considered an essential ingredient of creativity. Why then should women have the one but not the other? Lack of stamina in women seemed to provide one answer. Women were delicate; they were incapable of sustained creative effort. 'The main characteristic difference between the two sexes I should infer to be this—the male has the most energy, the female the most sensitiveness; and this distinction will, I believe, be found to rule the leading operations affected by those of each sex.'[13] Any creative or intellectual effort required constitutional resources that most women did not possess. There was no doubt about this, for it was a physiological fact (see Chapter 5).

Moreover, those few women who did possess the necessary stamina were said to be abhorrent to men. They could hardly be considered well-developed specimens of womanhood: 'The logical, philosophical, scientific woman is not the ordinary type; she frequently—we say it with all delicacy, and yet truthfully—departs from it in her physical as well as in her mental characteristics.'[14] Social disapproval of intellectual attainment in women claimed to be based on sound physiological sense; it was not, as some maintained, a new manifestation of hostility to women. 'Bluestockings' had long been abhorred, and the scorn of society only served to protect eager girls from jeopardising their womanhood to the gratification of the moment.

> Though good health be one of the greatest blessings of life, never make a boast of it, but enjoy it in grateful silence. We so naturally associate the idea of female softness and delicacy with a correspondent delicacy of constitution, that when a woman speaks of her great strength, her extraordinary appetite, her ability to bear excessive fatigue, we recoil at the description in a way she is little aware of.[15]

Women were not praised for intellectual attainments since these often went hand in hand with physical abnormalities. For fear of being thought abnormal many women of intellectual distinction denied their connection with intellectual work, even while continuing it.[16]

This dissimulation was reprehensible but necessary if normal young women were to be protected from the physiological effects of prolonged study. Before the 1870s these effects were merely hinted at in general literature, ostensibly from a feeling that propriety would be outraged if they were revealed: 'The physiological results of over-developed brains must not be lost sight of; but passing to points more capable of public discussion. . .'[17] Victorian prudery was an effective barrier to any analysis of the physiological objections to higher education for women. These objections were made in literature, and hints were given that they were based on sound reasons, but the reasons themselves were never mentioned; the reader was expected to know them and understand that they were too delicate to be spoken of. Despite the vagueness of these references, the idea was established that intellectual differences between the sexes had a physiological foundation that could not be denied.

To those who believed that men and women had different missions in life, there could be no justification for interfering with a differentiation that was part of nature.

> We believe that to apply the same systems of education and training to both sexes alike, and to open the same paths for both, would be to act in defiance of natural laws, and to diminish the usefulness and lessen the moral and spiritual influence which women unquestionably exert.[18]

Thus, intellectual differences between the sexes were accepted, though there was no consensus on how they originated. Women's brains were considered inferior to men's because women's inferiority in both mental and physical pursuits was obvious. Women's dilettante interests, their frivolous natures, and lack of physical and mental accomplishments were observable facts. What seemed to be so, was so. Men and women were as different intellectually as they were physically and attempts to change this fact of life would lead only to social unhappiness and ill health.

'Scientific Proofs' of Women's Intellectual Inferiority

Stimulated by Charles Darwin's *The Origin of Species* (London, 1859),[19] discussion in the 1860s of women's position in society changed its ground and became centred on attempts to account for the differ-

ences between the sexes through the theory of evolution. Comparative anatomists made detailed studies of the brains of men and women, studies which anthropologists and general writers used to elaborate their evolutionary interpretation. This suggested that men and women had evolved at different rates and in different ways, and that the higher the degree of civilisation, the greater were the differences between the sexes. A society organised its division of labour according to the characteristics of its men and women. Thus, 'the lower we go among savage tribes, the less of this diversity there would seem to be; so that it appears to be a direct retrogression to assimilate the work of the highly-developed woman to that of her mate; and if perfection is to be the aim of our efforts, it will be best advanced by further divergence of male and female characteristics.'[20]

Anthropologists, who themselves had discovered primitive societies in which men and women were still in the earlier stages of development, thought it doubtful that women had ever been men's equal, for had this been so there should have evolved on earth as many societies in which women predominated over men as there were those in which men predominated over women. Few, if any, such societies existed.

> I look around to the varying conditions of all parts of the world, and in no race, nor country, nor tribe, nor remote island, excepting one of doubtful authenticity, do I find an instance of woman having the upper hand, and reducing all the males to subjection. Now, if man and woman were born equal, out of every hundred of these remote races and peoples in islands and localities apart from each other you would find fifty races where the women had subjected the men, and fifty where the men had subjected the women.[21]

In primitive societies men and women often performed the same kinds of work; women were expected in some societies to do all the heavy carrying and even to continue their work while pregnant.[22] The natural delicacy of women was not appreciated, and they were little better treated than beasts of burden. Only gradually had civilisation differentiated the life and work of men and women over countless generations until, in nineteenth-century England, women were protected from the evils of the world and accorded the dignity their physique demanded. The change was not one of social organisation alone, for men and women during thousands of years had reacted differently to their instincts for self-preservation and propagation of the species, so that their responses now were as unlike as their roles in

society. These were the reasons why women needed a different education from men. Those who advocated that both sexes should receive the same education would have 'to undo the life-history of mankind' to achieve their ends.[23]

To reply that in England middle and upper-class women only were sufficiently protected, that factory women and domestic servants enjoyed no special consideration, was not to refute this argument.[24] The plight of the lower classes merely provided evidence that even the highest civilisation had far to go before all women were accorded their rightful treatment. It was hoped that in the future no women need do heavy work.

There was probably a 'natural law' which governed the way the mental structures of the two sexes had evolved, since it was 'universal throughout the human race, and still more because it was a good not an evil. Woman excelled in the faculties most useful to her, as man excelled in the faculties most required by him.'[25]

Evidence of the working of this 'law' could be found in anatomical studies of the human brain published during the 1860s. Evolution had stimulated interest in comparative anatomy, and attempts were made to find ways of measuring the growth of man's intelligence. Before any progress could be made in this work, some criteria had to be established for interpreting the data. Cranial measurement, or craniometry, as practiced by Adolphe Quetelet in Belgium, became widely discussed and practised. Gradually, a general agreement was reached on the most satisfactory lines and angles to use, and craniometry became an accepted way to define the differences in skull structure between various animals on the one hand, and between animals and human beings on the other. Anatomists then extended its use to describing the differences among human beings themselves. As well as measuring the skull, they calculated the volume of the brain by filling the cranial cavity with lead shot or Calais sand, deducting that fraction of the volume that in living organisms would be filled by tissue other than the brain.

Various other means of weighing and measuring skulls were devised, using skulls found in ancient burial sites and in Africa and India from peoples considered less civilised than Europeans.[26] European skulls were also analysed and identified by nationality. (*e.g.,* Irish, Scottish, English, German, and French). The number of skulls weighed was small, and the reasons they had been collected sometimes had no connection with the purpose for which they were being used.[27] However, although the anatomists themselves were

cautious in drawing conclusions from their studies, some anthropologists inferred from these experiments that intelligence was
directly proportional to the size and weight of the brain. From the
available cranial data they concluded that the highly civilised
European had evolved further from the ape than any other group of
humankind, and that the European man had evolved much further
from the ape than the European woman. The brains of men and
women varied sufficiently in respect to size and structure to suggest
that women were innately less intelligent than men. The male brain
was heavier than the female, both overall and in each of its parts; in
Europeans, the female brain averaged from five to six ounces less than
the male.[28] Other differences between the brains of men and women
showed that women's brains were more childlike in character and less
developed. The female skull was 'less tilted back on the condyles'[29] and
the average height of the female cranium was less than that of the
male.[30] Apparently women were being left far behind in the process of
evolution, since

> The difference between the sexes as regards the cranial cavity
> increases with the development of the race, so that the male
> European excels more the female than does the negro the negress;
> and hence, with the progress of civilization, the men are in advance
> of the women, so that the inequality of the sexes increases with
> civilization.[31]

These conclusions, of course, depended on the assumption that
anatomical descriptions of the skull and brain provided the key to
determining intelligence. A small skull (and, therefore, a small brain)
was assumed to show less intelligence than a large one, just as a child
was less intelligent than an adult. Idiocy could be diagnosed by cranial
formation were it not apparent without the diagnosis. The weights of
certain well-known persons' brains had been calculated after their
deaths and could be used to demonstrate these 'facts': 'Cuvier's brain
weighed rather more then 64 oz., that of the late Dr. Abercrombie 63
oz., and that of Dupuytren 62½ oz. On the other hand, the brain of an
idiot seldom weighs more than 23 oz.'[32]

With the translation into English of Carl Vogt's *Lectures on Man*
(James Hunt (ed.), [London, 1864]), the work of craniologists on the
Continent became widely known in England. The relevance of these
data to the general discussion of intellectual differences between the
sexes was suggested by John Stuart Mill. He rejected a direct relation-

ship between brain size and intelligence as being too simplistic. Were that the case, he wrote, 'A tall and large-boned man must be wonderfully superior in intelligence to a small man, and an elephant or a whale must prodigiously excel mankind.'[33] However, Mill did see the evidence of men's brains being larger than women's as providing support for the analogy of men's brains to powerful machines. Women, he suspected, had greater cerebral circulation than men.

> The results which conjecture, founded on analogy, would lead us to expect from this difference of organization, would correspond to some of those which we most commonly see. In the first place, the mental operations of men might be expected to be slower. They would neither be so prompt as women in thinking, nor so quick to feel. Large bodies take more time to get into full action. On the other hand, when once got thoroughly into play, men's brains would bear more work.[34]

The work of anatomists suggested that the intelligence of a human being depended upon the number of convolutions of the brain as well as upon its overall size, and there was some evidence that mental exertion could help to increase the number of convolutions.[35] If this were so, there was a question as to how far the differences between the sexes were the result of external social conditions (which could be changed), and how far they were innate. Although it could be argued that social conditions had helped to bring about the differences between the sexes, there was no reason to believe that a development that had already taken place could be reversed merely by altering those social conditions. Were that possible, however, it was argued that it would be highly undesirable to reverse the process of evolution merely to lessen differences between the sexes! Society had been well served by the process of sexual selection, which had always tended to strengthen mentally the males but not the females. Women had always been selected as mates on the basis of physical beauty not mental ability.

> In the struggle for the possession of the female, other things being equal, the man with the larger brain has the advantage. He must possess mental capacity of some sort to arrive at any position in the tribe or city, and without the possession of this position he has little chance of selecting his companion from the women held in the greatest esteem and highest estimation. . . Woman becomes

sought after for her beauty, as the varying standard of which may happen to be. . . . It appears that our standard of female beauty consists, amongst other qualifications, of a more or less perpendicular forehead, the result of a predominance of the cranial roof over the cranial base. In men we do not consider this the highest form of skull.[36]

To maintain the physical beauty of women, men had devised ways to prevent women having to cope with the vicissitudes of life. Necessity had forced men to develop intellectually so that women could be protected. This was thought to be part of the process of civilisation. At the same time it was claimed that differentiation of roles had brought enormous benefits to human society. Just as rabbits in the wild needed faculties that atrophied once they were domesticated, so women in barbarous societies needed faculties akin to men's that they lost as civilisation matured.[37] Yet, civilised women enjoyed benefits that far outweighed any losses they might have suffered over the centuries. Was there a woman in England now who would exchange her life for that of a Hottentot? Of course not. However close the mental capacities of men and women in primitive societies might be, there was no reason for European women to envy the lot of primitive women.

In sum, these interpretations of anthropological and anatomical studies attempted to show that in civilised society women could never expect to compete intellectually with men. Women should not be encouraged to believe that higher education could ever be of value to them, for their brains were less developed than men's. Nor was the difference between the brains of men and women the only reason that competition was impossible. Mental fatigue reflected adversely on the physical well-being of women, and there was a danger that too much education might make women incapable of producing children. No society could survive in which women had lost their true function in life — to reproduce the species. According to the *Saturday Review* the danger was so great that: 'The agitation for women's so-called emancipation should be strenuously resisted, lest we come to see such reversal of women's right action, as shall leave us, to quote eloquent words, a population of "unattached individuals, the fine dust of a social desert, incapable of being built into anything, and the prey of whirlwinds." '[38]

As mentioned earlier, the idea that mental strain could cause terrible repercussions was generally accepted as fact. The physical delicacy of women and their lack of staying power precluded a quest

for higher education by parents on behalf of their daughters, if only to prove their concern for their daughters' state of health. Written references to physiological details alluded obliquely to results 'we all know', leaving them unspecified. However, during the 1870s the restraints of prudery snapped, and opponents of higher education for women were free to write blunt descriptions of the gynaecological dangers awaiting the university-educated woman. It is to this subject we now turn.

Notes

1. 'Miss Becker on the Mental Characteristics of the Sexes', *The Lancet* (1868), p. 320.
2. 'Women of Business', *Tait's Edinburgh Magazine*, n.s. 1 (1834), p. 597.
3. Barrett to Browning, 4 July 1845, *Letters of Robert Browning and Elizabeth Barrett* (London, 1899), pp. 116-17. For an early refutation of the idea here expressed see M. L. G., 'Men and Women', *Tait's Edinburgh Magazine*, n.s. 1 (1834), pp. 101-3.
4. *The Times* (London), 30 June 1873, p. 6, col. 4.
5. *Ibid.*
6. 'The British Mother Taking Alarm', *Saturday Review* 32 (1871), p. 335.
7. *Ibid.*
8. Sarah E. Henshaw, 'Are We Inferior?', *The Galaxy* 7 (1869), p. 128.
9. *Ibid.*
10. 'Miss Becker', p. 321.
11. Oxoniensis, [pseud.], 'The Education of Women', *Christian Observer* 64 (1865), p. 547.
12. Remarks by Grazebrook in Emma Wallington's, 'The Physical and Intellectual Capacities of Woman Equal to Those of Man', *Anthropologia* 1(1874), p. 561. Isaac Taylor suggested that one of the specific intentions of female education was 'to render her the attractive companion of man, and to put her into communication with the world of mind; not indeed to explore it, but to tread its beaten paths in all directions' (Quoted by W. H. Davenport Adams, *Woman's Work and Worth in Girlhood, Maidenhood, and Wifehood* [London, 1880], p. 363.)
13. George Harris, 'On the Distinctions, Mental and Moral, Occasioned by the Difference of Sex', *Journal of the Anthropological Society* 7 (1869), p. cxcii.
14. 'Miss Becker', p. 321.
15. John Gregory, *A Father's Legacy to His Daughters* (London, 1828, originally published in 1774), p. 41.
16. 'It has been pointed out again and again how the mental acquirements of woman have proved of no pecuniary value, and how a strong mindedness has been considered as converse to attractive.' (W. L. Distant, 'On the Mental Differences Between the Sexes', *Journal of the Anthropological Institute* 4 [1875], p. 83.)
17. 'Feminine Wranglers', *Saturday Review* 18 (1864), p. 112.
18. 'Miss Becker', p. 320.
19. See also Charles Darwin, *The Variation of Animals and Plants Under Domestication* (New York, 1887, originally published in 1868).
20. 'The Probable Retrogression of Women', *Saturday Review* 32 (1871), p. 11.
21. Grazebrook in Wallington, 'Capacities of Woman', p. 561.
22. Emma Wallington ('The Physical and Intellectual Capacities of Woman Equal

to Those of Man', *Anthropologia* 1 [1874], p. 554) gave examples of hard physical labour by women in India, Abyssinia and other parts of Africa based on reports of observers in those countries. In the discussion following her paper, Gottlieb W. (von) Leitner described his own experiences in Thibet [*sic*] where female coolies had proved 'equal, if not superior' to the men in endurance. See remarks by Professor Leitner in Wallington, 'Capacities of Woman', p. 562.

23.   Henry Maudsley, 'Sex in Mind and in Education', *Fortnightly Review*, n.s. 15 (1874), pp. 470-1.

24.   Though women did not work in the mines in England after the 1840s, as late as 1869 several thousand were employed as blacksmiths, and 1,200 worked in brickfields carrying as much as 30,000 lbs. of clay in a day. See Wallington, 'Capacities of Woman', pp. 553-4. Elizabeth Garrett Anderson used the work of domestic servants as an illustration of how women could function at all times, and not need to rest at menstruation as was being claimed by some physicians, in 'Sex in Mind and Education: A Reply', *Fortnightly Review*, n.s. 15 (1874), p. 585.

25.   Remarks by Serjeant Cox as reported in W. L. Distant, 'On the Mental Differences Between the Sexes', *Journal of the Anthropological Institute* 4 (1875), p. 87.

26.   J. B. Davis discussed in some detail his own and other methods for weighing the brain in 'Contributions towards Determining the Weight of the Brain in Different Races of Man', *Philosophical Transactions* 158, pt. 2 (1868), pp. 505-27. Comparisons of ways of measuring skulls may be found in John Cleland, 'An Inquiry into the Variations of the Human Skull, Particularly in the Antero-posterior Direction', *Ibid.* 160, pt. 1 (1870), pp. 117-74.

27.   Davis, in 'Weight of the Brain', pp. 505-27, refers to the small number of skulls used by Dr. Thomas B. Peacock (see 'On the weight of the Brain of the Negro', *Memoirs of the Anthropological Society of London* 1 (1863-64), pp. 65, 520) who weighed the brains of only five Negroes and on this basis concluded that the average weight for the men was 44.34 ounces, and for the women, 43.5 ounces. Davis worked with larger numbers: e.g., 38 Negro men and 31 women; 21 English men and 13 women; 56 ancient Britons (male) and 10 females; etc., making a total of 1,139 for the whole world. Commenting on the purpose of his collection, Davis said, 'It should here be observed that the great design kept in view in forming the collection of skulls from which our data are derived was to acquire *exotic* crania' (p. 514). Distant cites statistics based on two thousand cases at St. Marylebone Parochial Infirmary and also uses results of smaller experiments carried out in France (Distant, 'Differences Between Sexes', pp. 78-80).

28.   Distant gives from four to six ounces as the average difference between the brains of men and women ('Differences Between the Sexes', p. 79). My figures are taken from Henry Gray, *Anatomy Descriptive and Surgical* (London, 1877), p. 473.

29.   'The female skull. . . being in this, as in various other respects, more child-like than the male skull.' (Cleland, 'Variations of the Human Skull', p. 161.)

30.   'It may be correct to say that in consequence of the persistence in the female. . . of the flatness of the roof found in childhood, the latest accession of height in the male skull is wanting in the female.' (*Ibid.*, p. 164.)

31.   Remarks by R. S. Charnock, president of the London Anthropological Society, in Wallington, 'Capacities of Women', p. 563. Distant, 'Differences Between the Sexes', p. 80, attributes this concept to Carl Vogt, who reported on cranial measurements made by European researchers.

32.   Gray, *Anatomy*, p. 473.

33.   John Stuart Mill, *The Subjection of Women*, World's Classics ed. (London, 1963, originally published in 1869), p. 503.

34.   *Ibid.*, p. 504.

35.   Distant, 'Differences Between Sexes', pp. 80-1.

36.   *Ibid.*, pp. 81-2. For a criticism of the idea of sexual selection see R. S. Charnock, 'President's Address', *Anthropologia* 1 (1874), p. 15. It was a woman author, George Eliot, who pointed out that the results of mating intelligence to beauty were not

always predictable: "It's the wonderful'st thing as I picked the mother because she wasn't o'er 'cute—bein' a good-looking woman too, an' come of a rare family for managing; but I picked her from her sisters o' purpose, 'cause she was a bit weak, like; for I wasn't agoin' to be told the rights o' things by my own fireside. But you see when a man's got brains himself, there's no knowing where they'll run to; an' a pleasant sort o' soft woman may go on breeding you stupid lads and 'cute wenches, till it's like as if the world was turned topsy-turvy." (George Eliot, *The Mill on the Floss*, Collins Library of Classics edn (originally published in 1860), p. 18.)

37.   Work by Darwin on differences between the brains of domesticated and wild rabbits is referred to by Distant, 'Differences Between Sexes', pp. 82-3.

38.   'Probable Retrogression of Women', p. 11.

5 | *Education and Sex*

In England during the 1870s opponents of higher education for women began to explain how mental strain affected the female reproductive system. Puritanical barriers with regard to sex broke down because the times demanded conclusive action: by 1870 women were already attending courses in London and Cambridge (albeit not officially as members of the universities), a few had even become doctors, and many others were being prepared to compete with boys for the university local examinations (see Chapter 1). Simply by doing what they had been assured they could not do, women were showing that many arguments used against them were illusory. Authorities had demonstrated that women's brains weighed less than men's, that the bone structure of their heads was less mature — in short, that evolution had passed them by — and yet, this had not deterred a few women from competing successfully with men. However, medical practitioners had evidence that although a woman might succeed intellectually if she so desired, she could do so only at great risk to her femininity. Since the chemical basis for sexual differentiation was unknown, physicians believed that how one behaved, dressed, worked, and played at puberty controlled the proper development of primary and secondary sex characteristics. Those who opposed the changes taking place in women's education decided they could be stopped only by an open discussion of medical details previously unacknowledged.

Recent educational achievements of women made anthropological 'proofs' of women's innate mental inferiority look doubtful. Perhaps the intellectual differences between the sexes were environmental after all. If some women, by education, could become men's equals intellectually, why should they be prevented from doing so? No one suggested that all women, any more than all men, should go to a university, but why should those who wished to do so be denied the opportunity?

The opponents of higher education for women felt compelled to answer these questions. Reluctantly, they began an open discussion of how women's reproductive organs worked and what dangers to them might ensue from prolonged and intensive mental work. They

intended to show conclusively that the Victorian ideal of modest womanhood was based on sound physiological principles that could be ignored only by endangering the human race. That the debate should be so hotly pursued by members of the medical profession was not accidental. They knew that the practice of medicine was considered an appropriate profession for women by some men as well as women. By recognising nursing as a respectable female occupation, men had acknowledged women's capacity to look after the sick in hospitals as well as at home. Though few people were prepared to take it, it was but a logical step to suggest that women could be successful doctors. 'What is there to make doctoring more disgusting than nursing, which women are always doing and which ladies have done publicly in the Crimea?' asked Elizabeth Garrett of her father when revealing her ambition to become a doctor.[1] In an age of reticence about sex, some people felt that women doctors would be very successful in gynaecology and obstetrics; a woman patient would discuss her symptoms more openly with another woman than with a man. This feeling was borne out in reality for, by 1871, Dr. Elizabeth Garrett Anderson's patients 'were increasingly women from all over London who wished to be treated solely by women for gynaecological conditions.'[2]

Medicine was the first occupation to be assailed by women in their drive to enter the professions, and it was medical practitioners who made the strongest attack against higher education for women. Specialists in gynaecology and obstetrics, who were the first to feel competition from women doctors, were prominent in the attack, claiming that the dangers of mental fatigue lay in its effects on women's reproductive system. Among those who joined verbally in the battle were John Thorburn, MD, FRCP, professor of obstetrics, Owens College, Manchester; Robert Lawson Tait, FRCS, LlD, honorary fellow and sometime president of the British Gynaecological Society; and William Withers Moore, MRCS, FRCP, DCL, sometime president of the British Medical Association, who had a large practice in Brighton that would have included gynaecological and obstetrical cases. Another leading contributor was Henry Maudsley, MD, FRCP, professor of medical jurisprudence, University College London.

In 1874 Maudsley published 'Sex in Mind and in Education', an article that introduced to the general literature in England a discussion of the physiological effects of higher education on women.[3] Maudsley's article owed much to a book by a Harvard professor, Edward H. Clarke, entitled *Sex in Education*, published the previous year in the United States.[4] There was some similarity between the

situation at Harvard when Clarke published this book and the situation at University College London when Maudsley published his article, for in the same year that each man wrote against women undertaking higher education, his institution agreed to allow women, for the first time, to take examinations under its auspices: the Harvard Corporation, in 1873, agreed to a request from the Women's Educational Association of Boston that women be permitted to take examinations similar to the Oxford and Cambridge local examinations, and University College London, in 1874, agreed to grant certificates, on the results of examinations, to women students attending courses at the college.[5] Although Julia Ward Howe in her attack on Clarke's book claimed that the reason Clarke saw diseases in American women 'is simply this, some of them wish to enter Harvard College, and some of them have already passed through other colleges',[6] no one accused Maudsley of the same prejudice. Elizabeth Garrett Anderson, writing at the request of Frances Buss and Emily Davies, rebutted Maudsley in the language of one medical practitioner to another;[7] the discussion was carried further in *The Lancet*, and later Robert Lawson Tait and John Thorburn took up Maudsley's arguments in their respective books, *Diseases of the Ovaries* (London, 1883) and *Female Education from a Physiological Point of View* (London, 1884). Finally, William Withers Moore made female education the subject of his presidential address to the British Medical Association in 1886.[8]

Few medical writers considered themselves conservative in their attitude toward women. Tait, for example, claimed that he was an 'advanced advocate of women's rights' although he could not 'help seeing the mischief women will do to themselves, and to the race generally, if they avail themselves too fully of these rights when conceded.'[9] Some deliberately dissociated themselves from earlier writers who had tried to prove the innate inferiority of women's brains. As men trained in science, physicians could not deny the evidence that women could compete successfully in examinations; they admitted that environment accounted largely for the differing intellectual capacity of the sexes. According to Thorburn: 'All the old-fashioned notions of women's brains being in some way inferior to men's are, I am convinced, utterly wrong. My experience shows me that they are equal if not often superior, but that this power is at present being frittered away by foolish attempts to ignore the physiological differences which exist between the two sexes.'[10]

Some doctors claimed they favoured a change in women's

education that would make women more rational beings, since there was medical evidence to show that the frivolous nature of women's education was responsible for some nervous disorders.[11] Yet this claim did not mean that they favoured the entry of women into higher education. On the contrary, they saw every reason, physiologically, why women should be denied it, at least on the terms it was offered to men. Earlier writers had mistaken environmental differences for innate differences in brain capacity between the sexes. Innate differences existed not in brain capacity but in the reproductive functions of the sexes, and it was differing reproductive functions that necessitated different education for men and women. Maudsley had no doubt that: 'There is sex in mind as distinctly as there is sex in body; and if the mind is to receive the best culture of which its nature is capable, regard must be had to the mental qualities which correlate differences of sex.'[12]

This discussion of higher education for women bore a different stamp from earlier ones, for lay people had no access to the medical data of doctors. Doctors' opinions on social matters bolstered as they were by medical evidence, were received with awe, and were almost impossible to refute. Only other doctors could offer new interpretations of medical evidence, and the prospect of physicians disputing with each other was highly discomforting to those accustomed to a consensus of medical opinion. Yet until lay people could draw on rival medical opinions they were unable to counter any of the arguments described below (rival opinions from doctors were forthcoming, however, and in the revaluation of the medical data, Elizabeth Garrett Anderson played a leading part).[13]

The medical attack concentrated on what would happen if women were encouraged to attend universities. The matter was urgent because at a women's college, founded in 1869 at Hitchin and moved in 1873 to Girton, Cambridge, a few women students were taking courses and examinations identical to those of men at Cambridge University. It was essential that they should be stopped, for the results would be irrevocable. There was enough evidence at hand from the United States to make such dangerous experiments in England unnecessary. Women had been admitted to some coeducational colleges in the United States since the 1830s, and evidence of the direful effect of higher education on the women students had been published. The time had come for doctors to make it better known in England.

Thus, British doctors used the opinions of some American doctors

on the effects of higher education on women to buttress their arguments, ignoring differences in teaching techniques between the two countries. In the United States it was general practice to require students to attend every class and to stand up to deliver recitations daily. Students were graded daily rather than being graded on occasional examinations. These practices, to which Clarke ascribed most of the ills befalling Misses A, B, C, D, and E, in *Sex and Education*, were not relevant in English higher education, and in the 1870s they were already being abandoned by some American colleges.[14] Nevertheless, British writers used American evidence to support their thesis that women were physiologically unsuited to strenuous intellectual work, that women lacked physical stamina. Physiologically, they claimed, the sexes were suited to different occupations: men for heavy work and women for the lighter duties of the home. Likewise, physiologically they were suited to different kinds of education: men for continuous concentrated thought, interspersed with the physical effort of organised games, and women for the lesser strain of general subjects and accomplishments, interspersed with periods of rest. Since women could not take part in organised games, necessary for men to counterbalance their mental exertion, any women undertaking higher education would be in danger of breaking down mentally.[15] According to Percy Gardner, who spoke out against women at Oxford and Cambridge, it was extremely improbable that the same education would fit men for their duties and women for theirs: 'Either sex is an appalling blunder, or else it must have been intended that each sex should have its own work to do, not merely in the physical economy of the race, but also in the social and intellectual world.'[16] No one could seriously believe that sex was a blunder on Nature's part, and therefore the constraints on women due to their physiology had to be respected. 'The aim of female education,' wrote Maudsley, 'should manifestly be the perfect development, not of manhood but of womanhood, by the methods most conducive thereto: so may women reach as high a grade of development as men, though it be of a different type.'[17]

Some had argued, as 'Justitia' in England and Caroline Dall in the United States, that women should be educated to combine marriage and a career in the way that men were educated to perform a broader function than merely to become husbands and fathers,[18] but to demand the same rights for women would be to ignore the true role of women in the home, and to deny the necessity of taking into account their physiology. 'The knowledge of the difference in their physical

structure, which we have acquired through science, proves this incontestably—man was created for strength, woman for beauty, whether of body or mind: man's life is of necessity active, woman's quiescent.'[19]

The joint training that boys and girls received in the nursery could not be continued once the early years of childhood had passed. Puberty brought sexual differentiation affecting boys' and girls' whole personalities; their education had to be differentiated too. 'The curves of separation swell out as childhood recedes, like an ellipse, and, as old age draws on, approach, till they unite like an ellipse again.'[20] Boys and girls, old men and women, were much the same, but men and women in the prime of life differed both in physical and mental characteristics. It was at puberty that the different mental characteristics of the sexes became apparent, as well as the different physical attributes. Both were the result of sexual development. 'To attribute to the influence of education the mental differences of sex which declare themselves so distinctly at puberty, would be hardly less absurd than to attribute to education the bodily differences which then declare themselves.'[21]

In each sex there was thought to be a close connection between mental and physical development. Women who were most perfectly developed physically manifested all those mental characteristics defined as feminine; the best physical specimens of manhood manifested to the fullest masculine characteristics. Aberrations from the norm illustrated the sexual link between mental and physical development: 'The mental qualities of mutilated men,' wrote Maudsley, 'approach those of women, while women whose reproductive organs remain for some cause in a state of arrested development, approach the mental and bodily habits of men.'[22]

It was an axiom of the times that physiological differences between the sexes entailed different kinds of behaviour and intellectual interests for men and women. Consequently, the most highly developed female, physiologically, would exhibit the most feminine type of behaviour and intellect, and conversely, the least highly developed female would exhibit the least feminine type of behaviour and intellect. Since the women demanding higher education were exhibiting masculine characteristics of intellect one could deduce that they were physiologically unfeminine. This immediately made them suspect in the eyes of the general public.

There were those who disagreed with the axiom, of course. John Stuart Mill had refuted it nearly forty years earlier in a letter to

Thomas Carlyle: 'The women, of all I have known, who possessed the highest measure of what are considered feminine qualities, have combined with them more of the highest *masculine* qualities than I have ever seen in any but one or two men, those one or two men were also in many respects almost women. I suspect it is the second-rate people of the two sexes that are unlike in both.'[23] This was an idea hardly flattering to those who prided themselves on their masculinity or femininity. When Mill expressed himself more fully in *The Subjection of Women* (London, 1869), he was attacked in the medical journal, *The Lancet*. The reviewer clearly stated the accepted medical view, later expressed by Maudsley: 'There are some women whose physical and intellectual powers are alike great; but these form the exception, and they are generally as remarkable for the masculine qualities of their bodies as for those of their minds.'[24] According to this view, if women were to remain true to their natures, physically and mentally, they had to be given an education that allowed for the differences between the sexes. At the latest, when girls reached puberty they had to be relieved of any kind of pressure, especially pressure from intellectual competition. Only by maintaining a balance between the input and output of nervous energy could a woman remain healthy.

When did the crucial period of development begin? William Withers Moore believed that the years preceding were as crucial as the years of puberty themselves:

> At no epoch of life is the necessity for maintaining the balance between construction and destruction of nervous energy greater than in the period immediately preceding adolescence; and it is just at this time that keen competition is most severely felt in subjecting. . . the latest evolved portion of the nervous system to a strain so great that only those possessing the best-balanced and strongest system can escape unscathed.[25]

Though Withers Moore argued here that the prepubescent period was the most crucial, other writers concentrated on the period of puberty itself. It was then that education became a serious factor in the lives of boys; preparation for the university local examinations took place during these years, and since girls were, after 1863, encouraged by teachers to enter these examinations, more and more were becoming subject to strain at this time. Such strain was detrimental to their health. According to Matthews Duncan: 'Amenorrhoea and chlorosis, and development of great nervousness, are frequent results of over-

pressure in education at or near the important epoch—fifteen to twenty years of age. To the same cause I have often attributed destruction of sensuality of a proper commendable kind, and its consequent personal and social evils.'[26]

Whether the results were the 'destruction of sensuality of a proper commendable kind', amenorrhoea, or chlorosis, over-pressure at puberty was disastrous, for each individual was thought to possess only a limited amount of energy. 'When Nature spends in one direction,' wrote Maudsley, 'she must economise in another direction.'[27] Here Maudsley echoed Herbert Spencer, who had described Nature as 'a strict accountant' and claimed that 'the amount of vital energy which the body at any moment possesses is limited; and that, being limited, it is impossible to get from it more than a fixed quantity of results.'[28] (This idea marked the introduction into human affairs of the principle of the conservation of energy, introduced into physics in the 1840s. Though doubtful physiology and erroneous physics, since the human body is not the closed system to which the conservation principle applies, the fixity of the individual's energy became a favourite theme for the remainder of the nineteenth century and was prominent in the writings of Sigmund Freud.)[29]

Nature provided sufficient energy for the body to function normally, but any excess used by one part had to be found by robbing another. At puberty women needed a great deal of energy to help the growth of their reproductive organs, consequently the energy they had left for learning was reduced. Only by robbing their reproductive organs of essential resources of energy could they continue serious study. It was folly to ask women, at this time, to increase the amount of energy they were using for study by making them prepare for examinations. As Maudsley explained: 'It is not that girls have not ambition, nor that they fail generally to run the intellectual race which is set before them, but it is asserted that they do it at a cost to their strength and health which entails lifelong suffering, and even incapacitates them for the adequate performance of the natural functions of their sex.'[30]

Through menstruation women's reproductive system made regular demands on their constitution, and mental strain was as dangerous to them as physical strain. Especial care had to be taken until menstruation was properly established; it had to become a regular bodily habit before any confidence could be expressed that the time of strain had passed. Ovulation was at this time thought to occur at menstruation, hence 'at each recurring period there are all the preparations for

conception, and nothing is more necessary to the preservation of female health than that these changes should take place regularly and completely.'[31]

Because of women's need for rest while menstruating, their education had to follow a different pattern from men's. The danger was that neither girls' schools nor the new colleges for women were organised to provide periods of rest. Thorburn felt that reform had to begin in the secondary schools, but that none could take place until mothers had been taught about their daughters' need for rest at menstruation: 'When this maternal education is completed on any considerable scale, it will compel the directors of such institutions to so far alter their arrangements as to permit on an average rate of general progress which will allow for an average loss of time by each individual girl.'[32] Thorburn went on to advocate that some British university should set up special courses of study leading to women's degrees. In England as in the United States, scheduling lectures and examinations without allowance for the periodicity of women's stamina would have disastrous results. As Clarke had pointed out with reference to the American experience:

> Those grievous maladies which torture a woman's earthly existence, called leucorrhoea, amenorrhoea, dysmenorrhoea, chronic and acute ovaritis, prolapsus uteri, hysteria, neuralgia, and the like, are indirectly affected by food, clothing, and exercise; they are directly and largely affected by the causes that will be presently pointed out, and which arise from a neglect of the peculiarities of a woman's organization. The regimen of our schools fosters this neglect. The regimen of a college arranged for boys, if imposed on girls, would foster it still more.[33]

The need for women to rest while menstruating did not cease once menstruation had become established. The period of menstruation was always one of heightened danger to the nervous system. Robert Barnes, MD reported in a series of lectures on the convulsive diseases of women that: 'Menstruation resembles pregnancy in giving rise to an exalted central nervous erethism, and ovulation is a primary cause of epileptic, vomitive, and hysterical convulsion.'[34] Whereas women's nerve-centres were always in a state of greater instability than men's, it was during menstruation that overwork was most dangerous.

There are few [physicians] who have not seen bright careers of

mental work and usefulness cut short, never to be resumed, after a few days of hard mental strain during a menstrual period. It cannot, therefore, be too strongly insisted on that, with the young and the delicate, at any rate, and to some extent with all women, the period of menstruation should be a period of comparative repose, mental and bodily, but especially mental.[35]

Lay people appear to have shared this fear of over-pressure. In 1874 Eveline, Countess of Portsmouth, confided in a letter to Mrs. T. H. Huxley:

I am sure you are right in not allowing your girl to do much work — I am grown very nervous about any forcing of the brain with young growing girls, I think it horribly capable of addling the brain instead of filling it — after all the quality of every work is a thousand times worth the quantity. My second girl is wonderfully better — I only allow her to do one hour of real work a day but she is always busy usefully.[36]

Belief in the need for women to rest at menstruation was maintained for many years. As late as 1926 the Air Ministry in Britain was in doubt whether women should be granted International 'B' Pilot's Certificates because of the strain of flying at menstruation.

To those who believed that menstruation was a pathological and not merely a physiological process, it was clear that the pattern of women's work as well as of education had to be different from men's. Women should be discouraged from thinking they could enter the professions. Who would want a doctor who was available only three weeks out of four? Or a barrister who might have to miss a case because she was 'indisposed'? The idea was preposterous. Yet this would have to happen if 'professional' women were to retain any chance of performing their role of child-bearers. They could never do the same amount of work as men, for women were physically unable to cope with continuous and regular effort:

This is a matter óf physiology, not a matter of sentiment; . . .not a question of two bodies and minds that are in equal physical condition, but of one body and mind capable of sustained and regular hard labour, and of another body and mind which for one quarter of each month during the best years of life is more or less sick and unfit for hard work.[37]

Menstruation continued for many years and the energy first diverted to it in puberty had to be maintained. Hence women, from puberty to menopause, lacked the strength for sustained mental effort. Their intellectual development of necessity was less than that of men, for they had to leave a considerable margin of nutrition for the processes of reproduction.

The conclusion that women were unsuited for the professions was of vast importance to those who opposed higher education for women, since the purpose of higher education was generally thought to be vocational. Thorburn went so far as to call for 'protective acts of parliament for the women of our educated classes' analogous to the protective legislation for women working in mines and factories.[38] As E. B. Duffey, a supporter of higher education for women, pointed out in a reply to Clarke, once women were thought of as creatures 'subject to and ruled by "periodic tides" the battle is won for those who oppose the advancement of women — the doors not only of education but of labor and any kind of physical and intellectual advancement are closed against her.' As Clarke well knew, claimed Duffey, labour had to be reliable and continuous to be valuable, and if women, by their nature, were unreliable, there was an end to the possibility of women competing with men for any kind of employment.[39]

Writers supported their conclusion that women should not enter the professions with assertions that mental effort affected women's reproductive capacity in many ways. Undue brain activity had a sterilising effect on both sexes, claimed Clarke, but its influence was 'more potent' upon women, because the physiological effort of reproduction was far greater for them than for men.[40] This point had been made several years earlier by Herbert Spencer who wrote that educated women not only suffered more frequently from sterility and the earlier cessation of child-bearing, but that they often were unable to breastfeed their children. 'In its full sense, the reproductive power means the power to bear a well-developed infant, and to supply that infant with the natural food for the natural period. Most of the flat-chested girls who survive their high-pressure education are incompetent to do this.'[41]

No woman could follow a course of higher education without running some risk of becoming sterile. Intelligent women made the best mothers, yet it was they who would be tempted to achieve intellectual success and endanger their fertility. Experience in the United States showed that, if education were allowed to interfere with the normal development of the menstrual cycle, a woman could expect

dire results, perhaps even permanent sterility. Clarke reported that he had seen instances 'of females in whom the special mechanisms we are speaking of remained germinal — undeveloped. It seemed to have been aborted. They graduated from school or college excellent scholars, but with undeveloped ovaries. Later they married, and were sterile.'[42] The country could not afford to lose potential leaders for lack of a mother; intelligent women had to be guided away from hazardous ambition and shown that theirs was the finest contribution that could be made to motherhood. For the good of the human race women had to be kept from intellectual competition with men. Such competition would 'hinder those who would have been the best mothers from being mothers at all, or, if it does not hinder them, more or less it will spoil them, and no training will enable themselves to do what their sons might have done.'[43]

Intelligent women, unspoiled by education, produced eminent sons. The country would benefit far more from such men than from a similar number of sterile but educated women who might otherwise have produced them. 'Unsexed it might be wrong to call the educated woman, but she will be more or less sexless. And the human race will have lost those who should have been her sons. Bacon, for want of a mother, will not be born.'[44] Whereas education did not deprive men of their virility, and could prove useful in helping them to earn more money to support their families, it was likely to disable women reproductively. Intelligent, well-trained mothers were the ideal; how many eminent men had proclaimed their debt to their mothers. Moreover, educators claimed that the early years of childhood were more important than they had previously thought; the role of a mother in the education of her child was becoming more important than ever before. Spencer, who was influenced by the work of Johann Heinrich Pestalozzi (1746-1827) and Phillip Emanuel von Fellenberg (1771-1844), claimed that parents' chief function with young children was to provide the conditions requisite for growth, and that this applied to the growth of children's minds as well as their bodies.[45] Intelligent mothers were needed to provide the kind of environment that would encourage mental development in their sons. An education that threatened to deplete the ranks of motherhood, and deny to it the most intelligent women, was as disastrous for the nation as for the women concerned. Every effort had to be made to get women to desist from their path of folly before it was too late.

Throughout most of the nineteenth century, people generally believed in the physical delicacy of the human female. Although the

physical stamina required by women of the labouring classes belied this, the ideal of womanhood rested in the prototype of the frail, protected woman of the middle classes. The mental and physical characteristics of the sexes were thought to be intimately connected and few would deny the influence of mental fatigue on sexual processes. Not only was hard work (as well as hard play) considered disastrous to the female, but mental strain was as bad, if not worse, in terms of maintaining adequate physical health. Medical 'proofs' of the negative effect of continuous intellectual work on the ability of women to reproduce only served to reinforce what opponents of higher education for women had been saying all along—women were unfit, emotionally and physically, to compete with men in the professional and business world. The ideal of womanhood was consistent with the medical facts.

So far, we have presented the major economic, mental and physical arguments used by the opponents of higher education for women. We now turn to the last, and perhaps the most influential, arguments against the entrance of women into the educational and professional realms—those arguments based on religion.

Notes

1.   Elizabeth Garrett Anderson, quoted by Jo Manton, *Elizabeth Garrett Anderson* (London, 1965), p. 73.

2.   Manton, *Elizabeth Garrett Anderson*, p. 226. The number of women who consulted Dr. Anderson is recorded on p. 227.

3.   Henry Maudsley, 'Sex in Mind and in Education', *Fortnightly Review* n.s.15 (1874), pp. 466-83.

4.   Edward H. Clarke, *Sex in Education* (Boston, 1873). In *A Century of Higher Education for American Women* (New York, 1959), p. 29, Mabel Newcomer comments, 'Dr. Clarke's statistical evidence was limited to six cases that had come to his attention. . . Even had all six cases been valid. . . they would hardly have proved his point. But the book confirmed prejudices; and the obvious fact that the great majority of women students enjoyed better than average health had to be bolstered up with special studies.'

5.   Samuel Eliot Morison, *Three Centuries of Harvard* (Cambridge, Mass., 1936), pp. 391-3, summarises the history of examinations and classes for women at Harvard; H. Hale Bellot, *University College London, 1826-1926* (London, 1929), pp. 369-71, summarises their history at University College London.

6.   Julia Ward Howe (ed.), *Sex and Education: A Reply to Dr. E. H. Clarke's Sex in Education* (Boston, 1874), p. 24.

7.   Elizabeth Garrett Anderson, 'Sex in Mind and Education: A Reply', *Fortnightly Review* n.s. 15 (1874), pp. 582-94.

8.   As reported in *The Lancet* 2, (1886), p. 315.

9.   Robert Lawson Tait, *Diseases of the Ovaries* (London, 1883), p. 91.

10.   John Thorburn, *Female Education from a Physiological Point of View*

(London, 1884), p. 10.

11. Maudsley, 'Sex in Mind', p. 482. Emily Pfeiffer, *Women and Work* (London, 1888), pp. 94-7, included testimony to the Schools Inquiry Commission (1867) on the education of girls by Dr. Charles B. Aldis: '*I am perfectly convinced* as the result of many years' practice that whatever tends to develop the minds of women will have the best effect on their moral and physical as well as intellectual health' (p. 95. Italics as found in Pfeiffer). Dr. Langdon Downe, in a personal letter to Pfeiffer, wrote, 'If there is anything more certain than another about the production of idiocy, it is the danger which arises from the culture of one side only of a woman's nature' (p. 96).

12. Maudsley, 'Sex in Mind', p. 468.

13. Anderson's reply to Maudsley has already been cited in note 7 above. Also see, Pfeiffer, *Women and Work*, pt. 4, entitled 'Medical Testimony and Statistical Evidence Favourable to the Advanced Education of Women', which gives a clear summary of the counter arguments.

14. The changes in American colleges are described by Thomas Wentworth Higginson in Howe (ed.), *Sex and Education: A Reply*, Chap. 2; Morison, *Three Centuries of Harvard*, pp. 341-9.

15. Educators, realising the importance of physical well being for intellectual success, introduced calisthenics, swimming, and later, gymnastics and organised games into women's educational programs. Details of their work may be found in: June A. Kennard, *Women, Sport and Society in Victorian England* (Ed. D. dissertation, Greensboro, N. C., 1974); Paul Atkinson in Sara Delamont and Lorna Duffin (eds), *The Nineteenth-Century Woman: Her Cultural and Physical World* (London, 1978), Chap. 4.

16. Percy Gardner, 'Women at Oxford and Cambridge', *Quarterly Review* 186 (1897), p. 543.

17. Maudsley, 'Sex in Mind', p. 481.

18. Justitia [Mrs. Henry Davis Pochin], *The Right of Women to Exercise the Elective Franchise* (London, 1855), pp. 14-15. See also Caroline Dall in Howe (ed.), *Sex and Eduation: A Reply*, p. 107.

19. 'The Education of Women', *Christian Observer* 64 (1865), p. 546.

20. Clarke, *Sex in Education*, p. 36.

21. Maudsley, 'Sex in Mind', p. 470.

22. *Ibid.*

23. Francis E. Mineka (ed.), *The Earlier Letters of John Stuart Mill, 1812-1818* (Toronto, 1963), p. 184.

24. 'John Stuart Mill, "The Subjection of Women" ' *The Lancet* 2 (1869), p. 511.

25. William Withers Moore, quoted by Emily Pfeiffer, *Women and Work*, p. 67.

26. Dr. Matthews Duncan quoted by William Withers Moore in his speech to the 54th annual meeting of the British Medical Association, Brighton, 1886, as reported in *The Lancet* 2 (1886), p. 315.

Amenorrhoea, according to *Webster's Collegiate Dictionary*, 5th edn, is the unnatural absence or suppression of the menstrual discharge; *chlorosis*, an anaemic disease of young women, characterized by a greenish hue of the skin, menstrual disorders etc.

27. Maudsley, 'Sex in Mind', p. 467.

28. Herbert Spencer, *Education: Intellectual, Moral and Physical* (New York, 1860), pp. 284-5.

29. See T. S. Kuhn, 'Energy Conservation as an Example of Simultaneous Discovery,' in M. Clagett (ed.), *Critical Problems in the History of Science* (Madison, Wis., 1958), pp. 321-56. 'The principles of the conservation of matter and energy. . . passed from safe guides for small empirical advances in knowledge into great philosophic dogmas of doubtful validity' (W. C. Dampier, *A History of Science*, 4th edn [Cambridge, 1948], p. 228.)

30. Maudsley, 'Sex in Mind', p. 473.

31.   Maudsley, 'Sex in Mind', p. 467. 'Nature has reserved the catamenial week for the process of ovulation, and for the development and perfection of the reproductive system' (Clarke, *Sex in Education*, p. 41). Cf. Frank Harris, *My Life and Loves* 1 (Paris, n.d.), p. 137. Further discussion of nineteenth-century medical views on menstruation may be found in Vern Bullough and Martha Voght, 'Women, Menstruation, and Nineteenth Century Medicine', *Bulletin of the History of Medicine* 47, no. 1 (January-February 1973), pp. 66-82; Elaine and English Showalter, in Martha Vicinus (ed.), *Suffer and Be Still: Women in the Victorian Age* (Bloomington, Indiana, 1972), chap. 3; and Lorna Duffin, in Sara Delamont and Lorna Duffin (eds), *The Nineteenth-Century Woman: Her Cultural and Physical World* (London, 1978), chap. 2.

32.   Thorburn, *Female Education*, pp. 15-16.

33.   Clarke, *Sex in Education*, p. 23. *Leucorrhoea* was defined as a morbid discharge of a whitish viscid mucus from the vagina; *dysmenorrhoea*, a difficult and painful menstruation; *ovaritis*, an inflammation of the ovaries; *prolapsus uteri*, the falling down of the uterus.

34.   Robert Barnes, MD, 'Lumleian Lectures on the Convulsive Diseases of Women', reported in *The Lancet* 1 (1873), p. 622.

35.   Thorburn, *Female Education*, p. 7.

36.   Eveline, Countess of Portsmouth, to Mrs. T. H. Huxley, 21 October 1874, Huxley Papers, Imperial College London.

37.   Maudsley, 'Sex in Mind', pp. 479-80.

38.   Thorburn, *Female Education*, p. 21.

39.   E. B. Duffey, *No Sex in Education* (Philadelphia, 1874), pp. 117-18.

40.   Clarke, *Sex in Education*, p. 137.

41.   Herbert Spencer, *The Principles of Biology* 2 (London, 1867), p. 486.

42.   Clarke, *Sex in Education*, p. 39.

43.   William Withers Moore, presidential address to the 54th annual meeting of the British Medical Association, as reported in *The Lancet* 2 (1886), p. 314.

44.   Withers Moore in *The Lancet* 2 (1886), p. 315.

45.   Spencer, *Education*, p. 108. Although Spencer here refers to *parents*, men had little time to spend with young children. According to Gottlieb von Leitner (commenting on Emma Wallington's 'The Physical and Intellectual Capacities of Woman Equal to Those of Man', *Anthropologia* 1 [1874], p. 563), 'The proper sphere for woman was to excel as a daughter, a sister, a wife, and a mother. The proudest position any human being could occupy was that of guiding and preparing the young for important stages of life.'

1. The Ideal Woman *The Duet. A Drawing-room study* 1872

2. Not All Can Achieve the Ideal. *Chainmakers— Single Bellows Worked at 3d a Day*

3. Work Within Women's Sphere. *Valentine makers c.* 1875

4. (Above) A Revolution of Gender Roles. *The Ladies of Creation* 1853
Naturally the Female Thinks Shopping Very Foolish and Tiresome
SUPERIOR CREATURE: For goodness' sake, Edward, do come away!
When you once get into a shop there's no getting you out again!

5. (Right) A Revolution of Gender Roles. *A Muscular Maiden*

A MUSCULAR MAIDEN.

"Thanks," she said, quietly; "I think I have arranged the matter."

6. A Revolution in Gender Roles. *The Parliamentary Female* FATHER OF THE FAMILY: Come dear, we so seldom go out together - Can't you take us all to the play tonight?
MISTRESS OF THE HOUSE AND MP: How you talk Charles. Don't you see that I am too busy. I have a committee tomorrow morning, and I have my speech on the great crochet question to prepare for the evening.

7. A Revolution of Gender Roles. *Robida caricature of 1880 forecasting women police in 1950 arresting a man for refusing to marry.*

8. Protecting the Ideal. *Demonstration at Cambridge against the Admission of Women as Students c.* 1897

6 | *Religion and Woman's Education*

Clergymen were among the most ardent supporters of the ideal of womanhood. They helped define it, adding to its secular characteristics a spiritual dimension unique to the period: the ideal woman was to be the moral guardian of society. Like the lay public, clergymen were divided about the best way to improve women's education. By the 1830s they expressed discontent with the shallow education offered women, urging parents to prepare their daughters for the sacred duties of running a home and raising children. Some, in the 1840s, took part in founding Queen's College for the better education of governesses and, later still, some clergymen suppported the founding of women's colleges in Oxford and Cambridge. They were among those who saw the need for women to become experts within their own sphere, to teach, to run hospitals for women, to organise services for the community. Theirs was a vision of women helping to preserve society.

Others among the clergy held a more conservative view of woman's role. They feared that intellectual competition would destroy the modesty of Christian women, and that careers would take them away from their duty of motherhood. It is their arguments that will be described below. Most clergymen argued in terms of the scriptures and of lofty moral concepts; they appealed to the religious beliefs of their audience. However, whether they recognised it or not, their arguments supported the political power of the churches, and, specifically, of the Church of England at the universities of Oxford and Cambridge. Just as some doctors opposed higher education for women because they felt their professional status would be threatened when women became doctors, some clergymen were influenced by similar motives. Not that there was an imminent threat of women becoming preachers—few reformers were so intrepid as to suggest that women be allowed into the pulpit—but the very presence of women students in Oxford and Cambridge was a potential threat to clerical power there. Though higher education for women was frequently attacked in the religious press during the 1860s,[1] nothing in these attacks could have prepared women for the vehemence expressed in

sermons by a few members of the clergy twenty years later. At that time women students in Oxford and Cambridge represented to those churchmen more than the antithesis of Christian womanhood: they were the last in a series of threats to clerical power in the universities.

In 1884 John William Burgon, one of the staunchest opponents of women students at Oxford, delivered a sermon that was rapidly published entitled: *To Educate Young Women Like Young Men, and With Young Men—a Thing Inexpedient and Immodest* (Oxford, 1884). This passionate sermon, prompted by the passing of a statute at Oxford to permit women to take (though not under university auspices) the first honours examinations in *Literae Humaniores* and the final honours schools in mathematics, natural science, and modern history, was probably the most forthright expression of clerical opposition to any of the changes within the universities of Oxford and Cambridge.

The opposition to women students of such churchmen as Burgon and Henry Liddon, and the ambivalent attitude of Christopher Wordsworth, has to be understood against the background of change within the universities. Between 1850 and 1895 endowments were redistributed, religious tests abolished for most posts, fellows permitted to marry, and several new subjects introduced into the curriculum. Clerical opposition to these changes was most vehement at Oxford. Liddon, select preacher to Oxford university, and Burgon, vicar of St. Mary's, Oxford and Gresham professor of divinity at Oxford university, both opposed most of the changes. They viewed them as signs of the decreasing power of the church in the university, as indeed they were, and they viewed the appearance of women students in the same light. Wordsworth, bishop of Lincoln, was a graduate of Trinity College, Cambridge. After his ordination in 1835 he had little direct contact with university politics, though before that time he had been a fellow of Trinity and a college tutor. Even though his daughter, Elizabeth, became the first principal of Lady Margaret Hall, Oxford, Wordsworth did not support claims for equality in education made on behalf of women. In his eyes such equality would destroy the essence of Christian womanhood. As early as 1852 Wordsworth preached against any form of public examination for women, and although he did not enter directly into the Oxford controversy, he dedicated to his daughter another sermon on womanly modesty shortly after the decision to admit women to the Oxford honours schools had been made.[2]

Women did pose a serious threat to clerical power at the universities

of Oxford and Cambridge. Were they to be allowed to become graduates of the universities, they would be entitled to a voice in university government. However, that voice would be permanently outside the clergy's domain, since women could not be ordained as ministers. Women graduates would never directly represent church interests in university affairs as did clergymen. Over the years, the number of women graduates would increase, and therefore their power would become greater. Herein lay the root of clerical opposition to women's educational aspirations at Oxford and Cambridge. Had this issue been raised openly clergymen might not have found such ready support as they did for their opposition to granting women degrees, since clerical power at Oxford and Cambridge had been challenged successfully on other issues. However, the threat women posed to clerical power was rarely mentioned in public. It was concealed within a broader issue on which clergymen were able to gather support from a large majority of graduates: male control of the universities. By marshalling the spiritual arguments against higher education for women, its clerical opponents became leaders of a movement to keep control of the two oldest universities entirely in the hands of men, and men only. Burgon, whose forthrightness seems to have embarrassed his allies, did not hesitate to bring these issues into the open in his 1884 sermon: 'Will you give [women] Scholarships and Fellowships? or shall they be eligible to those offices in the existing Colleges for men? Are they to have seats in Council, or will you give them a Council of their own?'[3] These questions were raised again in fly-sheets distributed at Oxford in 1896; so pertinent were they to the issue of the admission of women graduates to the universities of Oxford and Cambridge that it was not until 1925 that Oxford and 1947 that Cambridge voted for women's admission to the full privileges of the university.

Clergymen who were outspoken on the dangers of this kind of educational change based their teachings on the scriptures. Everyone knew the language of the Bible and religious opposition to higher education for women was buttressed by all the power of entrenched belief. Although some theological arguments could be disputed only by experts in the same way as some medical arguments, religious terminology was understood by all the educated community and most people felt capable of interpreting the Bible for themselves. The belief that it was God's will that women should lead a more circumscribed life than men lent a new dimension to the discussion of higher education for women, and added strength to clerical opposition. To

desire to change the order of society was a sin. Salvation lay with the conservative forces. Those who wished women to act as though they were men, and would educate them to compete with men, were flouting the divine will revealed at the beginning of time.

The religious arguments opposing higher education for women reinforced the nineteenth-century ideal of pure, undefiled women, sanctifying the home and guiding the family. The home became a spiritual haven, where women, as ministering angels, forgave the sins of their erring husbands and sons. 'Their kind services and their restraining improving influences make them men's guardian angels', wrote William Landels, a Baptist minister.[4] In this ideal, women played a crucial part in providing stability for men who were torn by doubts and faced by insoluble problems. Few people were prepared to confront social, economic and intellectual changes in society by changing their own terms of thought, which was what the psychological crisis of the age called for; most Victorians turned, instead, to an intensification of personal relationships and an exaggerated adherence to domestic virtues.[5] Religious writers, in their exaggeration of domestic virtues, described women as saviours of society. Men might be assailed by religious scepticism, but women never. Charles Darwin commented that his father had known 'during his whole long life only three women who were sceptics; and it should be remembered that he knew well a multitude of persons and possessed extraordinary power of winning confidence.'[6] In an attempt to prevent women from becoming sceptics religious writers urged them to accept their role as guardian angels. The subjection of women to such an ideal offered reassurance to those who believed that as long as women remained untouched by scepticism a line of retreat existed to the stability of the past. The ideal imposed impossible demands upon women, but while it lasted it drew strength from the spiritual crisis of the age.

The Bible as Evidence

Writers argued that the separate duties of men and women were divinely ordained. There was no need to ascribe physiological reasons for men and women doing different work (though they probably existed): the true reason, the fundamental reason, was to be found in the will of God. Whereas doctors, arguing against higher education for women, found a material necessity for women's mode of life, religious leaders found a moral one. It was God's will that women

should spend their lives as guardians of the home. By running the home and bringing up children women were fulfilling God's intention that men and. women should complement each other's work. The morals of society were secure in women's hands; their task was to guide the actions of their husbands and sons. According to this argument, when God created man and woman He created them for different purposes and, therefore, with different attributes. Men were strong, fitted to rough, hard work and continuous intellectual labour; women were gentle and weak, formed for work that demanded sweetness of temper and amiability. All individuals had to live according to these divinely implanted attributes; it was sinful to assume that they could be ignored or flouted.

From the Bible men and women could deduce what ideal pattern the Creator had in mind at the beginning of the world. God had placed Adam in the garden of Eden and made a woman from one of his ribs because "the LORD God said, *It is* not good that the man should be alone; I will make him an help meet for him."[7] Much discussion revolved around the interpretation of *help meet*. Some argued that since woman was created for man, as his help meet, God had forseen that woman's functions would complement man's; they would be different from but not inferior to his. In nineteenth-century England, the argument continued, middle-class society had almost perfected God's design for the divison of labour, for women were accorded the running of the home and the care of children, whereas men provided for the family financially: Men's and women's lives were entirely complementary.[8]

The validity of this argument was explained by Benjamin Parsons, a Congregationalist minister, in his book *The Mental and Moral Dignity of Women* (1842). He examined the root of the Hebrew word which in the Authorised version of the Bible was rendered help meet, and decided that the word כְּנֶגְדּוֹ (*kenegdo*) had as its root גָּד (*gad*) which sometimes includes in its meaning reference to rank and dignity. Parsons therefore maintained that Eve was ' "a help according to the rank and dignity of man" thus placing her on an equality with Adam.' This translation differed essentially from the term help meet which, according to Parsons, had the same root as the Latin *meteor*, *modius*, the Hebrew *madad*, and the Anglo-Saxon *metan*, and which had no meaning of dignity, but merely of 'proportion or correspondence'.[9]

According to Parsons, it was the 'vulgar' interpretation of the text in question that had led millions of people to believe that women had

no higher purpose in life than to gratify the desires of men and act as their servants. Parsons commented that Eve could hardly have been a household drudge in the garden of Eden since there was no wardrobe there to be looked after! God had evidently intended woman to be man's spiritual and intellectual companion.[10] Another writer with the pseudonym Emme Dee agreed, querying: 'Can the rib be inferior to the body from which it was taken?'[11]

Parsons' arguments were those of the clergy who wished to encourage a reform in women's education so that women could become teachers of morality to their children and intellectual companions to their spouses. However, other clergymen such as Burgon and Wordsworth held to an interpretation of the creation that 'proved' women's inferiority had been designed by God. For them, any pretention to equality between the sexes was anathema. Burgon claimed:

> Behold then, at the very outset, the reason of woman's creation distinctly assigned. She is intended to be Man's 'help' — Man's *helper*. . . Yet not a rival self: for, as the SPIRIT pointed out some 4,000 years later, 'the Man was not created for the Woman, *but the Woman for the Man*' and from this very consideration the SPIRIT deduces Woman's inferiority.[12]

This argument was echoed by laymen, who sometimes used the same Biblical cadences. 'Woman,' said William Withers Moore in his presidential address to the British Medical Association in 1886, 'was formed to be man's helpmeet, not his rival; heart, not head; sustainer, not leader.'[13]

The New Testament was used to elucidate the meaning of the brief account in Genesis. Man, who held his authority directly from God, should pray with head uncovered, but woman, who 'is the glory of the man', should pray with her head covered; man could learn through disputation, but woman should accept unquestioningly what man taught her. Her duty was to learn in silence; on no account was she to claim for herself the right to teach man: 'For Adam was first formed, then Eve. And Adam was not deceived, but the woman being deceived was in the transgression.'[14] Those who upheld the view that women should be subordinate to men in all things often followed St. Paul by basing their reasoning on the story of the Fall as well as the Creation. The events of the Fall, they argued, confirmed men's dominion over women. Because Eve tempted Adam to eat the fruit of the Tree of the

Knowledge of Good and Evil, Eve had been punished by God: 'In sorrow thou shalt bring forth children; and thy desire *shall be* to thy husband, and he shall rule over thee.'[15] St. Paul had described this subjection as it applied to Christians when he wrote: 'Wives, submit yourselves unto your own husbands, as unto the Lord.'[16]

Submission for women meant acceptance of their duties in the home. As wives and mothers their work was for their families and with their families; it was not with the wider world. Husbands had to face the problems of business life: the strain of negotiations, the problems of organising manufactures. Women came into contact with outside society only when disaster overtook the family and they were forced to earn their own living, or when they undertook acts of charity. A wife's duty was to promote the well-being of the man she had married. According to William Landels, Sarah Ellis, and others, most wives found happiness in tending their husbands when they returned home exhausted each evening and in guiding their children during the first years of innocent curiosity. There would always be some women who did not fit this picture, who wished for a more public life, 'but if we admit that the laws of life among us, such as they are, are good for the many, we should hardly be warranted, either by wisdom or justice, in altering them for the proposed advantage of a few.'[17]

The subordinate position portrayed in Genesis and in the Epistles called for self-restraint from women. They had to suffer silently whatever misfortunes life held in store; endurance was the foremost womanly characteristic. 'Bear to the end, and ye shall conquer; wait to the end and ye shall receive the crown,' one author urged.[18] Tied to the home with little variety of experience to divert their thoughts, women dwelt on misfortune in a way unknown and often unsuspected by their more active partners. In this atmosphere self-denial came to be preached as a virtue in itself.

Self-denial had to be practised by women in all aspects of their lives. As many possessed no money save that given by fathers, husbands, or brothers, they were often unable to obtain the things they desired. In middle-class families, where it was considered unladylike for unmarried daughters to work, dependence on male relatives was complete. Money for each dress, each pair of shoes, had to be asked for and might be denied. In the same way money might be denied for subscriptions to a library or attendance at a course of lectures.

When a woman married, all but her personal possessions became her husband's. Any money that she might earn as a married woman, whether living with her husband or separated from him, legally

belonged to him. Even if a woman received a marriage settlement, as those of the upper classes usually did, it applied only to land and stock settled on her at the time of her marriage; any subsequent gifts to her were legally her husband's. There was much agitation during the nineteenth century to change the law relating to women's property, beginning with the celebrated case of Caroline Norton, which led to a change in the law relating to custody of children. In 1858 by an Act relating to marriage and divorce, any property or money a woman inherited or earned after separating from her husband was deemed to be hers. Not until 1882 by the Married Women's Property Act were women living with their husbands granted the same rights. By subjecting herself to her husband, a wife had to understand that her time, as well as her person and her property, were at his disposal. Both wives and daughters expected their work or leisure to be interrupted by the demands of the men of the household.[19] Women's constant renunciation of doing what they wanted was perceived by John Stuart Mill to be the result of men's position of power and women's position of dependence.[20]

Whether young ladies were still tied to work in the household or were busy with accomplishments, they were taught that any desire they might have for book knowledge — for the kind of learning their brothers got at school — was an indulgence. To be reading was to be lazy and self-indulgent. At best, reading was a relaxation allowed only when all other duties had been performed. Virtue, as Charlotte Brontë acknowledged, lay in denying oneself such luxury:

Following my father's advice. . . I have endeavoured not only attentively to observe all the duties a woman ought to fulfil, but to feel deeply interested in them. I don't always succeed, for sometimes when I'm teaching or sewing, I would rather be reading or writing; but I try to deny myself; and my father's approbation amply rewarded me for the privation.[21]

Sarah Ellis, in her book *Education of the Heart: Woman's Best Work* (London, 1869) elaborated on these themes. Their families' approbation was most important to women for, unlike men, they could not gain honours from the world at large, they could not prove their success by earning a fortune or gaining renown for scholarship or creativity. Theirs was a more modest role; women gained their reward from their families, or from those others of society to whom they had rendered personal assistance.

For this reason women needed occupation that involved the whole of their being. Where their hearts were, there was their satisfaction. 'Heart work' was to be found in helping others, first at home and then if there were time and energy still left, in acts of charity abroad. The combination of the desire for 'heart work' and the possession of ample time made women of the middle classes ideal charity workers. Sarah Ellis was joined by others opposed to higher education for women in encouraging women's ambition to perform works of charity. Dedication to personal service, coupled with true Christian knowledge, they felt, made women a powerful moral influence in the world. A woman's beauty was complete only when pleasing features were joined to Christian sweetness. Women knew that outward trappings were of no value compared to the beauty of inner tranquility. 'Whose adorning. . . *let it be* the hidden man of the heart, in that which is not corruptible, *even the ornament* of a meek and quiet spirit, which is in the sight of God of great price.'[22]

It was to protect such a vision of Christian womanhood that Christopher Wordsworth preached against equality in education. How could women participate in any public displays of learning, such as public examinations, without jeopardising their modesty? Higher education for women would fling open the doors of feverish excitement in preparation for examinations and leave women with their beauty wilted. If this was what woman desired for herself she should be dissuaded:

> Let us endeavour to protect her from anything that would sweep away the graceful bloom and delicate hues of modesty; and which, in the place of her loveliest ornaments, may haply produce the hard features, the roving eye and bold stare, the loud speech, and the unquiet demeanour of a vainglorious display, of forward boldness and obtrusive effrontery.[23]

It was dangerous for women to believe that the cultivation of the intellect was an end in itself. Were they to act on their belief they would destroy the essence of their womanhood, become obsessed with worldly aspirations, and never reach the perfection God intended for them. 'The mind of woman cannot be trained and perfected except by the education of the higher faculty of her spirit, which rises upward to communion and union with God, the fountain of all Truth and Love.'[24]

The right education for women instructed their spirit as well as

their intellect. The question was how this should be done. Certain subjects, such as modern languages, were fashionable for women to learn but distracted them from their duties as homemakers. As the editor of the *Christian Observer* cautioned: 'To know something of herself, to love her Bible, and to love God, are worth all the languages of Babel: which in after-life often serve no better purpose than to make girls useless.'[25] Women, therefore, should be taught the fundamentals of homemaking, with sufficient Biblical and religious teaching to encourage them to undertake the moral education of their children.

The importance to women of spiritual understanding was underscored by the story of Martha and Mary in the Gospel according to St. Luke, which, like the story of the Creation, was subject to various interpretations. While Jesus was at their house, Martha spent her time preparing refreshments for him and waiting upon him, while Mary 'sat at Jesus's feet and heard his work.' With the indignation of one who feels exploited, Martha complained to Jesus that Mary was not helping her with the serving, and bade him tell her to do so. However, Jesus replied, gently, that Martha's priorities were wrong. She was fussing over trivia, but Mary understood the one thing that was important. 'Mary hath chosen that good part, which shall not be taken away from her.'[26] According to some interpreters the story of Martha and Mary showed that as well as learning how to manage a home, a woman had to develop her religious understanding. This did not entail her studying academic subjects as men did, however.

This attitude to the education of women was anti-intellectual. Those accepting it were prompted by fear that intellectual stimulus would cause women to lose their faith. Loss of faith for women would be catastrophic, they felt, since women transmitted the morals of society to each new generation. How could Christianity survive — how could English society survive — if mothers could not attend to the moral teaching of their children?

Even women who wanted to take courses of higher education were undermined by the fear that learning might destroy their faith. Constance Maynard had to be convinced before she entered Girton in 1872 that she could withstand temptation. Her cousin wrote to her reassuringly, for Constance, she knew, had a 'having' religion in the sense she spoke of:

In the present stir about Woman and her development, my heart would ache over an unspiritually-minded, unconverted girl going to a College, or even one who had merely a 'hoping' rather than a

'having' religion, heavenly and earthly *aspirations* get so easily confused together — while actual possessions assert their distinctness by their very nature and reality.[27]

Her experiences convinced Maynard that her mission was to found a college more truly Christian than Girton, where she herself could supervise the spiritual life of the students. In 1882 she became founding principal of Westfield College; its students were her living proofs to the world that education need not spoil Christian womanhood.

Not all who wished a woman to develop the spiritual side of her nature felt that any intellectual stimulus was undesirable. There was much difference of opinion about the meaning of the story of Martha and Mary. Some felt, as described above, that the spiritual life, exemplified in Mary, did not encompass learning. Others disagreed, claiming that the distinctive 'good part' of some women was to study and become teachers. However, it was not for women to choose this way of life for themselves; they were to take whatever God had given them — 'be it what others call drudgery' — and make it beautiful by the spirit in which they performed it.[28]

There was general agreement that 'Marthaism' had received too much emphasis in the past. This was one reason, writers suggested, for the degeneration of nineteenth-century society. If the moral tone of society were to be raised, women had to dedicate themselves to its spiritual regeneration. The world needed more Marys. Women had to be strengthened in their faith by education. If men were tempted by disbelief, women had to be strongholds of religious faith for them to return to. At all costs women had to remain faithful to Christianity, for only then could they fulfill their roles as guardians of the home. This attitude was one facet of conservative reaction to rapid social change, which left Victorians grasping the driftwood of their beliefs. Many believed that existing evils could be countered only by spreading more widely the moral values of their forbears. 'Among our own sex we want fewer "Marthas" and more "Marys"; less attention to, or rather less absorption in, the details and appliances of life and more in its principles and spirit.'[29]

With the feeling that there should be greater spiritual guidance from women went an increased respect for their nobility. Women, unassailed by the temptations of the world, living apart in the seclusion of the home, were described as men's superior conscience. Although women submitted to men in all the material aspects of life,

men knew they could never aspire to women's purity, and thus were willing to submit to women's spiritual guidance. In purity lay women's nobility. So long as women were considered merely as agreeable amusements for men, theirs was but a frivolous existence. Christian ethics, however, offered woman a higher ideal, to be the conscience of man. It was for this role that she should be educated.

These arguments redefined woman's role in society to make her the guardian of Christian morality and the repository of virtue. At a time when great numbers of men and women were moving from country to cities religious writers felt a duty to redefine woman's role. What model did the woman of the upper classes offer her less fortunate sisters? The frivolity of life amongst the aristocracy before 1840 was no fit model for them, yet there was evidence, by that date, that aristocratic ways were already being copied by the middle classes. Who could say where such copying would end? Only by woman's returning to the simple ways of her forbears could society be saved from decadence. Whereas men were increasingly being differentiated, as individuals, according to their education and occupation, those who wished to halt this process tried to do so by defining a role for 'woman', as though the multitude of individual women formed one unit whose role in life was the same no matter what class they belonged to, or what aspirations they had.

In this definition woman's submission to man was justified by Biblical injunction. It was clearly sinful for a woman to claim for herself the authority of a man; her true duty would be neglected if she did so. English society cried out for an intensification of woman's care for the moral well-being of her children. Wealthy mothers were neglecting their duties, leaving the moral training of their children to nurses incompetent to teach them. Parents were corrupting children by their obsession with material comforts and their carelessness for religion. What was needed was a return to a religious life. Women should not hanker after university education, which some men acquired. Learning would cripple them for their true work in life; it would seduce them with ephemeral truths and leave them without belief, without modesty, without purity.

And when our virtuous women are all made free-thinkers and free-doers, and the feminine millenium looked for among the faithful of the advanced sect has set in, we plain folk who believe in the mutual interdependence of the sexes, but in the natural inferiority and consequent subordination of women, must look elsewhere than at home for the *tacens et placens uxor* of our dreams and desires.[30]

Sexual Morality

The 'plain folk' described above found the religious definition of woman's role exceedingly persuasive by the 1860s when the ideal of purity in sexual behaviour had become sacrosanct to the middle classes.[31] Virginity was the standard for both sexes, though women were punished more severely than men for infringing it since, unlike men, they were said to lack sexual desires, and their action could, therefore, result only from their vanity or their greed for money. Hence Landels claimed, 'Speaking of the sexes generally, we believe it will be found that good women as a rule exceed good men in goodness, and that bad women equally exceed bad men in their peculiar line.'[32]

The Pre-Raphaelites gave most graphic expression to the ideal of feminine purity, harking back to a romantic medieval chivalry. Dante Gabriel Rossetti portrayed the dilemma posed by the ideal in his love for Elizabeth Siddal. Theirs was an unworldly, even mystical romance. Rossetti, at least, could admit to sexual passion, but his standards forbade him to sully the romance with such 'impure' desires. While he was courting Lizzie he formed a liaison with a professional model, Fanny Cornforth, which he continued after he and Lizzie were married.[33]

The belief that 'love of a noble kind' was separate from and superior to sexual desire, and that its expression should be through virginity and continence was analogous to the practice of thrift and parsimony in economic affairs. Peter T. Cominos has described persuasively the spread of a normative standard of thrifty sexual behaviour among men, which condoned sexual intercourse only for the propagation of the species in the state of matrimony.[34] Although, as Patricia Branca suggests in *Silent Sisterhood*, there must have been women who experienced pleasure from their own sexuality, this was not what society expected them to experience.[35] The spread of a belief in the superiority of asexual love had serious social consequences because, in accepting it, men and women came to develop feelings of guilt for every sexual desire and for every sexual experience, including those they experienced with their marriage partners. Husbands brought up to accept the new ideal of woman, and trained from puberty to be ashamed of their own sexual drives, tended to feel guilt perpetually for the sexual demands they made upon their wives; providing them with financial support was one means of assuaging this guilt, a kind of *quid pro quo* not very different from the money paid a prostitute.

Some writers of the time claimed there was a connection between

changing marriage patterns and an apparently growing demand for the services of prostitutes.[36] There is evidence that by 1870 fewer children were being born into each middle-class family than in the previous decades. *Coitus interruptus* and abstention from sexual intercourse were probably the most prevalent methods of birth control used at the time. The latter was no doubt congenial to a generation of women brought up to believe that virginity should be forfeited in marriage only for the sake of procreation—it was not theirs to experience pleasure from sexual intercourse, but to accept it in dutiful submission. Women brought up with an exalted belief in their own purity had a vested interest in maintaining it. 'Girls know absolutely nothing until they are married,' wrote Lady Emily Lutyens. 'They are taught that everything is wrong, and then suddenly plunged right into the middle of it.'[37] Women were likely to punish their husbands or themselves for any pleasure they found in sexual intercourse. They were expected to look on sex as a necessary evil, a symbol of the subjection meted out to women by God because of Eve's transgression. Rather than abase themselves further in the eyes of their wives and detract from the nobility of marriage, some husbands resorted to prostitutes for sexual satisfaction. Although little was written at the time about the number of married men who paid for the services of prostitutes, there is no doubt that they formed a substantial part of the clientele.[38] At the same time, the age of marriage for middle-class men increased. As mentioned earlier, parents in the last decades of the nineteenth century demanded higher incomes from prospective sons-in-law than formerly, so that their daughters might begin married life at the standard of their fathers' homes when they left them. As a result, many young men had to postpone marrying until they had established themselves financially. Although there was strong pressure on young men to remain celibate during their years of bachelorhood, there was ample evidence that celibacy was difficult to sustain. To some young men, women of the so-called demi-monde, who had been trained neither to repress their sexuality nor to accept a position of subordination, were more attractive than the eligible women they were expected to marry.[39]

There was an inherent contradiction in an ethical code that urged men to consider women both as spiritual mothers and as physical wives. A sensitive man might find no release from the overwhelming sense of guilt that accompanied his sexual feelings for a woman of his own class. Some men, therefore, rejected the idea of marriage, and formed semi-permanent relationships with demi-mondaines. The rise

in age of marriage for men, and the increase in the number of permanent bachelors can be seen to have contributed to an increasing demand for prostitutes.[40] Towards prostitutes middle-class men might feel a great deal of disgust, but little guilt, for these women were thought to have chosen their course freely, in spite of evidence offered by Josephine Butler and her associates that freedom of choice for most prostitutes was fictitious.[41] Society treated prostitutes as outcasts for good reason, Landels claimed, for,

> Men who lead loose lives are not so abandoned in general character as women of the same class. This may, indeed, be partially accounted for by the different treatment which the sexes meet with in society; the men being welcomed to respectable circles notwithstanding their vice, while the women are treated as outcasts, and driven by the strength of the feeling against them into greater defiance of, and departure from social proprieties. . . But that difference of treatment has itself to be explained. . . Society treats vicious women more rigidly than vicious men, partly because it recognizes in them, already, as certainly as it tends to produce in them, a greater degree of wickedness.[42]

In becoming prostitutes women forfeited the respect to which they were entitled as members of the weaker sex. They renounced purity, the essence of womanhood.

Sexual promiscuity was believed to be far more abominable in women than in men. There were sins, such as promiscuity, which, though equally heinous in the sight of God, even Christians felt were worse when committed by a woman than a man, 'because in committing them she violates, as it were, the very law of her nature in a sense in which he does not.'[43] Society therefore punished severely any woman who committed a sexual indiscretion. There was no reason to feel this was unjust. Through the punishment of vice, woman's purity was protected, and the majority saved from sin. 'It would be well for men if they also were ruled by a severe opinion,' wrote Winwood Reade in *The Martyrdom of Man*,[44] but their more bestial nature made it unlikely that such severity would be adopted.

There was an ambiguity in the attitudes towards women described above. Whereas they were lauded as men's consciences and the repositories of virtue, they were also held to be easily corruptible. Society had to protect women from themselves. Eve, not Adam, had been tempted by the serpent; only by constant exhortation could her

descendants be kept from sin. Consequently, the education of women had to be carefully supervised. Their reading had to be prescribed so as to protect their virtue and strengthen their faith. Women should be kept out of universities because they would be tempted to follow any examples of vice they found in pagan literature or any atheistic ideas they found in science. University courses were designed for men who could withstand such temptations, or who, if they could not, would be excused by society. Sexual lapses were understandable in men, they could never be condoned in women. Agnosticism might be tolerated in men, but society could not tolerate it in the mothers of future generations.

Some people made a further assumption about women: Eve's succumbing to the serpent's temptation showed that women were *innately* sinful. This was an added reason for not allowing them to attend universities, since they would be a constant distraction to men. Margaret Murray, an Egyptologist who had been a student in the 1880s, wrote of her student years: 'Everyone knew that women were anathema in a university, not only because of their inferior intellect but also on account of their innate wickedness they would be a terrible danger to the young men.'[45] Thus, no matter whether men considered women temptresses or merely easy prey to sexual license, they questioned the prudence of allowing them to attend lectures with men, or of opening colleges for women in towns populated largely by young male students. To do so would not only put women—and men—in the way of temptation, it would make exceptions of certain women and thus undermine the role assigned 'woman': 'It is certainly time to condemn every step towards the individualization of women lest they become viragoes, and their orphaned children the *gamins* of the gutter.'[46]

Given the belief that seems to have been widespread by mid-century that women had no sex drives of their own, that they subjected themselves to men's demands for sexual intercourse merely for the sake of perpetuating the human race, in return for which men provided women with financial security, it is not surprising that women's desire to undertake higher education in order to earn their own livings led to panic among those who wished to conserve marriage and the family. Once women were financially independent would they have any reason to endure sexual relations that they found distasteful? If women were able to support themselves, at a similar standard of living to which they had been accustomed, might not many choose to do so and thereby abandon marriage and the bearing of children? This, of

course, would be disastrous socially. 'If women can do without marriage, can men do so?' Asked Anthony Trollope. 'And if not, how are men to get wives if the women elect to remain single?'[47] Men would be forced to rely on prostitutes for sexual gratification, and so the 'Social Evil' would reach unbounded proportions. The birthrate, especially of the middle classes, would drop dramatically; the next generation would provide but a meagre supply of men and women capable of governing the country, and carrying on its illustrious business enterprise. Britain would decline from international pre-eminence.

Thus, the moral and religious arguments used against higher education for women not only reinforced the nineteenth-century ideal of womanhood, but denied women their individuality with all the power and influence wrought by the word of God. In the mind of believers it was a sin to change the relationship God had ordained between man and woman, and those advocating change in women's position in the home and in standards of women's education were considered sinners. The times were conducive to these beliefs, and many felt they had God on their side in opposing women's aspirations. To go against the Lord's directives was to court disaster. As Burgon warned: 'For the creature to set himself in opposition to the revealed mind and will of the Creator is plainly sinful, and can only be attended by disastrous consequences. Let the relation of the sexes be the matter in hand, — and it is clear that you are touching foundations.'[48]

In the next chapter, we discuss the nineteenth-century ideal of womanhood in relation to historical fact. The economic, medical, and religious arguments used to oppose higher education for women were based mainly on this ideal, rather than on the realities of the times. The discrepancies between the real and the ideal were great and caused enormous psychological conflicts within women seeking opportunities for educational and professional advancement. The religious arguments just presented manifest some of these discrepancies. Let us now consider them all in more detail.

Notes

1.   One letter on women's education appeared in 1834 in the *Christian Observer*, an influential Anglican evangelical journal, but the 1860s and 1870s was the heyday of the discussion in religious journals. The *Christian Observer*, *Evangelical Magazine*, *Eclectic Review* (Non-Conformist), *Christian Life* (Unitarian), and the *Unitarian Review* all ran articles at that time on the education of women.

2.   Christopher Wordsworth, 'On Intellectual Display in Education', *Occasional Sermons*, 3d ser. (London, 1852); and *Christian Womanhood and Christian Sovereignty* (London, 1884).

3.   John William Burgon, *To Educate Young Women Like Young Men, and With Young Men a Thing Inexpedient and Immodest* (Oxford, 1884), p. 23. The sermon was preached on Trinity Sunday, 1884.

4.   William Landels, *Woman: Her Position and Power* (London, n.d.), p. 130. There were two further editions in 1859 and 1870.

5.   Humphry House, 'The Mood of Doubt', *Ideas and Beliefs of the Victorians* (London, 1949), p. 77, discusses this reaction to the tensions of society described in chapters 1 and 7.

6.   Charles Darwin, *The Autobiography of Charles Darwin 1809-1882*, Lady Nora Barlow (ed.) (New York, 1959), p. 95. Darwin went on to compare his father's experience with his own: 'At the present time, with my small acquaintance, I know (or have known) several married ladies, who believe very little more than their husbands' (p. 96). 'Nothing is more remarkable,' Darwin claimed, 'than the spread of scepticism or rationalism during the latter half of my life' (p. 95).

7.   Gen. 2:18, 21-22.

8.   See 'Mill on the Condition of Women', *Christian Observer* 68 (1869), pp. 625-6.

9.   Benjamin Parsons, *The Mental and Moral Dignity of Women*, 2d edn (London, 1849), pp. 19-24. This book was first published in 1842. A third edition appeared in 1856.

10.   Parsons, *Dignity of Women*, p. 22.

11.   Emme Dee, *Woman: Her Mission and Education* (London, 1876), p. 30.

12.   Burgon, *To Educate Young Women*, p. 15.

13.   As reported in *The Lancet* 2 (1886), p. 315.

14.   1 Tim. 2:11-14. See also 1 Cor. 11:7-9; 14:34.

15.   Gen. 3:16.

16.   Eph. 5:22.

17.   Anthony Trollope, *Higher Education of Women* (London, [1868]), p. 76. A similar attitude was expressed in 'Queen Bees or Working Bees?' *Saturday Review* 8 (1859), p. 576. Sarah Ellis, supervisor of a school for young ladies (Rawdon House) and wife of a missionary, wrote a series of books on the moral duties of women.

18.   W. H. Davenport Adams, *Woman's Work and Worth* (London, 1880), p. 167. This book was reprinted in London, 1882: several editions also appeared in the United States. Self-denial was also a theme in novels of the period.

19.   See Emily Davies as quoted in Barbara Stephen, *Emily Davies and Girton College* (London, 1927), p. 30; Pamela Horn, *The Rise and Fall of the Victorian Servant* (New York, 1975); Theresa McBride, *The Domestic Revolution: Modernization of Household Service in England and France* (New York, 1976); Ann Oakley, *Woman's Work: The Housewife, Past and Present* (New York, 1974), chapter 3; J. A. Banks and Olive Banks, *Feminism and Family Planning* (Liverpool, 1964), p. 65; and J. A. Banks, *Prosperity and Parenthood* (London, 1957), pp. 76-7 discuss changes in household arrangements in this period.

20.   John Stuart Mill to Auguste Comte, 1843, Francis E. Mineka (ed.) *The Earlier Letters of John Stuart Mill*, (Toronto, 1963), p. 607.

21.   Brontë to Robert Southey, 1837, James Aitken, (ed.) *English Letters of the 19th Century*, (Harmondsworth, Middlesex: Penguin Books, 1946), p. 154.

22.   1 Pet. 3:3-4.

23.   Wordsworth, *Christian Womanhood*, p. 27.

24.   Wordsworth, *Christian Womanhood*, p. 39.

25.   Editor's note, 'On the Education of Girls', *Christian Observer* 65 (1866), p. 94.

26.   Luke 10:38-42.

27.   Constance L. Maynard, 'Green Book Diary for 1871-72' (MS Westfield College, London). The letter was copied into the diary; 4 July 1872, entry.

28. ' "The Good Part"; or, Mary and Martha: A Word for Young Women', *Evangelical Magazine* n.s. 39 (1861), pp. 223-8.

29. Justitia [Mrs. Henry Davis Pochin], *The Right of Women to Exercise the Elective Franchise* (London, 1855), p. 33.

30. 'The British Mother Taking Alarm', *Saturday Review* 32 (1871): 335.

31. For discussion of Victorian attitudes towards women and sexuality see Peter T. Cominos, 'Innocent Femina Sensualis in Unconscious Conflict', in Martha Vicinus (ed.), *Suffer and Be Still: Women in the Victorian Age* (Bloomington, 1973), pp. 155-72; Jean L'Esperance, 'Doctors and Women in Nineteenth Century Society: Sexuality and Role,' in John Woodward and David Richards (eds), *Health Care and Popular Medicine in Nineteenth Century England* (New York, 1977), pp. 105-27; Carl Degler, 'What Ought To Be and What Was: Women's Sexuality in the Nineteenth Century,' *American Historical Review* 79, no. 5 (1974): 1469-90.

32. Landels, *Woman: Her Position and Power*, p. 124.

33. See William Gaunt, *The Pre-Raphaelite Tragedy* (New York, 1942), pp. 46-7; William Bell Scott, *The Autobiographical Notes of the Life of William Bell Scott, R.S.A., LL.D., and Notices of His Artistic and Poetic Circle of Friends, 1830 to 1882,* vol. 1 (London, 1892), p. 101.

34. Peter T. Cominos, 'Late-Victorian Sexual Respectability and the Social System,' *International Review of Social History* 8, nos. 1,2 (1963): 18-48, 216-50.

35. Patricia Branca, *Silent Sisterhood* (Pittsburgh, 1975), chapter 7.

36. Cominos, 'Late-Victorian Sexual Respectability,' p. 230, refers to comments by several authors, and quotes Grant Allen: 'Our existing system is really a joint system of marriage and prostitution in which the second element is a necessary corollary and safeguard of the first.' ('The Girl of the Future', *Universal Review* (1890), p. 58.)

37. Lady Emily Lutyens, née Emily Lytton, to Rev. Whitwell Elwin, *A Blessed Girl: Memoirs of a Victorian Girlhood Chronicled in an Exchange of Letters, 1887-1895* (Philadelphia, 1954), p. 68.

38. The significance of effective teaching of sexual repression to the breakdown of the Victorian ideal of woman has yet to be explored fully. The demands of married men for the services of prostitutes is discussed briefly by E. M. Sigsworth and T. J. Wyke, 'A Study of Victorian Prostitution and Venereal Disease', in Martha Vicinus (ed.), *Suffer and Be Still*, pp. 86-7.

39. James Laver in *Manners and Morals in the Age of Optimism 1848-1914* (New York, 1966), pp. 46-83, describes the attractions of the demi-monde. See also, Cominos, 'Late Victorian Sexual Respectability', pp. 233-4. Jonathan Gathorne-Hardy, *The Unnatural History of the Nanny* (New York, 1973), claims that upper class Englishmen acquired their regard for the sexuality of lower class women from their nannies: 'Nannies gave baths and tucked up in bed. It was Nanny's arms that went round little boys, Nanny's breasts and lips they felt, Nanny they smelt. And Nannies were lower class' (p. 98).

40. See Banks and Banks, *Feminism and Family Planning*, chapter 3.

41. Laver, *Manners and Morals*, pp. 84-116, and Constance Rover, *Love, Morals and the Feminists* (London, 1970), pp. 76-7, discuss the relationship between poverty and prostitution; Butler's opinions were discussed also in her letters.

42. Landels, *Woman: Her Position and Power*, pp. 134-5.

43. Oxoniensis ['One who belongs to Oxford'—pseud.], 'The Education of Women: Comments on *Essays and Pursuits of Women* by Frances Power Cobbe (London, Emily Faithfull, 1863)', *Christian Observer* 64 (1865), p. 547.

44. Winwood Reade, *The Martyrdom of Man* (1872), Thinker's Library edn (London, 1945), p. 366. By 1884 this book was in its eighth edition in England. It was also published in the United States.

45. Margaret Murray, *My First Hundred Years* (London, 1963), p. 154.

46. 'The Probable Retrogression of Women', *Saturday Review* 32 (1871), p. 11.

47. Anthony Trollope, *North America*, vol. 1 (London, 1862), p. 398.

48. Burgon, *To Educate Young Women*, p. 18.

7 | The Ideal of Womanhood Confronts Reality

Opponents of higher education for women attempted to prove that the Victorian ideal of womanhood was based on sound moral, social, and intellectual principles, and that to go against these principles was to destroy the fabric of society. The most conservative opponents relied on Biblical authority and conventional wisdom. Others drew on the latest scientific evidence in comparative anatomy and physiology. Still others based their arguments on the dire consequences any change in the social structure with respect to sex roles would have on the economic stability of the country. As the movement for higher education for women gained momentum and women began to take courses previously provided only for men, opponents were forced to admit that some of their assumptions were wrong. Yet their defeats never shook their support for the ideal of womanhood; they merely proceeded to defend it in different terms.

The ideal took shape in the first decades of the nineteenth century; although it was modified over time, the broad outlines fixed relationships between the sexes, at least for men and women of the middle classes. Within the family it meant that the man, as paterfamilias, controlled family finances, enforced discipline, and had the final say in decisions relating to members of the family; the woman, as wife and mother, set the moral standard of the family, organised the household, and supervised the up-bringing of the children. Family income might come partly from real property or investments, and partly or entirely from the father's earnings, augmented in later years by contributions from the adult, unmarried sons. Neither wives nor daughters were expected to earn money, though wives had usually contributed a dowry to the family's property at marriage. As Tilly and Scott pointed out in *Women, Work, and Family* (New York, 1978) employed children of the lower classes acquired power and a voice in decision-making within those families which depended for support on the earnings of individual family members. Similarly, in those middle-class families which depended entirely on earnings, employed sons acquired power, but girls, deprived of the right to contribute to the family income, were denied it.

The ideal of urban middle-class life turned out to be different from the life of the aristocracy on which it was patterned. Leisure, based upon income from property, had been a gentleman's prerogative for generations. There never was any question among the aristocracy that it was as desirable for men as it was for women not to work. (Indeed, members of the gentry followed the aristocracy in this regard.) Wealthy women might spend much time at home while their husbands were out shooting or they might spend time and money on acts of charity, but they were never expected to be the sole repositories of virtue. Aristocratic society was in some ways uncultured and even brutish, but it provided a rough equality in the lives of the sexes, a companionship between them, which few of the middle classes in the nineteenth century could attain. Leisure for middle-class women was made possible only by the unceasing work of men.

Nineteenth-century writers preached that women should find fulfillment in the home, thinking nostalgically of the homes of their parents and grandparents in the villages and small towns of pre-industrial England. They failed to comprehend that these homes could never be reproduced in the cities of their own time. The part these writers urged women to play was not based upon reality. Life was not the same as it had been. It was the dichotomy between reality and the model or ideal set for women that precipitated their struggle for higher education.

Most responsible citizens of the middle classes accepted separate roles for men and women. They took it as a matter of course that women should find their occupation in the home, and saw no possible role for them in business or in the professions. Yet, after the middle of the century, they found their opinions challenged by a growing number of people, including their own and their friends' daughters. We shall now look more closely at the reasons behind this challenge and at some of the people who disapproved of the ideal of womanhood.'

Economic Realities

The belief that men alone should provide for their families and women should be protected from having to earn money placed a heavy burden upon men. As husbands, fathers, brothers and sons, men were called upon to provide for a galaxy of female relatives. During the nineteenth century, an increasing number of women remained single, so that the

burden of providing for them throughout their lives fell on their male relatives.[1] The 1851 census revealed what people knew from experience—many middle-class men were failures in terms of the ideal. They failed to earn incomes large enough to support their female relatives. Events beyond the control of any individual—illness, death, or business failure—claimed their victims and destroyed the financial security of whole families. Although some 500 life insurance offices were established between 1800 and 1870, many were unstable and even fraudulent. Only after the passage of the Life Assurance Companies Act of 1870 was more protection afforded to policyholders, while the Married Women's Property Act of 1870 (reaffirmed in the Married Women's Property Act, 1882) enabled women to take out policies on their own account, or husbands to make wives the beneficiaries of their policies.[2] Many families were impoverished by the major depressions which began in 1836 and 1873. Others were affected by less significant fluctuations, and business failures took place all the time. Moreover, with the best will in the world, many tradesmen, lawyers, clergymen, and merchants were unable to earn sufficient money to provide daughters with incomes for life.

Women also paid a high price for being relieved of the need to support themselves. Some fathers transferred the locus of their anxiety from fear that they themselves would be unable to provide for their families to fear that their daughters would fail them by becoming old maids.

> The daughters of professional men, whose incomes average from £500 to £1,000 a year, cannot but feel themselves a burden and a drag on the hard-won earnings of their fathers, they must know—if they allow themselves to think at all—that they are a constant cause of anxiety, and that should they not get married, there is every probability of their being, sooner of later, obliged to enter the battle of life utterly unprepared and unfitted for the fight.[3]

Young women, therefore, as well as their male relatives, became obsessed by the need for them to marry well. Parents expected a girl's education to make her as attractive as possible in the marriage market. Failure in a man was defined as his inability to provide for the women of the family. Failure for a woman was to remain unmarried and thereby be a financial burden to her father and brothers. This accounts for the extreme displeasure of relatives when a girl refused an eligible match, and for the acceptance of match-making as a duty by

relatives and friends of unmarried girls: 'It is as much a duty in regard to a girl as to seek a profession for a boy. Marriage is a woman's testing and highest function, and it is a culpable remissness not to use the means for the end.'[4] Despite the vigilance of their friends, however, the number of women who failed to attain the married state envisaged for them increased as the century progressed. Reasons for this increase among women who were unmarried through necessity, not choice, included a rise in the age of marriage, demand from parents for sons-in-law with sound financial position, rise in the number of permanent bachelors, and higher emigration among men than women.[5]

To some people the custom of leaving women ignorant of how the economy worked appeared dangerous. Women of the middle and upper classes lived in an artificial world; money was always provided for them, and they had no suspicion that one day they might have to provide it for themselves. For many respectable women, however, that day did arrive, and they were left to face it alone, uncomprehending, and untrained.

Men and women themselves secure financially, but sympathetic to those who were not, saw the danger most clearly and led the way in demanding a new kind of education for women. The insecure could not afford to look openly at the economic facts; they shut their eyes to the possibility of failure and fought to maintain the status quo.[6] They feared lest they hasten defeat by admitting its possibility. How could a man retain the respect of his business colleagues if he allowed his daughters to train for any kind of work? How could a girl so trained expect to find a wealthy husband? The answer seemed to be that there was no way, and this was why those who most needed to take action refused to do so.

Preparation for Work

Those who dared face reality knew that preparing women for work was the only way to safeguard them from penury. But preparation presupposed that families of the middle classes were willing to anticipate the need for women to earn their own livings, something they were unlikely to do as long as holding a job entailed a woman's loss of status. This dilemma was particularly acute for upper middle-class families, and it lasted throughout the nineteenth century: professional skills were needed for high-status jobs that paid well, yet those families whose daughters would have to work were least likely to allow them to

acquire the necessary education. Once well-established families, especially from the aristocracy, allowed their daughters to attend courses of higher education, it became possible for the needy among the middle classes to allow their daughters to do likewise without losing face. For this reason, the support of aristocrats such as Lady Stanley of Alderley,[7] and distinguished families such as the Gurneys[8] and the Wedgwoods,[9] immensely assisted the development of higher education for women.

Through a series of changes in commercial, professional, and industrial organisation, women had been replaced by men in many responsible jobs by the beginning of the nineteenth century. The number of women working with their husbands in trades or skilled crafts had declined. Fashions of gentility made it unladylike for a wife to spend her time working in the family business, (or, as it came to be phrased: to spend her time *assisting* her husband with *his* business), and this change of fashion was accompanied by a clarification of the separate role of women (see Chapter 2). Some wives still kept accounts or managed the transactions of their family businesses, but more women than formerly spent their time visiting, shopping, keeping up accomplishments and arranging evening entertainments. Although in the past it had been customary for a woman who was widowed to take over the family business, which she had always helped to run, by the beginning of the nineteenth century few widows had had sufficient experience to do so. Their lack of business experience remained a cause of distress for widows and their families throughout the century, and indeed became more widespread with the acceptance of the Victorian ideal of womanhood.[10]

As the distinction between amateur and professional came to be more rigorously drawn, women lost other opportunities they had possessed to participate the economic life of the community. Professional qualifications came to be defined in terms of courses and examinations; women, with their lack of formal education, were automatically excluded from professional status. Until the mid-eighteenth century some occupations had traditionally fallen to women. During the next hundred years, however, single as well as married tradeswomen withdrew, or took unskilled employment. Few remained skilled artisans. Women had traditionally been hairdressers and wigmakers, but the elaborate fashions developed during the later eighteenth century needed, so it was claimed, the skill and strength of a man to create, so women were gradually ousted from hairdressing.[11] Other occupations traditionally open to women, such as medicine,

dentistry, midwifery, and pharmacy, became professionalised, and, because they were not allowed to train or qualify for professions, women were excluded from work they had previously done. For none of these occupations in the past had women (or men) needed formal schooling; they had learned what was necessary through experience on the job, and through personal contact with other practitioners. They had little or no feelings for the general applicability of their techniques; mothers had taught their daughters the family's traditional remedies, but few had seen fit to write books for the benefit of the public as a whole.[12] Only when family networks broke down, with the migration of large numbers of people from rural areas to the towns, did the need for a more public knowledge of health care techniques become clear.

Midwifery, in particular, was a pragmatic art since those who practised it were often quite uneducated, and unable to generalise their experiences in writing however skilled at their work. When medicine, pharmacy, and midwifery became intellectualised, qualifications for their practice included attendance at courses designed for men only. Women practitioners of these occupations all but disappeared. Margaretta Grey wrote the following in her diary during 1853:

> I have always regretted that they [women] have suffered the whole of the medical offices, with the knowledge and applications of simples, which used to lie in the province of mothers of families, to pass out of their hands, and that the practice of midwifery, so obviously appropriate to women, should be given up by them. Medical men in want of occupation lay claim to this as a province of theirs and decry all household dabbling in medicine as derogatory to science.[13]

Women were squeezed out of industrial trades, also, as technological changes increased the capital investment needed to set up as a craftsperson. Few women had sufficient capital to do so, and women found it far more difficult than men to borrow capital. A steep rise in apprenticeship fees discouraged women from applying to the few guild trades that remained open to them.[14] In the old handicraft system women had rarely received any training, but had managed to pick up the skills of the craft on the job. However, 'with the increase of skill and new technique, such conditions were no longer possible.'[15]

Lack of skill among women was exaggerated because of a common

belief that men should manage large machinery. Analogies were drawn between the working of men's minds and bodies and the working of large machines. Belief in the affinity between men and machines was shared by many of the men who formed trade unions during the nineteenth century. In 1868, Josephine Butler wrote to Frederic Harrison that she wished she could publicise the effects of trade unions on women's employment. Women could testify to the discrimination they experienced: '*Thousands* could come forward with their own sad tales—of exclusion, perpetual exclusion—but if you examine *men*, as I have done, a little privately, you will get such dodging reasoning as I hear from many a tradesman here. "Women can't or won't, or are unfit." '[16]

With the increasing distinction between amateurs and professionals, people's qualifications for jobs came to depend not on who they were but on what skills they possessed. The change gathered momentum in the 1850s, but already in the first decades of the nineteenth century pressure from aspiring middle-class families had led to a strengthening of the examination systems for men at Oxford and Cambridge.[17] Graduates from these universities, who had been successful under the new examination system, later urged its extension to the practice of medicine, and admission to officer training establishments, the Indian Service, and the Civil Service.[18] The middle years of the nineteenth century saw the proliferation of qualifying associations which monitored the qualifications and practice of engineers, actuaries, pharmacists, architects and others.[19] Entry through merit—gradually defined as academic merit—became the keystone of Victorian philosophy:

> The principle of the modern movement in morals and politics, is that conduct, and conduct alone, entitles to respect: that not what men are, but what they do, constitutes their claim to deference; that, above all, merit, and not birth, is the only rightful claim to power and authority.[20]

Since women had no access to universities or professional schools and declining access to skilled trades, they were condemned to amateur status in each area. At the moment when avenues of upward mobility were opening for men, they were closing for women.

Already by the 1840s, however, men and women of the middle classes began to concede that those women forced by lack of money to seek employment should be provided with training for the good of the

society they aimed to serve. For example, many indigent gentlewomen became governesses, yet their only qualifications were their indigence and their gentility. Neither gave them skills for their job. Many governesses were unhappy failures who clung to their jobs for the sake of security, enduring the taunts of their charges and the contempt of their employers. Despite the increasing supply of applicants for positions as governesses, employers were dissatisfied with the quality of education they offered and the lack of any way to tell which applicants possessed adequate qualifications. As a response both to this dissatisfaction and to their own desire to help the needy, F. D. Maurice and his supporters founded, in London, Queen's College (1848) for the training of governesses.[21] Queen's College, and the Ladies College, Bedford Square, founded in the following year, prepared women teach in a society that, educationally, was far more sophisticated than it had been a generation earlier.

The two women's colleges in London opened their courses to other women than merely those who were training to be governesses or teachers. The courses were well subscribed. Women showed a growing interest, also, in attending public lectures on academic subjects.

Women's newly awakened interest was frustrated, however, when the dispute between amateurs and professionals resulted during the 1860s in several learned societies closing their meetings to women. Professionals wished to convert these societies into places where those working on scientific and philosophical problems could exchange views and work out a consensus of opinion. Amateurs, on the other hand, looked on the learned societies as places for the dissemination of ideas to those eager to learn; they resented the suggestion that because they were amateurs (no matter how great their enthusiasm) they should be excluded from discussions.

The question of whether women should be allowed into the learned societies embittered the dispute between professionals and amateurs. There were some professionals who favoured the advancement of education for women, yet rejected the idea that women should become members of learned societies on the grounds that as women they were, *ipso facto,* amateurs. Thomas Huxley, a prime mover in attempts to professionalise learned societies, believing that women were, at best, intelligent amateurs, opposed their membership in the Ethnological and Geological Societies. Although he was a constant supporter of better education for women, to make them fit 'companions of men in all their pursuits', he did not believe that other people would follow his plans for educating his daughters in the same way as his son:

You know as well as I do that other people won't do the like, and five sixths of women will stop in the doll stage of evolution to be the stronghold of parsondom, the drag on civilization, the degradation of every important pursuit with which they mix themselves— 'intrigues' in politics and 'friponnes' in science.[22]

Charles Lyell had written to him hinting that women should be allowed into the Geological Society rather than leave half of the human race to gain its interpretation of creation from '60,000 sworn teachers of endowed opinions';[23] Huxley replied:

The Geological Society is not, to my mind, a place of education for students but a place of discussion for adepts: and the more it is applied to the former purpose, the less competent it must become to fulfil the latter—its primary and most important object. . . If my claws and beak are good for anything they shall be kept from hindering the progress of any science I have to do with.[24]

Huxley took the same attitude towards discussions at the Ethno-logical Society of London, of which he became president in 1868. His opposition to the custom of allowing women to attend meetings called forth an impassioned plea from Eliza Lynn Linton, which is intriguing because she herself, at a later date, scorned the aspirations of women reformers. 'When we are admitted into Societies then we are admitted into something that infinitely enriches and enlarges our horizons,' she wrote to Huxley. 'I pray you with all my strength to keep us as attendants at the Ethnological meetings, and when you are going to discuss hazardous papers give us warning, and we will stay away. Else, let us be free still to attend.'[25] Huxley remained adamant, however, and the proposal to ban women from the scientific meetings of the society (inviting them only to special meetings of a 'popular nature') was approved in 1869.[26]

Getting Good Jobs

The exclusion of women from occupations requiring professional qualifications and from learned societies coincided in time with the development of the ideal described earlier. Women were to find fulfillment in the home; they were not to work outside. However, in reality many middle-class women could not rely on male relatives to

support them; they themselves had to earn money. Some sympathisers ventured to help them by founding colleges for their education. Others publicised and sought to alleviate their exploitation — their low pay, long hours and squalid working conditions in a society that forbad women to train for professional occupations but welcomed them as cheap labour in unskilled ones.

A group of women reformers from headquarters at Langham Place in London began a journal (1858) and an employment society (1859),[27] in order to open to women of the middle classes jobs commensurate with their intelligence and their status in society. The task was formidable because new types of jobs were evolving whose respectability was in doubt, and because women seeking employment came from families of disparate status, even within the middle classes. Bessie Parkes, Jessie Boucherett and their colleagues at Langham Place believed that if men from the middle classes were opticians and shopkeepers, doctors and lawyers, their sisters and daughters should be able to find work of equal standing, even if this meant that women had to undertake professional training. They were appalled by the number of pleas for help they received. The 'Langham Place ladies' dealt with reality. Men might cling to an ideal of woman as the angel of the home, but in London, Leeds, and Manchester hundreds of 'angels' were starving while society ignored their plight. Organisations similar to the one at Langham Place were formed outside London to open new jobs for women as skilled workers such as bookkeepers and printers. In Leeds, new jobs were opened in draughtmanship; in Sheffield, in metal decoration and the needle trades. The programmes offered for more than ten years at Queen's College and the Ladies College, Bedford Square, had raised expectations for the educational qualifications of governesses and, as a result, many governesses with less education became redundant. 'Registers for Governesses were opened, and an effort was made to find other employment for those least suited for teaching, as housekeepers, companions, bookkeepers, clerks, and, in conjunction with the emigration societies, to draft abroad some of those who wished to go to the colonies.'[28]

Such concerted efforts by women to improve their employment opportunities were timely. According to the census of 1851 a large number of women worked. While the majority came from the lower classes, a sizeable proportion were women of the middle classes. The census listed separately, but nevertheless counted as part of the workforce, more than 450,000 'wives and daughters (above 20) of farmers, innkeepers. shopkeepers, shoemakers &c.' who worked alongside their

husbands and fathers, thus maintaining the traditional work pattern of the family unit. However, more than two million women were 'engaged in independent industry or possessed of independent means.' (The latter, who must have belonged to the middle or upper classes, appear to have numbered about 173,000.)[29] The vast majority of working women were unmarried, but approximately one-seventh of all married women worked, and in some areas, such as the lace, silk, and ribbon-making districts in the Midlands, the fraction was much higher.[30]

Several hundred thousand independent women workers were from families of the middle classes. There was a bitter irony in their position, because they were downwardly mobile in an age that offered men unprecedented opportunity for upward mobility. Women from the middle classes lost status when they worked because 'ladies' were not expected to earn their own living. The problems of middle-class working women were compounded by the menial nature of the jobs open to them. Their biggest complaint was that they were forced to take low-paying, low-status jobs when their families' positions should have entitled them, as it entitled their brothers, to jobs demanding skill and good manners. Constantly, and with reason, they faced the danger that their loss of status would spiral, that they would end up as milliners or slopworkers condemned to illness and early death, or driven by low wages and overwork to seek an easier life through prostitution.[31] An early supporter of better education for women saw a link between profligacy in her own sex and lack of education: 'The injustice that confined woman to inferior cultivation, extended to man superior freedom. No fiend could have devised more productive sources of human misery; for, in their mutual reaction, they have doomed man to degraded intellect — woman to degraded morals.'[32]

The growing interest after 1860 in controlling prostitution, and even eliminating it by rehabilitating prostitutes and opening alternative avenues of employment to women, may have reflected the power of the middle classes to impose their values on the poor — who regarded prostitution as one form of seasonal labour[33] — but it was also an indication of people's awakening to women's economic and sexual exploitation. The causes of prostitution seemed to stem most obviously from the social condition of women. Thus the *Westminster Review* claimed that it was not seduction that accounted for the large number of prostitutes infesting the streest of English towns, but the desire of ordinary working women to escape from the drudgery of their lives. 'To such the temptation to vice is as strong as the inducements to

continue chaste are to the class which has all to lose by a dereliction from what is in their case as much the path of interest as of virtue.'[34]

In 1864, concern over the spread of venereal diseases led to the passage of the first Contagious Diseases (Women) Act by which, in certain garrison towns in the south of England, women known to be or suspected by the police of being prostitutes were required to undergo fortnightly internal examinations, and to be hospitalised if they were found to have gonorrhea or syphilis. The act was renewed in subsequent years and medical examinations were extended to women in other towns. The Contagious Diseases Act brought vociferous opposition from those who claimed women's personal liberties were violated by their terms and that prostitution should be abolished not regulated. Led by Josephine Butler, the movement to repeal the acts was eventually successful, but in her fight for repeal Butler had to chide some reformers for their blindness to the consequences of their protective attitudes towards women. To Frederic Harrison, who preached a humanism that would prevent all women from working and make them guardians of home she wrote, 'Thousands are actually now starving: I do not mean of the *lower* classes, but of the middle classes. Thousands are driven to prostitution, a profession which theories such as yours, do more to encourage than any amount of actual profligacy.'[35]

There remained many who, like Harrison, opposed the opening of new fields to women. The opposition was particularly vehement when women demanded an end to their exclusion from high-status jobs. Such opposition was bitterly resented by those who knew the hardships endured by working women. From the beginning of civilisation women had taken up the 'fag-ends of work', exhausting themselves for little pay. This, men were prepared to allow. But to have women 'competing for the higher rewards of cultivated faculty has proved too much for the justice, to say nothing of the "chivalry," not indeed of individual men, but of men in the aggregate.'[36] Contemporaries were faced here with two challenges: the first was a challenge to the notion of separate spheres for men and women; the second was a challenge to the notion that women (even within their own sphere) should remain untrained amateurs rather than trained professionals.

As we have already seen, most Victorians thought of men and women as having separate spheres, each made up of those tasks, behaviours, and attitudes appropriate for their sex. The response to the changes of industrialisation had been to protect the separation of the spheres. The ideal was for women to remain in the home. Where

they could not do that, but had to work, separation was obtained by having women perform different tasks from men, where possible in a separate location. But physical separation of the sexes could not always be maintained.

In the 1880s, for instance, with the introduction of the typewriter, there was serious discussion of whether women typists should be allowed to work in business offices.[37] Although wives had traditionally dealt with correspondence and balancing the books in family businesses, men were usually employed for these jobs in firms large enough for a separate office. Copyists and ledger clerks were the 'Bob Cratchits' of the business world, steadily employed at meagre wages. The pressure from women to be employed as typists met with opposition from middle-class employers brought up to believe women's function was to be socially attractive, not economically useful. An unmarried woman's task was to find a husband, not a job for herself. If she took a job her interest in it could only be temporary; she would use her position to help her in her search for a husband. Women in business offices were a danger, therefore, to the young unmarried men there who might be tempted to marry below them, and a danger to the married men who might be tempted to flirt with them. As with women in the professions, there was concern that unmarried women in businesses, working with men who were married, would form liaisons with them, and thus put new strains on marriages and families. Neither men nor women of the middle classes were brought up to relate to one another outside a social-sexual context. As a result, Victorians were only comfortable with work patterns that separated the sexes, and suggestions for mixing the two sexes at work met strong opposition.

Fear of the sexes working together was one source of opposition to women obtaining professional qualifications. Another source was the challenge women professionals posed to the notion that women should remain untrained amateurs. Loopholes in regulations that allowed women access to certain professions existed not because women were welcomed, but because it was inconceivable that they would apply. Once women dared to do so, the regulations were changed to bar them. The Society of Apothecaries changed its regulations after Elizabeth Garrett had passed its qualifying examinations in 1865, and the Royal Academy forbade women to become Associates because, according to John Stuart Mill, 'they were so distinguishing themselves, they were assuming so honourable a place in their art. . . No sooner do women show themselves capable of competing with men in any career,

than that career, if it be lucrative or honourable, is closed to them.'[38]

However, those who demanded that women should be trained to become professionals did not necessarily envisage the break down of separate spheres. Within women's sphere, as within men's, a new hierarchical structure of work meant that women needed training, as did men, to perform their tasks. Some women, for instance, were needed to head girls' schools and women's hospitals. There was no justification for training them less well than their male counterparts.

Thus, by the last decades of the nineteenth century, many upper and middle-class people came to accept the reality of unmarried women working in semi-professional or even professional jobs, while still believing in the ideal of married women remaining in the home. New fields of work were opened to women but these remained as consistent as possible with the ideal of womanhood, and came to be defined as women's jobs. The ideal, therefore, changed over time: in content, as it embodied new ideas on the importance of rational learning for both sexes, and in extent, as reluctantly it came to be applied to married women only.

Opposition to women working as men's colleagues, in the same jobs, remained strong. William Landels, while advocating equal pay for equal work, wished to see men turn back to 'manly' occupations and leave the lighter work to women. 'Counting buttons and measuring tape, selling tea and sugar in small quantities, issuing tickets and making entries of the simplest kind. . . these. . . are not of a nature either to require or to develop any manly quality.' Such jobs should be made available to women while men found 'more suitable and worthy pursuits.'[39] In a similar vein, *The Lancet*, which stead-fastly opposed women's entry into the medical profession, was happy to support the entry of women into less prestigious fields. 'An effort is now being made to introduce women into the hairdressing trade. . . Surely this is an employment to which women are perfectly suitable. . . We desire to see women displacing men from all those employments which do not rightly belong to them.' Four years later, it reported that, in one sub-district of London, a woman had been appointed deputy registrar of births and deaths. 'Why not?. . . Many women have great aptitude for routine duties, which men commonly find so irksome.[40] Two strands of thought appear here: that men should not begrudge handing over their least prestigious jobs to women, since the reduction in job opportunities for men that resulted was justified because such jobs were unmanly; and that men and women could not both be employed in the same kind of jobs. One sex

was bound to drive out the other. It was this belief that motivated much of the opposition to women in their struggle to obtain professional training.

The Ideal as Reality

As well as those who challenged the ideal because it proved economically unrealistic were men and women, particularly of the wealthy middle classes, who had turned the ideal into reality but soon became disillusioned with it. Why did the ideal of womanhood prove intolerable to some people as a reality?

Part of the answer lay in the emptiness of women's lives as they lived out the ideal. Their homes were to occupy all their energies, but homes that could do so existed only in the minds of writers. In the real homes of wealthy city dwellers, maids and cooks did the work wives and daughters were supposed to do. It was a sign of ill-breeding in a lady to spend much time attending to household duties. She had social obligations that demanded her attention.

Home, also, was changing its character. Its role as a unit of production was shrivelling. First, manufacturing and business transactions moved away from the home to their own premises. Then, the home, especially the city home, became less important as a producer of foods and household supplies. By 1870, commercial production of jams, butter, and bread was well established; although people might still prefer to make their own (or have their cooks make them), they did not have to do so.[41] In the same way household supplies, such as soap, could be bought readily.

Clothing, too, began to be produced outside the home. A result of wealth was that families could afford to employ dressmakers to make clothes for all the women. As with housework, there was a social stigma attached to the *necessity* of making one's own clothes. Not that sewing was abandoned by ladies—the ability to sew was a definite asset for a marriageable young woman—but sewing for an every day purpose was considered unladylike. Despite their aspirations to gentility, however, many married women of the middle classes spent a considerable part of their time sewing for the family.

When the sewing machine was introduced in the middle of the century the method of producing clothing changed dramatically. First, people of the middle classes could purchase sewing machines to

use at home, and, since a seam could be machined quickly, the time taken up by sewing was halved. At the same time that the sewing machine was successfully marketed, commercial patterns for clothes were developed.[42] No longer did women have to learn how to make or copy a pattern, a complicated mathematical problem. Instead, they could buy patterns in shops, choosing from a variety of styles undreamed of before, and these they could hand to their dressmaker to make up for them, or run up for themselves on the sewing machine. A second effect of the sewing machine was that readymade clothes could be produced rapidly in workshops. Although readymade clothes were frowned upon by the wealthy, who had always been able to employ others to make their clothes for them by hand, they were welcomed by the majority of the population.[43] Sewing machines revolutionised other household work as well as the making of clothes. Making and mending curtains, sheets, and towels, all these activities when done by machine, took less time, or were performed outside the home.

By the last decades of the nineteenth century many interesting and productive tasks traditionally carried out by women in the home — as well as some that were dull and unproductive — had disappeared from there. Men, also, had left the home to follow their work: those of the middle classes to manage factories, organise large-scale buying and selling, or run law offices. In most occupations the scale of operations increased during the century making it the rule for men to work away from home all day. Some women, deprived of both meaningful work and the companionship of their spouses, began to resent the insignificance of their lives.

When so many complicated, time-consuming tasks had been eliminated from the home, women were encouraged to concentrate on bringing up their children. Indeed, writers in the nineteenth century suggested that women's especial duty was to develop their children's character. Protected from the sins of the world, women were to be the true guardians of morality. There was irony in this belief because women's education did not prepare them to be teachers, and society paid scant attention to women's opinions on moral and ethical issues. Sons, particularly, grew to despise their mothers' ignorance. Boys and men developed a 'sultan-like' sense of superiority to all women which, according to John Stuart Mill, perverted their whole existence, as individuals and as social beings.[44] Men's sense of superiority was rooted not only in women's lack of education, but in the contempt men held for women's opinions. It was this contempt that women reformers such as

Mrs. Pochin sought to combat, 'How can our youth respect that maternal judgment which they see publicly despised and rated below par?' At no age, Pochin argued, should sons have to feel ashamed for the influence exercised over them by their mothers.[45]

There was irony also in the very suggestion that mothers should concentrate on bringing up their children, since childcare was work that those who could afford it handed over to others — to women of lower economic status than themselves. Nannies were employed to care for babies; governesses to supervise the early education of boys and, in some families, the whole education of girls. Older boys left the house to attend school and, after the founding of the Girls' Public Day School Company in 1872, it became more usual for girls to attend school also.[46] At the same time that responsibility for educating children was transferred from the home to the school, the number of children born into each family was decreasing.[47] In a smaller family each individual gained psychic space, and more money was available for each child's education. Formal education grew more important as people came to accept stratified occupational structures, and as the individual was recognised as the unit through which changes in family status could be most easily effected.

Victorian insistence on the sanctity of the home and the family represented an attempt to preserve those institutions from changes already taking place. By the end of the nineteenth century, the factory and sweatshop had displaced the home as the primary unit of production, while the school was displacing the family as the guardian of morality and culture. These changes shrunk the significance of women's lives. Writers might exhort women to exercise their moral power over their families, but wives and mothers of the middle classes could find few ways to do so.

Their unmarried daughters felt even more frustrated. The wealthier the family, the greater was their frustration. Many had no function in the home. They were not needed to help with housework since maids were employed to do it. Supervision of the servants was the mother's task. Even if there were trouble with inefficient or insubordinate maids, that was not an issue that daughters could help resolve. Unmarried daughters, therefore, were the first to revolt against the ideal set for them by society. 'The home is woman's realm' — but not the home of their experience. The one they lived in had no use for them; they were not needed there. Etiquette bound them to a round of visiting. Their days were spent in drawing rooms, practising a musical instrument, embroidering, drawing, watching

hopefully for a marriageable beau.

> It is not easy for those whose lives are full to overflowing of the interests which accumulate as life matures, to realise how insupportably dull the life of a young woman just out of the schoolroom is apt to be, nor the powerful influence for evil this dullness has upon her health and morals. There is no tonic in the pharmacopoeia to be compared with happiness, and happiness worth calling such is not known where the days drag along filled with make-believe occupations and dreary sham amusements.[48]

While men idolised hard work, and earned respect from their peers through their industry and financial success, women earned respect from being idle and non-productive. A woman who could lounge on a sofa all day reading or embroidering was obviously wealthy. Her husband or father had provided servants to cook and clean; *he* was a success economically and consequently *she* was a success socially. However, this situation was potentially full of strain, for idleness was never considered a virtue by the middle classes. It was difficult for parents to exhort their sons to find a goal in life towards which to work, while at the same time encouraging their daughters to be idle.

Some young women, despising the idleness imposed upon them by their family's status, decided to seek jobs for themselves, despite the censure of respectable society. They rejected the example set for them by the outstanding women of earlier generations — the learned savant, poet, letterwriter, or playwright — and turned instead to paid professional work. In work, they had learned, lay the true purpose of life, and only successful work would receive the rewards of society. 'The case of the modern girl is peculiarly hard in this, that she has fallen upon an age in which idleness is accounted disgraceful. The social atmosphere rings with exhortations to act, act in the living present.'[49]

Daughters of Evangelical families, particularly, despaired at the meaninglessness of their lives. They had been taught the need to combat evil in the world; they watched with envy as their brothers trained for useful work while they sat idle at home waiting to get married. They had been taught the practice of scrupulous soul-searching; they knew how to analyse their motives to be sure that God was behind them and not the Devil. Their Evangelical beliefs were a call to action, yet society said that women should not leave the home. How could they carry out their mission of curbing vice if they were not allowed to find out what vice was? Many Evangelical daughters were

certain they had a mission, that God had called them into the world for a purpose. They believed it was their duty to find out what that purpose was. Constance Maynard, for instance, became convinced that she was to help establish a truly Christian college. She rejected opportunities to develop two colleges because neither seemed to fit her chosen path. On 12 February 1882, she wrote in her diary, 'Another thread slips into the cord. A day or two ago I heard that Miss Dudin Brown "wished to start a college", means and influence being in her hand, and yesterday she asked me to the first Council meeting. I went. . . and the discussion flew to the mark at once. . . By this day fortnight something will be settled that forms a definite outlook, the grasp of my life may be near and yet one holds back.'[50] A month later, 19 March 1882, recording her last meeting with her admirer, Mr. Robertson, she wrote, 'I spoke gently, assuring him it was all of no pleasure or use to me, save as bringing glory to God and true blessing to the girls of England. . . He said it was "taking the veil", — so it is perhaps, but in a noble cause, and some one should do it whose heart is in it.'[51]

Society claimed that a woman's mission lay in the home, but these young women found that their homes were organised to function without them; woman's mission lay in marriage and motherhood, but some women, like Maynard, saw a broader mission for themselves, while others felt the opportunity for marriage had passed them by. Were they to spend the rest of their lives in idleness, waiting for a husband who might never come? Perhaps society was wrong. These women had intellects equal to their brothers'; why should they remain untrained and useless? God's work needed to be done; surely He did not mind if it were done by women instead of men? By such reasoning women raised in the Evangelical, humanitarian tradition, valuing learning only as it applied to God's work, decided that their fulfillment lay outside the home; Elizabeth Garrett Anderson, Emily Davies, Sophia Jex-Blake, and Constance Maynard were all from Evangelical families. Others, motivated not by religious feelings but by the boredom of the lives, followed their lead. Such a one was Margaret Murray, an Egyptologist who early in her life decided to train as a nurse because of 'the sheer boredom at home.'[52]

There were other reasons why the nineteenth-century ideal proposed for women was found intolerable. It claimed that women were purer than men. The sexual implications of this attitude led many husbands to join the ranks of those discontented with the ideal. Some women became too 'pure' to enjoy sexual relations in marriage,

and husbands felt driven to gratify their sexual desires elsewhere than with their wives.

The notion of purity spilled over into the whole marital relationship. In some families, husbands dared not reveal the details of business transactions to their wives for fear of censure or, more disastrous, fear that their wives would cease to respect them.[53] When men did find topics of public or private interest that were safe to discuss with women they were often reluctant to open the subject for fear that women, by their lack of education, would misunderstand the issues or divert the argument to personal matters. Social intercourse between the sexes was therefore reduced to a series of vacuous conversations. Moreover, tension between some husbands and wives increased because wives did not share the exhaustion their husbands felt from their work. Often servants performed all the physical work in the house, so that when their husbands returned in the evening wives were ready to exert themselves and enjoy the companionship they had been deprived of all day. As a result men became exasperated by the constant chatter of their wives who, in turn, were exasperated by the silence of their husbands.

Marriages between businessmen and the prototype of the ideal woman were disastrous in other ways. Girls were raised to believe that their minds were inferior, their bodies delicate, and their fate predestined. The poor opinion women had of themselves, of their ability to function as independent adults, was reinforced again and again by the artificial standards embodied in the ideal of womanhood. The resultant emotional distress of women was a constant theme in novels of the period. Early in the century Jane Austen wrote, 'We certainly do not forget you, so soon as you forget us. It is, perhaps, our fate rather than our merit. We cannot help ourselves. We live at home, quiet, confined, and our feelings prey upon us.'[54] And later, Charlotte Brontë, 'Can labour alone make a human being happy? No; but it can give varieties of pain, and prevent us from breaking our hearts with a single tyrant master—torture. Besides, successful labour has its recompense; a vacant, weary, lonely hopeless life has none.'[55]

Marriage was thought to be an escape from the emotional anxiety seen in many contemporary young women. Too often, it was claimed, unmarried women degraded themselves by prying into other people's affairs and spreading scandal. 'All this is owing to an exuberant activity of spirit, which, if it had found employment at home would have rendered them respectable and useful members of society.'[56] In reality, however, married life offered the wealthy middle-class woman

little employment. The ideal woman, once married, received little respect for her accomplishments and found herself unnecessary to the successful running of her home or of her husband's life.

Opponents of higher education for women supported an ideal that few women could live up to, and some who did found to be frustrating and vacuous. The Christian legacy, the higher ideal of providing moral support for husbands, children, and society at large was supposed to be their duty and their most important contribution, especially in marriage. 'The gain of society, therefore, will be, not in depreciating woman, in treating her as a puppet and plaything, as an inferior tool through whom children are born, and houses kept swept and garnished. . . but as, in truth, the conscience of man and society, the household minister, the national monitor, through whom the ideas of society may be kept high and pure.'[57] Yet society did depreciate women and only theoretically did it respect those who lived the ideal. The moral duties accorded women were impossible to carry out because their sphere of influence was so limited. To hope that women would influence society simply by their example was naive, since their families were out of reach much of the time, and charitable work to be effective often required a life that was too worldly to be considered moral.

The claims of those who had experienced the ideal and found it unworkable were the most difficult for society to face. To have accepted their validity would have meant jettisoning the accepted ideal for woman and formulating another. The claims had to be denied.

> We sometimes hear in well-to-do homes that the women in it are dying of *ennui*, want of occupation, and objectless lives. Such homes are the creation of an artificial society. The immense mass of the people in city or in country would smile in derision to have the like imputed to them. . . It may be that in classes, sufficiently rich to be freed from labour yet not rich enough to enter the arena of society, time may hang heavy on the hands of many women. . . But this is surely the prejudice of an age. . . whose true education is still so deplorably short of our hopes and our ideals.[58]

Opponents of higher education for women were certain that the demands of reformers from whatever source they arose would in the end lead to a revolution in the relationship between the sexes. They worked strenuously to show why the existing relationship had to

remain unchanged. They did this by emphasising innate differences between the sexes, and by describing the political as well as social anarchy that would result from the type of society envisaged by reformers. In the 1830s feminism had been associated in people's minds with the Saint-Simonians,[59] and throughout the century equality of the sexes was regarded as an offshoot of French revolutionary thought. The Paris Commune was seen by the *Saturday Review* as an example of the political anarchy caused by the feminist revolution in society.

> The insurgence of women is a fringe of the red flag that has been flying so insolently over the city where marriage has been decreed unnecessary, fatherhood obsolete, and where women have fully attained those hideous rights for which they blindly clamour. . . The latent folly which would destroy family ties is but an introduction to the madness of the Paris incendiaries.[60]

Reformers pressing for higher education for women were circumscribed by the beliefs and prejudices of society. They could not advocate an overthrow of existing mores, even had they wished to see it. They could not admit that opponents were possibly right in suggesting that higher education would eventually take women away from their realm of the home. They stated that the majority of women would always stay there. They were concerned only with a small minority, many of whom found themselves unable to marry, even though they wished to do so. And, insofar as women based their claims to higher education on their need to earn a living in jobs commensurate with their status and intelligence, they gained support in spite of the strength of arguments against them.

On other issues they were less successful. The right of women to a liberal education for the sake of their development as individuals, a theme well developed in the twentieth century, gained little support in the nineteenth. Middle-class society did not favour learning for its own sake, nor did it yet define the rights of the individual in terms of equal opportunity to education. Nor was society prepared to relinquish an ideal for womanhood that seemed so close to realisation. Even if unmarried women workers had to be tolerated, there was no reason for married women to work, and those who were still employed had to be discouraged from continuing their employment. Therefore women's attempts to enter the professions continued throughout the century to be opposed by people who felt that any professional woman would

pave the way for a reckless increase in married women workers. The economics of professional education made it unlikely that women would want to retire from professional work on marriage. Those who supported the idea of women combining marriage and career, as Elizabeth Garrett Anderson had done, were seen to be advocating the overthrow of one of the pillars of society.

> We are defending the principle of the womanliness of woman against the anarchic asserters of the manliness of woman. There is a passionate part of so-called reformers, both men and women, who are crying out for absolute assimilation as a principle. . . In the name of mercy let us all do our best with the practical dilemmas which society throws up. But let us not attempt to cure them by pulling society down from its foundations and uprooting the very first ideas of social order.[61]

The example of Elizabeth Garrett Anderson, a professional and a wife and mother, did not have as great an effect in her own generation as in later ones, for there were few men and women prepared to follow the example she and her husband set and replan relations between the sexes. Higher education for women came to be accepted by society merely because it was expedient, in spite of warnings that it must in the end undermine the ideal of woman in the home.

The terms of the debate over higher education for women only changed (insofar as they have changed at all) when education came to be seen, in the twentieth century, as something broader than occupational training, when the middle classes abandoned their single-mindedness about business and professional success and broadened their vision to include the general cultural development of each individual.[62] By that time, however, women were accustomed to fighting for higher education within the framework of established societal values, and they had come to embrace the idea of higher education as professional training with the same ardour as their erstwhile opponents. We now turn to a discussion of that fight.

Notes

1.   This trend changed between 1901 and 1921. In 1901, of every thousand women in England and Wales, 395 were single, 497 married, 108 widowed. In 1921, the figures were, respectively, 368, 520, and 112. See Sylvia Anthony, *Women's Place in Industry and Home* (London, 1932), chapter 1.

2.   See Lee Holcombe, 'Victorian Wives and Property: Reform of the Married

Women's Property Law, 1857-1882', in Martha Vicinus (ed.), *A Widening Sphere*, (Bloomington, 1977), pp. 3-28.

3. Miss Downing, 'Work as a Necessity for Women', as reported in *Victoria Magazine* 18 (1872), p. 221.

4. Reverend Whitwell Elwin to Emily Lytton, 24 April 1892, in Lady Emily Lutyens, *A Blessed Girl* (Philadelphia, 1954), p. 97.

5. See J. A. Banks and Olive Banks, *Feminism and Family Planning* (London, 1964), chapter 3.

6. A series of pamphlets was printed to persuade parents to educate their daughters. The first, Emily Faithfull, *How Shall I Educate My Daughter?* (London, 1863), dealt with parents' fears.

7. Lady Stanley was Henrietta Maria Dillon, who married Edward, 2nd Lord Stanley of Alderley. According to Nancy Mitford (*The Ladies of Alderley* [London, 1938]) 'She loved him so much in spite of everything that during his lifetime her personality was completely suppressed. . . When he died, however, she became the terror of all who were in contact with her. She threw herself with unbounded energy into the championship of women's rights and higher education, and was among the founders of Girton, Queen's College, London, and High Schools for girls.' This account of the sudden change in Lady Stanley on the death of her husband is an exaggeration. Even during his lifetime she was an ardent supporter of women's education.

8. Russell Gurney, MP, Recorder of the City of London, and his wife, Emelia, were active in aiding Elizabeth Garrett (Jo Manton, *Elizabeth Garrett Anderson* [London, 1965], pp. 78-9, 115, 139, and 173.) They were also friends of Emily Davies. In Parliament, Russell Gurney actively supported opening the professions to women. Emelia Gurney was a member of the first executive committee of Girton College.

9. Hensleigh Wedgwood, grandson of Josiah Wedgwood, was a philologist. The Wedgwoods were associated with the Ladies' College, Bedford Square, he as a trustee, she as a council member. The Wedgwoods were cousins of the Darwins; Erasmus Darwin was also a trustee of the Ladies' College, Bedford Square.

10. Ivy Pinchbeck, *Women Workers and the Industrial Revolution, 1750-1850* (London, 1930), p. 283.

11. *Ibid.*, pp. 290-2; Neville Williams, *Powder and Paint* (London, 1957), pp. 87-9. Women seem first to have become hairdressers during the seventeenth century.

12. For the few pharmaceutical books written by women between 1650 and 1760 see Myra Reynolds, *The Learned Lady in England, 1650-1760* (Boston, 1920), pp. 433-4.

13. Diary of Margaretta Grey as quoted by Josephine E. Butler, *Memoir of John Grey of Dilston* (Edinburgh, 1869), 326n.

14. Pinchbeck, *Women Workers*, pp. 292-3.

15. *Ibid.*, p. 304.

16. Butler to Harrison, 7 May 1868, Josephine Butler Collection, Fawcett Library, London.

17. R. J. Montgomery, *Examinations* (London, 1965), pp. 16-17.

18. *Ibid.*, pp. 21-30; Raymond Williams, *The Long Revolution* (New York, 1966), pp. 137-40.

19. See Geoffrey Millerson, *The Qualifying Associations: A Study in Professionalization* (London, 1964).

20. John Stuart Mill, *The Subjection of Women*, World's Classics edn (London, 1963, originally published in 1869), p. 525.

21. Josephine Kamm, *Hope Deferred* (London, 1965), chapter 12.

22. Huxley to Sir Charles Lyell, 17 March 1860, Huxley Papers, Imperial College, London.

23. Lyell to Huxley, 16 March 1860, Huxley Papers, Imperial College, London.

24. Huxley to Lyell, 17 March 1860, Huxley Papers, Imperial College, London.

25. Linton to Huxley, 11 November 1868, Huxley Papers, Imperial College,

London.

26. 'Report of the Council of the Ethnological Society of London. May 1869', *Journal of the Ethnological Society of London*, n.s. 1 (London, 1868-69), pp. x, xiv. To ensure larger professional participation, Huxley suggested the amalgamation of the Ethnological Society with the Anthropological Society of London. His proposal met opposition but was eventually effected in 1871 under the title, The Anthropological Institute of Great Britain and Ireland. In 1873, despite prognostications of failure through lack of professional support, a dissident group broke away and founded the London Anthropological Society, to whose ordinary meetings women were admitted and invited to present papers. This society was dissolved in 1875 (see *Journal of the Ethnological Society of London*, n.s. 2 [1869-70], p. xvi; *Anthropologia* 1 [1874], pp. 1-17.)

27. *The Englishwoman's Journal* was launched in March 1858. Thirteen volumes were published between that date and 1864 when it was succeeded by the *Alexandra Magazine*. Bessie R. Parkes and Barbara Leigh Smith opened the office at Langham Place. They were joined by Jessie Boucherett (who began the Society for Promoting the Employment of Women), Jane Crow, Adelaide Proctor, Sarah Lewin, Ida Craig, Emily Faithfull and others. A lively description of their work is in Kamm, *Hope Deferred*, pp. 179-85.

28. Annie T. Eddison and Eleanor Thompson, *Origin and History of the Yorkshire Ladies' Council of Education and of its Branches* (n.p. [1892]), p. 25. Barbara Leigh Smith (*Women and Work* [London, 1856]) suggested types of work women could be trained for; a decade later, Bessie Rayner Parkes (*Essays on Woman's Work* [London, 1865]) described jobs opening to women. For a recent study of the Female Middle Class Emigration Society, see A. James Hammerton, 'Feminism and Female Emigration, 1861-1886', in Martha Vicinus (ed.) *A Widening Sphere*, (Bloomington, 1977), chapter 3.

29. [John Duguid Milne], *Industrial and Social Position of Women, in the Middle and Lower Ranks* (London, 1857), pp. 165-8.

30. *Ibid.*, pp. 207-8. Much work by married women was carried on in the home, despite the claim of Andrew Ure, an opponent of factory legislation, that low wages for women in factories encouraged them to leave work and look after their families (*The Philosophy of Manufactures* [London, 1835], p. 475). Peter Gaskell's response was that these women, rather than looking after their families, worked at home for even lower wages than in the factory at 'fustian cutting, hand-loom weaving, or some other less unbroken labour' (*Artisans and Machinery* [London, 1836], p. 174). Louise A. Tilly and Joan W. Scott, (*Women, Work and Family* [New York, 1978], p. 68) estimate that in 1851 40% of women in manufacturing were in 'non-mechanized, homebased garment trades.'

31. 'The Dressmaker's Life', *Englishwoman's Journal* 1 (1858), pp. 319-25. For a discussion of the precariousness of women's respectability see Duncan Crow, *The Victorian Woman* (New York, 1972), pp. 29-31, 66-70.

32. M.L.G., 'Men and Women', *Tait's Edinburgh Magazine*, n.s. 1 (1834), p. 103.

33. See Judith and Daniel Walkowitz, 'We are not Beasts of the Field: Prostitution and the Poor under the Contagious Diseases Acts', *Feminist Studies*, 1 (Winter, 1973), pp. 73-106, and Judith Walkowitz, 'The Making of an Outcast Group: Prostitutes and Working Women in Nineteenth-century Plymouth and Southampton', *A Widening Sphere*, pp. 72-93.

34. 'Review of [Henry G. Jebb], *Out of the Depths* (Cambridge, 1859),' *Westminster Review*, n.s. 16 (1859), p. 303.

35. Butler to Harrison, 7 May 1868, Josephine Butler Collection, Fawcett Library, London.

36. Emily Pfeiffer, *Women and Work* (London, 1888), pp. 25-6.

37. Bernard de Bear, 'Commercial Education in England and America', United States Commissioner of Education, *Annual Report for 1898* (Washington, 1899), p. 332.

38.   John Stuart Mill in *Hansard*, 189 (1867), p. 827.
39.   William Landels, *Woman: Her Position and Power* (London, n.d.), pp. 110-11.
40.   *The Lancet* 2 (1869), p. 794; and 1 (1873), p. 618.
41.   T. N. Morris, 'Management and Preservation of Food', in Charles Singer *et al.* (eds), *A History of Technology*, vol. 5, (London, 1958), pp. 26-52.
42.   During the 1850s paper patterns were distributed free with each issue of the *English Women's Domestic Magazine* which, during those years, was publishing in monthly instalments Isabella Beeton's book of cookery and household management. These patterns seem to have been the first to be commercially produced.
43.   By 1860 sales of the Singer sewing machine in Europe was higher than those in the US. See Sir Alexander Fleck, 'Technology and its Social Consequences', in Singer *et al.* (eds), *A History of Technology*, vol. 5, p. 819. 'Pre-eminently a labour-saving device, it effectively ended the traditional bondage of women to the needle' (D. A. Farnie, 'The Textile Industry: Woven Fabrics', in Singer *et al.* (eds), *A History of Technology*, vol. 5, p. 590).
44.   Mill, *Subjection of Women*, p. 523. An analogy can surely be made here with the mental conflict of whites brought up by black women in societies that deny blacks equality with whites.
45.   Justitia [Mrs. Henry Davis Pochin], *The Right of Women to Exercise the Elective Franchise* (London, 1855), p. 11.
46.   The Girls' Public Day School Company, later called the Girls' Public Day School Trust, had established 37 schools before the end of the century and provided secondary education for more than 7,000 girls (see Josephine Kamm, *Indicative Past: A Hundred Years of the Girls' Public Trust* [London, 1971], pp. 188, 207-15; for details of other secondary schools for girls see Kamm, *Hope Deferred*, pp. 215-17).
47.   This is briefly discussed by R. C. K. Ensor, *England, 1870-1914* (Oxford, 1936), pp. 270-2. For a detailed discussion see J. A. Banks, *Prosperity and Parenthood* (London, 1954), p. 142, and Banks and Banks, *Feminism and Family Planning*, chapter 7.
48.   Elizabeth Garrett Anderson, 'Sex in Mind and Education: A Reply', *Fortnightly Review*, n.s. 15 (1874), p. 590.
49.   Emily Davies, as quoted in Barbara Stephen, *Emily Davies and Girton College* (London, 1927), p. 143.
50.   Constance L. Maynard, 'Green Book Diary for 1882', (Ms. Westfield College Library, London), pp. 56-7.
51.   *Ibid.*, pp. 64-5.
52.   Margaret Murray, *My First Hundred Years* (London, 1963), p. 79. Lady Caroline Jebb wrote to her sister in Philadelphia, 27 April 1879: 'Edith Reynolds says that Julia, her sister, is so much better and happier now that she really has something to do after college, than when she was fretting because she did not somehow get married. She was pretty, too, but as long as the law is against two wives, there are scarcely men enough to marry half the women, and with the best of qualifications, one half must turn to something else' (Mary Reed Bobbitt (ed.), *With Dearest Love to All* [London, 1960], p. 149).
53.   This dilemma for husbands provided the theme of Oscar Wilde's *An Ideal Husband* (London, 1899).
54.   Jane Austen, *Persuasion*, World's Classics edn (London, 1957, originally published in 1818), p. 267.
55.   Charlotte Brontë, *Shirley*, Everyman's Library edn (London, 1943, originally published in 1849), p. 179. Emily Pfeiffer, *Women and Work*, pp. 90-7, detailed some comments by doctors on the effects of women's brooding on misfortunes.
56.   John Gregory, *A Father's Legacy to His Daughters* (London, 1828), p. 80.
57.   'Studious Women', *Eclectic Review* 14 (1868), p. 269.
58.   Frederic Harrison, *Realities and Ideals* (New York, 1908), pp. 108-9.

59.   For a discussion of the association made between feminism and the Saint-Simonians see John Killham, *Tennyson and 'The Princess'* (London, 1958), chapter 2.

60.   'The Probable Retrogression of Women', *Saturday Review* 32 (1871), p. 11.

61.   Harrison, *Realities and Ideals*, p. 74.

62.   The evolution of the idea of the individual is discussed in Williams, *Long Revolution*, pp. 141-2, and, at greater length, in chapter 3.

8 | *The Opposition's Influence on Higher Education for Women*

The opposition to higher education for women was strong because it drew support from many groups: doctors defending their professional status, clergymen protecting clerical influence in university government, social reformers fighting the exploitation of working women, and idealists planning to ennoble women's lives. Each group used different arguments to support the same thesis, women did not need and should not have higher education as it was provided for men.

The opposition was never overcome by debate. When opponents were proved wrong, either logically or empirically, they might retreat into silence, but they rarely changed their belief that higher education for women was unnecessary and undesirable. However, many of the opponents' children and grandchildren came to accept an idea which, in their parents' generation, had been held by only a few: that higher education would enable women to support themselves, when necessary, in jobs of which they and their families could be proud. The need for higher education had to be believed in before the arguments against it were overridden. Only then was previously disdained evidence in favour of higher education for women found to be acceptable.

Opponents of higher education for women did not succeed in stopping its development, but they did effectively influence the people working for it and the institutions they established. Twice, opponents strove to differentiate women's education from men's: in the 1860s by initiating special examinations for women, and in the 1880s and 1890s by suggesting a separate women's university. In the first endeavour they were successful, partly because they found allies among supporters of improved education for women. In the second they were unsuccessful, partly because by the time a separate women's university was canvassed most of those engaged in higher education for women opposed the idea.

The overt influence in these two instances was at least equalled, however, by opponents' indirect influence at all times through social pressure, interpretation of scientific data, medical opinion, and religious teaching. We shall turn first to an evaluation of opponents'

indirect influence on higher education for women.

Indirect influence of the opposition: Religious arguments

Few people were willing to support higher education for women as long as it meant flouting social convention, incurring God's wrath, or both. That social convention was often founded upon religious teaching added to its strength. For instance, the belief that women should not address public meetings matched the Biblical injunction that women should be silent in public places. Only gradually did people's attitude change towards women speaking in public; by the end of the nineteenth century women still could not become lawyers or clergymen. Medicine, the one learned profession to which women did gain access, rarely called for their speaking in public. Although in the last decades of the nineteenth century women served on school boards, and became Poor Law guardians, it was not until the Sex Disqualification (Removal) Act of 1919 that a woman was first called to the bar, and some religious denominations still do not ordain women.[1] As Kathleen Bliss, historian of women's service in the churches has pointed out, the opposition to women ministers has been strongest in those Christian denominations where the concept of the ministry is sacerdotal; in those denominations where the minister is regarded chiefly as 'pastor, preacher and prophet, set aside for a special function among believers who are all in some sense priests', women ministers have been accepted.[2]

The injunction that women should be silent in public was part of the wider belief, expounded by opponents of higher education for women, that they should be modest in all things, including intellectual attainments. This belief had to be respected by reformers, who did not necessarily agree with it, because it was a social convention accepted by some of their supporters as well as by opponents.

More complex in its effect on higher education for women was the belief that women should practice self-denial and humility. If reformers tend to suffer guilt from the process of criticising society, because, as critics, they reject what they have been taught to accept and set their opinions against those of the majority,[3] women who urged others of their sex to change their role in society must have experienced more guilt than most reformers, because they challenged the teaching of their religion as well as of society. As Christians these women had been taught to resign themselves with humility to a subordinate role;

instead, they fought against it and urged other women to do the same. The conflict between their religious upbringing and their ambition in some cases generated anxiety and guilt that handicapped their efforts at reform.

The conflict was most severe in women from Evangelical families, though in a society permeated by Evangelical attitudes all women must have felt the conflict in some measure. Evangelicals accepted a personal commitment to Christ and to serve society, but women, unlike men, were expected to fulfill their mission in the home. When unmarried women yearned to exchange trivial accomplishments and unsystematic acts of charity for the purposeful education and professional life allowed their brothers they were reproached for being unwomanly. They were claiming equality with men in intellect and the right to a public life which their religious training forbade them. In their persistent efforts to make careers for themselves, some women experienced agonies of mental torment trying to reconcile their femininity with their desire to serve society.[4]

Since being pliant and modest were attributes of femininity, women with professional ambitions, and even those who were less ambitious but desired to serve society at large, considered themselves, in some ways, masculine. Perhaps the belief that they were like men gave women such as Sophia Jex-Blake the strength to undertake 'masculine' work. Had they thought themselves to be average women, and had they accepted the conventional estimate of women's strength, they would have felt incapable of undertaking professional work. As it was, they had to be even stronger than their male counterparts because they had to overcome societal assumptions about their mental and physical inferiority, start in the race without adequate preparation and gain 'what training they had been able to obtain in an atmosphere of hostility, to remain in which has taxed their strength and endurance far more than any amount of mental work could tax it.'[5]

The historian finds it difficult to ascertain whether these women perceived themselves to be part of a movement to redefine the roles of *all* women, or merely as opening new options for others as 'deviant' as themselves. Few combined marriage and career, as did Elizabeth Garrett Anderson. Though some may have felt slighted when young at being overlooked in marriage, they came to regard spinsterhood as their deliberate choice. Given the attitudes of society towards sexual promiscuity in women, we can assume that most unmarried professional women did not have sexual relations with men. Some appear to have repressed or redirected all heretorsexual desire and relied only on

other women to provide them with emotional support and, in some cases, sexual gratification.[6]

The opponents of higher education for women were not slow to argue that education would unsex women and make them unmarriageable. Once women's colleges were established, opponents pointed to the low marriage-rate among women students to prove their point. Of the first 41 students at Girton College, only 16 married, and of the first 750 students at Lady Margaret Hall, Oxford, only one quarter married.[7]

Women reformers scoffed at the claim that women, any more than men, needed an education solely for their responsibilities as wives and mothers.

> We do not teach our sons that the sole subject of their existence is to get married, and prove good husbands and fathers, according to a narrow conventional standard. . . Marriage with them puts no stop to the career previously marked out and offers no check to the concentration of mind necessary to the advancement of knowledge.[8]

Despite the logic of this argument, women who wished to combine career and marriage faced tensions, (that still exist in our own day), which derived from the definition of male and female roles accepted in nineteenth-century society.

Another dilemma presented to reformers by the opponents of higher education for women was the argument that higher education would make women infidels. Before reformers could proceed with any plans to change the education of women they had to demonstrate that education did not lead women to lose their faith. Higher education would have been thwarted had the opponents' contentions seemed true. Reformers asked for and received support from individual clerical leaders in the foundation of women's colleges. Their influence can be seen in the prescriptions for religious observance adopted by several colleges. At Lady Margaret Hall in Oxford, a Church of England residence, 'prayers in the chapel began and ended the day, and on Fridays and Sundays Miss Wordsworth [the first principal and herself the daughter of a bishop] conducted a Bible class.'[9] At Girton, where instruction according to the Church of England was given but was not obligatory, the Girton Prayer Meeting was established by Constance L. Maynard when she was a student there in the 1870s. 'Here was the very first college for women starting on its life,' she wrote, 'and I had been sent there quietly to stand for God in the midst

of it.'[10] The religious affiliations of women's colleges and the care taken by them to maintain religious observance among their students was an acknowledgement of both women's students' own desire to retain their religion, and the power of their opponents' arguments.

Indirect influence: Scientific and medical arguments

As well as being used to support direct intervention in the design of women's education, scientific and medical arguments against higher education for women had an indirect influence on the thinking of reformers. They found themselves obliged to defend, and therefore to conceptualise, their work in terms defined for them by their opponents.

Those who believed women should be accepted as university students and as professionals felt that individual choice was paramount. It could be exercised only if people, male or female, could undertake whatever occupations they chose. However, those who opposed women's entry to colleges and professions viewed individual variations as aberrations from a norm. They perceived all women to be members of a scientific class or group called woman. Thus they sought to define *woman's* role in the home, and they spoke of *woman's* intellectual capacity as being inferior to *man's*. Scientific and medical studies that purported to find general laws applying to all members of the scientific class of woman, such as those described in chapters four and five, were particularly welcomed as grist for political and social arguments.

The response of reformers to scientific and medical studies was two-fold: to change working conditions for women students in order to forestall the illnesses predicted, and to gather data on the health of women students in order to refute the arguments entirely. The founders of women's colleges were eager to protect their students from mental fatigue. They encouraged walking, rowing, riding, swimming, and calisthenics. A majority of students at women's colleges in Oxford and Cambridge, as reported up to 1887, took between one and two hours' exercise a day.[11] According to an American student at Newnham College, Cambridge, in 1890, 'between 12:30 and 3:30 p.m. the students set off for long walks, or they crowd to the tennis and five courts; wet or fine everyone tries to go out somewhere. On wet days the gymnasium is a great resort.'[12] The author was struck by the good health of women students during her four-year stay at Newnham.

Educators protected the health of women students by supervising their social lives as well as by organising their physical education. College doors closed in the early evening, and students could only stay out later with special permission. At first, women students were chaperoned to lectures; later, chaperons were used only for social functions. Physicians argued that too much dancing and party-going was a hazard to women's health; educators guarded against this hazard with especial care because an amalgam of exhaustion from studying and 'over-excitement' from social activities would have proved fatal to their aspirations for women students.

The medical arguments against higher education for women had been drawn from experience in the United States as well as England. In both countries, therefore, educational reformers were eager to gather data with which to refute them. To the surprise of many who had read Edward Clarke's *Sex in Education* (Boston, 1873), the Association of Collegiate Alumnae in 1885 published evidence that college-educated women in the United States were *not* less healthy than other women of their age.[13] Women educators in England were impressed. When, in 1887, a committee from the women's colleges in Oxford and Cambridge decided to carry out a similar study of their students, they used the Association of Collegiate Alumnae's questionnaire as a model, amending it to fit British conditions. The committee decided to obtain information from a similar group of women who had not attended college, so they sent each student a second questionnaire to be filled out for the sister (or female cousin) closest in age to her, so long as she had not attended college. In all, 566 students responded, and 450 sisters or cousins in the comparison group who had not attended college.[14]

The Sidgwick report on the results of this study should have allayed fears for college women's health. It did not do so immediately because conventional wisdom in medical matters was hard to override. According to the report, students at all stages of their lives reported better health than their sisters. The rate of marriage for students and sisters between the ages of 20 and 30 was remarkably similar, although it was low in both cases, while the average age at marriage was 26.7 for students as against 25.53 for sisters. Most remarkable, however, from the point view of refuting medical prognostications, were the statistics on child-bearing. Students had a *lower* proportion of childless marriages than their sisters (28 per cent compared to 40 per cent), and a *higher* average number of children born per year of marriage (0.36 to 0.27). 84 per cent of the students' children but only 59 per cent of

the sisters' children were reported in excellent or good health.[15] These figures, based on a well-defined sample, contradicted the evidence previously offered by physicians who opposed higher education for women.

Despite the report, conventional wisdom on the danger of higher education to women's health persisted. And though reformers had refuted the charges of their opponents, they had paid a price in terms of their original way of thinking. They had begun by claiming the need to consider each individual's aspirations; they had spoken out against constraints on women as a group. In response to their opponents, however, they made regulations for all students that left little freedom for individual variation, and they gathered data on women students as a group in order to justify their work.

Direct influence of the Opposition: Special Examinations for Women

Physicians who were forthright in opposing women's claims to the same higher education as men, gave technical expression to beliefs that were widespread in society. Few people dared to oppose popular opinion where the health of their daughters was concerned. Without knowledge of the hormonal basis of sexual development, the English middle classes in the nineteenth century place extensive faith in environment for developing sexual maturity. Physical exercise and rigorous mental stimulation was the prescription for making men out of unruly boys; girls had to be treated differently. Puberty put such demands on their physiques that mental stimulation had to be avoided; physical exercise had to be moderate at all times, and abandoned altogether during menstruation. The acquisition of modest learning in an atmosphere of tranquillity was the only course to be recommended for girls. It was these opinions, supported by biological and medical evidence, that prompted opponents of higher education for women to recommend special examinations and, later, a separate university for women.

The period bristled with controversy over examinations. As on the issue of professional versus amateur in the learned societies, whether or not to admit women merely added a new complication to a debate already raging among men. The university local (or lower) examinations had been established in 1859 as part of a movement to make academic competition the means of selection for government jobs.

From the beginning the examinations were opposed in principle by those who believed academic competition was an unsuitable means of selection, and in practice by those who felt that examinations forced schools into too narrow a curriculum which emphasised Latin and Greek at the expense of science, literature, modern languages, and history.[16] When, early in the 1860s, it was suggested that women should be allowed to enter for the university local examinations, the whole issue was reopened. Those who objected to examinations in principle were adamant that women as well as men should refrain from taking them, as the principle of competition was wrong. The pressure from women was seen to be an indication of the radical tendencies of the whole plan, which in the detractors' opinion should never have been introduced in the first place.

Those who were against examinations as they were at that time constituted for men felt they had an even stronger case against women's taking the examinations. While it could be argued that the examination syllabus had not changed the curriculum in boys' schools, since boys had been forced to spend their time on Latin and Greek for centuries, the same argument did not hold in the case of women, who only then were to be forced to undergo a pernicious education in order to pass the local examinations, instead of being free, as before, to explore the new fields of history, modern literature, languages, or science. Thus many who favoured the reform of women's education denounced the idea of women being tied to the outdated curricula of men, and welcomed the educational opportunities that seemed to exist in establishing special courses and examinations for women. They even proposed more advanced courses than those for the university local examinations. A number of men, wishing to reform education at Oxford and Cambridge by broadening the curriculum and abandoning the lowest level of pass, or poll, degree, foresaw a way to harness women's ambitions to their own plans for university reform, and to use women students as the pilot group for these changes. At Cambridge, Henry Sidgwick led a group of men and women who pressed for special college level courses for women different in content from those of men.[17] James Bryce expressed to Emily Davies the views of these reformers when he commented on her plan for founding a college for women,

> I doubt rather as to the propriety of holding examinations exactly similar to the Cambridge examinations for a degree. These examinations — so far as they are pass or poll examinations — are

really very bad. . . . It would be much better for a new institution not only to set up a higher standard than the contemptibly low one of Oxford and Cambridge, but to let that examinations be in subjects and on text-books better chosen and of more educational value.[18]

Davies and her supporters scorned these views. They rejected courses in new subjects, however exciting they promised to be, in favour of those accepted as criteria of success for men. Their insistence that women study Latin and Greek, already under fire as inappropriate for nineteenth-century men, and their rejection of innovations illustrate the fallacy of expecting those who aspire to enter existing social institutions to embrace avant-garde policies. Women were underprivileged, in our terminology; many who wanted to help them hoped that they would branch out into new fields and become the vanguard of educational change for both sexes. However, Davies and her friends saw danger in women's accepting an untried pattern of education. They could receive no guarantee that men would accept the pattern for themselves. If they did not, women would be left with a separate kind of education, which would be considered inferior to men's, and women would never be able to prove it was equal to that of men. Davies wrote in 1869, 'perhaps I exaggerate, but I think it is discouraging to see so many of the new things for women started on the basis of separation. It seems like getting into more of a *system* of separateness, and it makes one suspicious of anything like a step in that direction.'[19]

Despite the opposition of Davies and her supporters, the movement to establish special examinations for women grew, because it was favoured for many reasons. Those who deplored anything that smacked of competition between the sexes, those who believed the standard of teaching in girls' schools to be too low to produce successful candidates for the university local examinations, and those who wished to prevent women from becoming qualified for the professions added their voices in favour of special examinations.

The desire of women to enter the professions was real. During the 1860s Elizabeth Garrett persuaded some physicians to allow her to take courses with them, and in 1865 she succeeded in qualifying as a physician through the Society of Apothecaries. Those who opposed Garrett's success expected that special examinations, with the certificates to be issued for passing them, would divert women's ambitions by providing them with recognition for their efforts, while not providing

them with qualifications for careers.

That the intention of special examinations was, indeed, to divert women from professional training may be judged from the fact that at the University of London, where matriculation was the prior qualification for degree examinations of the university, women were provided with special examinations in lieu of both matriculation and the degree examinations. However, at Oxford and Cambridge, the university local examinations (comparable in level with matriculation) were *not* qualifications for a degree, and were opened to women in 1870 and 1863 respectively. These universities instituted special examinations for women in lieu of the undergraduate degree examinations only.

Whether to establish special examinations for women was a question first dealt with by the University of London, and appears to have arisen directly as a consequence of Elizabeth Garrett's application in 1862 to be allowed to matriculate at the university. She was told firmly, as Jessie Meriton White had been told six years previously, that the charter of the university forbade women to enter for the examinations of the university.[20] In reply her father, Newson Garrett, sent a memorial to the Senate of the university asking that the charter be changed to allow women to have all the privileges of the university. The University of London was in a unique position, according to the memorial, because candidates for degrees would probably come from the two existing women's colleges in London, and because the university, unlike the colleges at Oxford and Cambridge, required no residence of its candidates for degrees. Since 'the examinations involve nothing which could in the slightest degree infringe upon feminine reserve, we believe that by acceding to our wishes you would be conferring an unmixed benefit.'[21] When the memorial was presented to the Senate, George Grote, the Vice-Chancellor, moved that the Senate try to obtain a modification of the charter to allow women to take the same examinations as men but not allowing them, as graduates, to become members of the Convocation, one of the governing bodies of the university. That is, women graduates were not to be allowed to have any part in the governance of the university. The motion was defeated by the casting vote of the Chancellor.

George Grote's speech in support of his motion was outstanding for its clarity. In later years the issue became clouded, and both sides resorted to emotive language in presenting their case. Grote, however, spoke dispassionately and questioned the right of any group to bind another to its opinions concerning the proper education of women. He

claimed,

> The *onus probandi* lies on those who contend that the female
> minority should be excluded from our examinations, and none but
> members of our own sex admitted. . . and that to admit women to
> the studies suitable for men would be confounding a distinction
> important to uphold. Gentlemen who hold this opinion have
> undoubtedly a full right to judge for themselves on the type of
> female education, and I am quite aware that a very respectable
> portion of the community judge as they do about it. But *I* dissent
> from them: I hold the opposite opinion; and another portion of the
> community, equally respectable, hold the opinion along with me. I
> believe that the studies included in our curriculum are improving
> and beneficial in their effect upon the minds of women, where
> women are disposed and able to appropriate them, as well as upon
> the minds of men. Now those females who hold the same views as I
> do on feminine education, and their fathers or guardians, are
> powerfully interested in the admission of women to our examina-
> tions; but those who adopt the same opinion as Lord Overstone
> have really no interest in the question at all. Whether the University
> is open or closed to women, these females will pursue their own
> educational march in a different direction, without being affected
> by our regulations. They have a full right to do this; but they have
> no right to make their own opinions upon female education
> binding on all, whether assentient or dissentient; they have no *locus
> standi* entitling them to insist on closing the doors of our University
> against all those other females who approve and desire to pursue
> the studies which it prescribes.[22]

This was not language likely to appeal to men who felt it their duty
to protect women as a group. Nor was the language calculated to allay
the fears of physicians for whom Elizabeth Garrett had raised the
spectre of women graduating in medicine.

In the years immediately following the Senate vote against allowing
women to enter for degrees, Convocation of the University of London
regularly discussed the question of university examinations for
women. No attempt seems to have been made to get the Senate to
reverse its decision of 1862. Instead, in 1866, a motion from Convocation was approved by the Senate for establishing an examination for
women 'special in its nature.' As finally set up, the examination had
two levels corresponding to matriculation and inter(mediate) B.A.
respectively.[23]

The modifications which the Senate have introduced into the Programme being such as they deem likely to bring it into conformity with the course of study ordinarily pursued by the class of Females who may be expected to become candidates.[24]

But the examination for women would not have aided Elizabeth Garrett one whit in her attempt to become a doctor; only matriculation would have qualified her to take the university examinations for physicians. While protectors of women took pride in having provided intellectual stimulus for women without endangering their health or femininity, professional men, especially physicians, were equally pleased at having diverted women from entry into the professions.

Their complacency was short lived, however. The University of London's examinations for women were not a great success. The numbers entering were few, comparing unfavourably with the increasing entry for the Cambridge local examinations. Those who did enter excelled in the 'masculine' subjects of classics, mathematics, and science, and not in those which had been specially included for them.[25] Apparently women candidates did not wish to benefit from the broader curriculum offered them. From Cheltenham Ladies' College came an additional complaint. 'We think that the questions set on the same subjects are usually more difficult in the women's examination, whilst the public is ready to say that a woman's examination must be a poor one.'[26]

In 1874, Convocation, representing the graduates of the university, resolved that women should be permitted to take degrees at the university. The Senate, at that time, was not prepared to apply for a new charter for this purpose, but in 1875 it did decide to abolish the special general examinations for women and allow women to matriculate. The issue was of great interest because a number of women medical students, who had been turned out of Edinburgh University, were seeking permission to take degrees from other British institutions.[27] In 1873 their cause had been championed by several influential members of parliament including Russell Gurney, a long-time supporter of women's higher education, and Robert Lowe, member for the University of London. In 1876 Parliament passed a law 'to remove Restrictions on the granting of Qualifications for Registration under the Medical Act on the ground of Sex,'[28] and on the strength of this act, Edith Shove applied to be admitted to the University of London for medical examination and degree. Without consulting Convocation, the Senate accepted Shove's application in February 1877. The action

of the Senate to take advantage of the enabling Act of 1876 without consulting Convocation, which had already urged the admission of women to *all* degrees, brought about a power struggle between the two bodies over the rights of Convocation.

As at Cambridge University in later years, some physicians had a leading role in opposing women's entry to the university, although their tactics were indirect. Although the historians of Convocation, Percy Dunsheath and Margaret Miller, did not discern this strand in the struggle, it appears that a number of physicians who opposed women's entry into medicine supported Convocation's more radical and more controversial proposition, to admit women to *all* degrees, in order to delay the immediate admission of women to medical degrees, as had been decided by the Senate. When, in June 1877, John Storrar, MD, chairman of Convocation, proposed 'that the Senate concur in the opinion of Convocation [See Minutes of Convocation, 8 May 1877] "that it is inadvisable for this University to admit Women to the Degrees of Medicine before it shall have considered the general question of their admission to the Degrees of all Faculties" '[29] his motion was defeated, and among those voting against it were such supporters of higher education for women as Joshua Fitch, Robert Lowe, and also Sir James Paget, a physician who had assisted Elizabeth Garrett. Dunsheath and Miller described how the power struggle between Convocation and the Senate continued, with Convocation, late in July 1877, requesting that the Senate desist from action under the enabling Act. The opinion of Convocation was that the university should apply for a new or supplemental charter to be approved by both bodies.[30] On the surface this appears a more radical stance than the Senate's, but in fact it was not. At a Senate meeting on 4 July 1877, prior to this action by Convocation, the Senate had adopted a motion (apparently, since their votes are not recorded, in the absence of Dr. Storrar and the other physicians who had supported him the previous month), to obtain a new charter extending the power to grant degrees to women as already possessed in the faculty of medicine, to all other faculties.[31] Thus Convocation's request later in the month has to be interpreted as an attempt to postpone the *immediate* admission of women to degrees under the enabling Act, and the furor over the Senate's affront to Convocation's prestige by acting without consulting that body as a smoke screen to disguise the medical profession's opposition to women physicians. To the chagrin of opponents, a supplemental charter was drawn up and adopted within a year; women were admitted to degrees of the university in

1878, and all separate examinations for women at the University of London came to an end. In 1882 women graduates were admitted to Convocation, and thus to governance of the university.

The University of London had not been alone in providing special examinations for women during the 1860s. In 1869 they were begun at Cambridge, which already permitted women to take the Cambridge local examinations. The new examinations, for women over eighteen, provided recognition for a standard of work between the poll degree and the (honours) tripos. Pressure for such examinations came from several sources, including women who had organised lecture courses in several cities. Their views were presented by Josephine Butler who was at that time president of the North of England Council for promoting the Higher Education of Women. Butler went to Cambridge with a petition signed by more than five hundred women teachers and three hundred other women. For them, the way to proceed was to accept that which seemed feasible. They were concerned with the immediate issue of improving the standard of women's education. In terms of the Piagetian framework suggested in Chapter one, these women, and their male supporters at Cambridge, seem not to have adopted a new category of thought that accepted one public-and-private sphere open to men and women, but merely to have assimilated the notion of improving women's education to their ideal of womanhood. This is not surprising because girls had competed with boys in the university local examinations for only six years, and few schools existed that provided girls with a systematic education. And yet, as we shall see later, there were others who already perceived the illogicality of accepting special examinations if women's professional aspirations were to be fulfilled.

Among the supporters of Josephine Butler and the North of England Council were Henry Sidgwick and other reformers at Cambridge who believed that women undertaking higher education should be subjected neither to the antiquated course for the poll (or pass) degree, nor the strenuous course for the tripos. Sidgwick's arguments were remarkably successful, and after the examinations had been established by the university, lecture courses were instituted in Cambridge itself for women living within a radius of eighty miles of the city who wished to prepare for the examinations. So great was the response that a formal lecture committee was formed, the Association for Promoting Higher Education of Women in Cambridge. Within two years a house of residence for the students was needed in Cambridge, and, since the Association did not wish to add to its

responsibility, Henry Sidgwick proceeded on his own initiative to establish Newnham Hall under the guidance of Anne J. Clough.[32]

Sidgwick's policy did not go unchallenged, however. Emily Davies, struggling to achieve higher education for women on the same terms as men, felt it to be a sad mistake which threatened the success of the college she had established at Hitchin. She was aware of the short-comings of the Cambridge curricula and the obstacles faced by the unprepared students at Hitchin, but her opinion did not waver: women had to demonstrate that they could follow the same courses of study as men in the same length of time if they were ever to be admitted to the universities. Any changes in curricula would have to be insti-tuted by the university for both sexes at the same time. With great persistence she maintained that the college at Hitchin should associate itself with Cambridge University and the students take *all* the examinations expected of men students. The college opened in 1869. A year later some students were ready to take the 'Little-go' and at the end of 1872 the first three passed their tripos examinations, one in mathematics and two in classics.[33] The founders of Girton (the college moved from Hitchin to Girton, outside Cambridge, in 1873) 'had a great fact to prove, and a great principle to vindicate.'[34] The principle was that women had a right to the highest culture, and the fact was that women like men had the ability to attain it. Success in special examinations could provide no proof that women could pass university degree examinations; only by taking the men's examinations could women prove their ability.

After a few years the special examinations for women established by Cambridge University were transformed into the higher local examination which was opened to men as well as women. It was especially popular among women who had attended lecture courses away from Cambridge, and men attending university extension courses.[35]

The question of allowing women to take Cambridge University degree examinations was thornier. As in the earlier discussions, the issue was complicated by the desire of university reformers to use women as the vanguard for changes that would later be extended to men. In 1881 the Senate of Cambridge University agreed to allow women to take the previous and tripos examinations on the same conditions as men, with the proviso that women might, if they so desired, substitute parts of the higher local for the previous examination and thus not have to learn Latin or Greek. At the same time the Senate agreed that the poll degree examination would in

future be closed to women. As a result of the new policy Newnham and Girton drew closer in their aims because the substitution clause allowed Newnham students with no Latin or Greek to study for the degree examinations if they so desired. Over the years, however, fewer women students left school unprepared in the classics, and thus practically all chose to take the triposes. Those people who had, with noblesse oblige, fought to make special allowances for women found their charity unneeded.

Women's exclusion from the poll degree was another issue. Even Emily Davies was swayed by arguments that women should prove their excellence and thus eschew the 'gentlemen's degree'. But from our perspective more was at issue than intellectual excellence. Graduates governed the university; a low standard for the degree examinations, meant a large number of students were likely to graduate. Although women did not at that time have the right to obtain degrees from the university, there was a possibility that they might in the future. The University of London's action to allow women to graduate could not have gone unnoticed. By closing poll degrees to women, while maintaining them for men, the Senate was ensuring that women, if ever they were allowed to graduate, would be a small minority indeed, and thus an insignificant pressure group in the governing body of the university.

At Oxford the passage of special examinations for women was similar to that of Cambridge. Somerville College and Lady Margaret Hall both opened in 1879. Students attended lectures directed towards special examinations, established in 1875, through the Oxford local examination machinery for women over eighteen whether or not they had studied in Oxford. St. Hugh's College, founded 1886 for students of limited means, and St. Hilda's, founded 1893 for students from Cheltenham Ladies' College, were able at once to take advantage of the Oxford Statute of 1884 which enabled women to take honours examinations in mathematics, natural science and modern history. However, the Statute did not require residence from women, 'nor did it allow them to sit for any of the intermediate examinations on which the qualification for a degree depended.'[36]

At Oxford and Cambridge, as at London, special examinations for women lasted only a decade. At London, when the examinations were abolished, women gained the right to graduate and become members of the governing body of Convocation. At Oxford and Cambridge women gained only the right to demonstrate their ability through examination; they were denied both the right to graduate and

membership in university governance. Girton was the only women's college established in Oxford or Cambridge during the nineteenth century with the firm intention that its students should follow the same courses, at the same pace, as men at the universities. The institutional pattern of higher education for women at both universities reflects the strength of the opposition to women joining men in their degree courses.

Direct Influence of the Opposition: A Women's University

Once residences for women students had been founded in Oxford and Cambridge opinions about higher education for women polarised. The universities of Oxford and Cambridge were very different from the University of London which at that time was an examining body only. To obtain an Oxford or Cambridge degree was not merely to pass the necessary examinations, as at London; it was also to live for three years within a collegiate environment, which derived from monastic life its emphasis on male comradeship. Women had no place in the intellectual life of such a university. When the suggestion was made that women students should be granted degrees, opponents pointed out that participation in the environment of a university was as important an ingredient for a degree as passing examinations. They did not feel that women savoured authentic collegiate life in the so-called 'women's colleges'. How could they, since colleges at the universities embodied male culture? Only a women's university could embody female culture. 'Let those who wanted this sort of training for women found a University for women, conducted by women, devoted to the objects and duties in life which belonged to women.'[37] Opponents pointed, also, to the effects on university governance of granting degrees to women, who would then be entitled to vote on university policies. This issue was discussed at Oxford in 1884 and at both Oxford and Cambridge in 1896 and 1897 when there was a flurry of flysheets and letters to the press about the issue.[38] The opposition of clergymen to women graduates was particularly strong, because the last vestige of clerical control in the universities lay in the graduate bodies. No women could expect to become ordained, and therefore no woman graduate could augment the clerical interest in university government.

Inviolable masculine control of the universities of Oxford and Cambridge proved to be a strong weapon for opponents of higher

education for women; they brandished it for over fifty years. Once the constitutional effects of granting women degrees were understood, opponents tried once more to interfere directly in the institutional development of women's education, as they had tried earlier through special examinations. This time they suggested that women should have a university of their own.

Plans for a women's university were canvassed particularly eagerly by clergymen and physicians. The Reverend Charles L. Dodgson (Lewis Carroll), for instance, felt 'the real "way out", from our present perplexity, is to be found in some such course as that. . . Oxford, Cambridge, and Dublin, should join in a petition to the Crown to grant a charter for a Women's University.'[39] Some men who had supported the first moves for higher education of women at Oxford and Cambridge joined those suggesting a separate women's university once women asked to be granted degrees. Their request showed clearly that they wanted *the same* higher education as men. George Forrest Browne, Disney professor of Archaeology at Cambridge, later Bishop of Stepney and then of Bristol, and an early supporter of higher education for women at Cambridge, was among the leaders of the drive to establish a women's university.[40] In 1887 he pleaded for the setting up of a degree granting institution for women.

> The operations of such a body would be not local in scope, but national; possibly even imperial. It would become rich and powerful. . . Whatever the future of women's education may be, it would be guided with a sole view to the interests of women. And all would go on here [Cambridge] as now, smoothly and pleasantly.[41]

The plan gained support in the 1880s from doctors who had also added their voices in favour of special examinations for women twenty years earlier. Medical opinion in favour of a women's university held that there women would not be tempted to overstrain themselves. The belief that human activity was regulated by the law of the conservation of energy meant that women who diverted energy to intellectual activity were thought to have less available for menstruation. Some physicians construed this to mean that women who undertook prolonged courses of higher education might become sterile. At a women's university, students would be expected to rest during menstruation and thus conserve their energy for that task. Medical opinion on the issue of energy conservation carried much weight because people were well aware of the dangers of mental strain even in

men. Mental collapse, which seemed to be associated with unremitting intellectual work, could be avoided, apparently, by physical exercise. Men found walking a great antidote to mental strain. Leslie Stephen and his friends went on long walks; Thomas Huxley, though unable to compete with others in the distance he walked each day, took short walking tours as his favourite way "of recruiting from the results of a spell of overwork."[42] The historian G. M. Trevelyan claimed that in his youth he walked as many as forty miles in a day to counteract the debilitating effect of overwork.[43] Women, however, could not do that. They were doubly endangered by mental strain because they had few opportunities for physical exercise to alleviate it.

A women's university was first seriously discussed at Cambridge in 1887 when the Council of the Senate refused to consider a memorial asking that degrees be granted to all who satisfied the requirements regardless of sex. No one promoted the scheme at that time, but in 1896 it was revived and gained adherents in Oxford as well as Cambridge.[44] A year later the governors of the Royal Holloway College called a conference in London to discuss the scheme which appeared to fulfill the wish of the founder of the college. A clause in the deed of foundation expressed the wish that the college eventually ask for power to grant its own degrees. Here, according to supporters of a women's university, was the chance to establish it as an institution.

The scheme never matured, however; it was opposed by the conference without a vote. Educators argued that degrees would lose their value if the number of degree-granting institutions were increased; and that women's colleges could maintain their status as colleges of higher education only if they attached themselves to an existing university. Had there been any educational advantage to the scheme it would still have had to be abandoned because of lack of financial support. No one at the conference could foresee where the necessary endowment would have come from. The scheme for a women's university was dropped, and the Royal Holloway College later became a constituent college of the University of London.

With this episode ended the last attempt by opponents of higher education for women to divert its growth and render it different in kind from that men.

It would be naïve, however, to perceive the subsequent history of women's education as a steady march towards equality with men. Carol Dyhouse has shown the fallacy of such a whig interpretation.[45] Her study outlines the changes in elementary and secondary school

curricula for girls during the first decade of the twentieth century in response to fears that other countries, especially Germany, were producing a larger number of intelligent and healthy people than the English. Women of the middle classes were prime targets for persuasion because they, it was claimed, were the potential mothers of intelligent sons who would become officers in the armed forces. The mood of those who urged that domestic science be taught in secondary as well as elementary schools was often antagonistic to women's aspirations for equality. Such 'masculine' subjects as mathematics and science were thought unnecessary for girls, who would better spend their time on laundry work and cooking. Women aiming to go on to college could hardly have been unaffected by such claims, or the pressure to marry and have children rather than to pursue a career of their own.

Such pressure was a continuation of the tactics used by those who opposed higher education for women from its inception. For over a decade they successfully diverted women from taking the same examinations as men, they prevented women from gaining the right to graduate from Oxford until 1920 and Cambridge until 1921[46] and, most importantly, they forced those who wished to reform women's education to defend their work in terms defined for them by others. Those terms were based upon the ideal of womanhood, and the separation of men's and women's spheres.

Notes

1. In 1870 the first women, Elizabeth Garrett Anderson, Emily Davies, and Lydia Becker were elected to school boards; in 1875 the first woman, Miss Merrington of Kensington, was elected as a Poor Law guardian. (See *Advancement of Women in Public Life and Professions* [Fawcett Society, London, 1967.]) According to information received by the author from the late Vera Douie of the Fawcett Library, in 1922 Dr. Ivy Williams was the first woman to be called to the bar, although she had obtained her LL.D. (London) in 1903 and had taken the B.C.L. examination earlier in Oxford.

2. Kathleen Bliss, *The Service and Status of Women in the Churches* (London, 1952), pp. 135-6.

3. For a further discussion of this see Stanley M. Elkins, *Slavery: A Problem in American Institutional and Intellectual Life* (Chicago, 1959), p. 161 ff.

4. See Constance Maynard's diaries (Westfield College Library, London); Jo Manton, *Elizabeth Garrett Anderson* (London, 1965), p. 53; and Margaret Todd, *Sophia Jex-Blake* (London, 1918), pp. 50-8.

5. Elizabeth Garrett Anderson, 'Sex in Mind and Education: A Reply', *Fortnightly Review* n.s. 15 (1874), p. 589.

6. Evidence for this suggestion is contained in the diaries of Constance Maynard; C. B. Firth, *Constance Louisa Maynard* (London, 1949); and Todd, *Sophia Jex-Blake*.

7.   See *Girton College Register* (Cambridge, 1946), pp. 1-7; and Vera Brittain, *The Women at Oxford* (New York, 1960), p. 232.

8.   Justitia [Mrs. Henry Pochin], *The Right of Women to Exercise the Elective Franchise* (London, 1855), pp. 14-15.

9.   Brittain, *Women at Oxford*, p. 75.

10.   Firth, *Constance Louisa Maynard*, p. 133.

11.   Mrs. Henry [Eleanor] Sidgwick, *Health Statistics of Women Students at Cambridge and Oxford and their Sisters* (Cambridge, 1890), pp. 48-50.

12.   Eleanor Field, 'Women at an English University: Newnham College, Cambridge', *Century Magazine* 42 (n.s. 20) (1890), pp. 290-1.

13.   American Association of University Women, *Health Statistics of Women College Graduates*. Report of a special committee of the Association of Collegiate Alumnae, Annie G. Howes, chairman, together with statistical tables collated by the Massachusetts Bureau of Statistics of Labor (Boston, 1885).

14.   The comparison group contained 382 sisters, and 68 cousins. The results from this group were not as reliable as those from the students, since the sister or cousin did not have to fill out the questionnaire herself. (Sidgwick, *Helath Statistics*, pp. 7-8.)

15.   Sidgwick, *Health Statistics*, tables 25-9 on pp. 61-5.

16.   Between 1850 and 1875 *competitive* examinations were introduced (e.g., for the civil service and the India office), which aimed to select the ablest, unlike qualifying examinations, which merely set minimum standards. Competitive examinations resulted in the founding of cramming schools and the narrowing of curricula to cover only examination material. (See R. J. Montgomery, *Examinations* [London, 1965], pp. 24-30.)

17.   See Rita McWilliams-Tullberg, *Women at Cambridge: A Men's University—Though of a Mixed Type* (London, 1975), chapter 4.

18.   Letter from Bryce to Davies, 4 June 1867, as quoted by Barbara Stephen, *Emily Davies and Girton College* (London, 1927), p. 155.

19.   Letter from Davies to H. R. Tomkinson, 6 January 1869, as quoted by Stephen, *Emily Davies and Girton College*, p. 195.

20.   Manton, *Elizabeth Garrett Anderson*, p. 125.

21.   Memorial of Newson Garrett to the senate of the University of London, 28 April 1862 (University of London, *Minutes of the Senate* [1859-62], S.M. 98.)

22.   George Grote, as quoted by Alexander Bain, *The Minor Works of George Grote with Critical Remarks on his Intellectual Character, Writings, and Speeches* (London, 1873), pp. [164-5].

23.   See Percy Dunsheath and Margaret Miller, *Convocation in the University of London* (London, 1958), pp. 53-7. In order to establish the special examinations for women, a supplemental charter had to be obtained which was then accepted by both the Senate and Convocation of the university. (*Minutes of the Senate* [1867] S.M. 173-4.)

24.   William B. Carpenter to The Right Honourable William Gathorne Hardy, MP, 20 July 1868. University of London Archives, 'Letters 1868', p. 407.

25.   Dunsheath and Miller, *Convocation*, p. 57.

26.   Unsigned, undated document from Cheltenham, attributed to Dorothea Beale, 'Memorial to be laid before the Senate respecting the assimilation of the Women's Examination to the Matriculation Examination', University of London Archives.

27.   See Todd, *Sophia Jex-Blake*, pp. 392-6.

28.   *The Statutes: Revised Edition*, 18 (London, 1885), 39 & 40 Victoria.

29.   *Minutes of the Senate* (1877), S.M. 151.

30.   Dunsheath and Miller, *Convocation*, pp. 58-9.

31.   *Minutes of the Senate* (1877), S.M. 184.

32.   At first the plans for the residence were very modest: 'It is proposed to open a house in October for the reception of students attending these lectures [for women in Cambridge]. The regular payment for each student will be £20 a term, but a reduction

of one-fourth will be made for persons preparing for the profession of Education'
(*Cambridge University Reporter*, 10 May 1871, p. 344); See also Blanche Athena
Clough, *A Memoir of Anne Jemima Clough* (London, 1897), pp. 148-55.

33.   These were Sarah Woodhead, mathematical tripos; Rachel Cook and Louisa
Lumsden, classics tripos. The three became known as the Girton pioneers. For details of
Girton's philosophy see H. M. Stanley of Alderley, 'Personal Recollections of Women's
Education', *Nineteenth century* 6 (1879), pp. 308-21.

34.   Stanley of Alderley, 'Personal Recollections', p. 314.

35.   The connection between the ladies educational associations and the development of university extension lectures is discussed by J. F. C. Harrison, *Learning and
Living 1790-1960* (Toronto, 1961), pp. 222-32; Edwin Welch, *The Peripatetic
University: Cambridge Local Lectures, 1873-1973* (Cambridge, 1973), chapters 1-5;
and by Clough, *Memoir of Anne Jemima Clough*, pp. 103-46.

36.   Brittain, *Women at Oxford*, pp. 66-7.

37.   Beresford Hope, *Hansard* 219 (12 June 1874), p. 1550.

38.   See for example the letter from Percy Gardner in *The Times*, 31 January 1896,
and the reply from A. Sidgwick, *The Times*, 11 February 1896. The Fawcett Library has
a collection of pamphlets which includes the *Report of the Degrees for Women
Syndicate*, 1 March 1897 and a discussion of the report as reprinted from the *Cambridge
University Reporter*.

39.   Charles L. Dodgson (Lewis Carroll), 'Resident Women-Students (1896)', *The
Complete Works of Lewis Carroll* (New York, 1936), pp. 1185-8.

40.   Browne (1833-1930) was the first editor of the *Cambridge University Reporter*.
In 1871 he was appointed secretary of the local examinations syndicate, and in 1874
began to serve on the council of the Cambridge University senate.

41.   George Forrest Browne, *The Recollections of a Bishop* (London, 1915), p. 310.
These remarks were part of a proposal issued by Browne to the senate of Cambridge
University, 10 October 1887.

42.   Leonard Huxley, *Life and Letters of Thomas H. Huxley*, I (London, 1916),
pp. 154-5.

43.   G. M. Trevelyan, *An Autobiography and Other Essays* (London, 1949), pp.
25-6.

44.   See Stephen, *Emily Davies and Girton College*, p. 333; Browne, *Recollections*,
pp. 310-11; Brittain, *Women at Oxford*, p. 109.

45.   Carol Dyhouse, 'Social Darwinistic Ideas and the Development of Women's
Education in England, 1880-1920', *History of Education* 5, no. 1 (1976), pp. 41-58.

46.   As noted on p. 101, women were admitted to full membership of Oxford
University in 1925 when they became eligible for election to the Hebdomadal Council.
Women at Cambridge were admitted only to 'titular' degrees in 1921; in 1947 they were
admitted to full membership of the university.

9 | Conclusion

This book has been a study of ideas. It has dealt with a range of arguments against higher education for women expounded by those who supported the Victorian ideal of womanhood. They perceived that higher education threatened not only the ideal, but the belief in separate spheres which the ideal was designed to protect. The task they set for themselves was to fend off a revolution in relationships between the sexes.

Only briefly have we caught sight of the people who developed these ideas, or been concerned with their tactics to obtain public support. The politics of opposition would be another study, less easy to formulate than the politics of the anti-suffrage movement, but involving people who shared the same constellation of beliefs as the anti-suffragists.[1] The radical challenge of the suffrage movement, like that of the movement for higher education, was to the structure of gender roles.[2]

This study suggests that the ideal of womanhood, based upon the notion of separate spheres, represented more than an expedient response to conditions in early nineteenth-century England. It expressed deep-rooted beliefs about the relationships of men and women that proved impervious to changes in the conditions of English society. Chief among them was the belief in male supremacy.

Contemporary feminist scholars have examined the expression of this belief in different societies, using the word patriarchy to describe the hierarchical ordering of society based on male supremacy. They have concluded that industrialism intensifies the divisions between men's and women's spheres, and increases the exploitation of women.[3]

In previous chapters we have discussed the Victorian practice of having men and women work at separate activities. Where women undertook paid work they were, as often as possible, assigned to jobs performed only by women, which were paid less than men's jobs. The economic rationale for this segregation was that, because women were satisfied with lower wages than men, the two sexes could not compete for the same jobs. If they did, all wages would be driven down to the

level of those acceptable to women. Because of the wage differential, people could understand why women might aspire to men's more highly valued jobs, but could not understand why any man would want a woman's job. As with their paid work, women's unpaid work in the home was also valued less than men's work in factory or office. Despite exhortations from clergymen and social reformers for men and women to revere women's work as wives and mothers, no concrete measure could be made of a woman's success at this work; it did not bring status or material goods to the family as her husband's or sons' work did. Because women's household work did not bring such rewards, people could understand why women might want to obtain paid work, but could not understand why men would want to do housework or look after the children.

The concept of patriarchy explains the lack of reciprocity in these situations because, in a society bound to a system of male domination, men, irrespective of their economic roles, are accorded higher status than women. Two corollaries of this are that men who take on women's tasks lose status, and any task that women perform drops in rank in the hierarchy of desirable tasks because it becomes tainted with women's low status. Had there not been a system of male domination in nineteenth-century England, women's aspirations to enter the male sphere would likely have been matched by men's aspirations to enter the female sphere, and thus there would have been no barriers to a change of conceptualisation from separate spheres to one unified private-and-public sphere, shared by men and women alike.

In a unified sphere, women would expect to have, and would be obliged to have, equal access to all activities in what nineteenth-century writers called the male sphere; reciprocally, men would expect to have, and would be obliged to have, equal access to all activities in the female sphere. Mutual obligation is used here to explain the logic of the concept of one unified sphere. The concept hypothesises *a reality* in which men and women alike share in all activities. Were obligation not implied, the reality would not be conceivable because women would be free to choose *not* to share in men's activities, and men would be free to choose *not* to share in women's activities. In that case, the reality would be separate spheres, although the hypothetical construct was a unified sphere.

In nineteenth-century England, where separate spheres were accepted, what was feared most in a revolution of relations between the sexes was not the acquisition of status by women working at men's jobs, although that was a controversial issue as we have seen, but the

loss of status among working women's husbands who would be expected to take over some tasks in the home. This fear was so profound that it was rarely written about; instead, it was expressed through cartoons and caricatures such as those which illustrate this book. In cartoons the threat of change was parried by ridicule.

Nonetheless, the Victorian age was one of change in the roles of men and women. Despite the perpetuation of separate spheres, women's legal rights increased as a result of individual challenges to the law. In politics, by 1870 women had established their right to become Poor Law guardians and to serve on school boards. In education, despite the prognostications of opponents, some women undertook courses in higher education without suffering harmful effects, becoming desexed, or challenging the mores of society. By the end of the nineteenth century a growing number of women had completed a college education, and were occupied outside the home in jobs which were useful to society and satisfying to themselves.

The opposition to higher education for women illustrates some general themes about the process of change in society. First, the emancipation of women, in which their higher education was a vital factor, cut across political alignments founded on other issues. The historian finds the distinctions useful for describing political events irrelevant when describing reactions to the threat of a revolution in relations between the sexes. On that issue a new distinction arose between those who favoured a change in relations and those who did not; each side drew its supporters from among Conservatives as well as Liberals, members of the Church of England as well as nonconformists.

Secondly, the history of the movement for higher education for women suggests that so long as the discontented members of society voice their discontent in general terms, the opposition to them remains general and diffuse. Once the discontented formulate a call to action and plan to found new institutions or change old ones, the opposition becomes specific. In the nineteenth century, whenever an interest group felt itself threatened by the intrusion of women, members of the group wrote articles and gave lectures to show why women should not be allowed to participate in their particular activity on equal terms with men. When they were sufficiently powerful politically, opponents of women amended the rules governing entry into their societies or professions to exclude women.

Thirdly, the constant factor that holds together opponents to a particular social change is the belief that such a change is undesirable.

The belief has to remain constant, although the arguments used to support it may change. On the issue of higher education for women opponents remained constant in their defence of the ideal of womanhood and the separation of men's and women's spheres of life; however, their arguments in defence of the ideal changed. For example, at one time the arguments were drawn from evolution, which allegedly proved that women's brains were inferior to men's; when this 'proof' was shown empirically to be wrong—that is, when some women passed the highest examinations designed for men—it was abandoned and replaced by another argument. Such changes in argument are essential if an opposition is to remain effective for any length of time. So long as people believe a particular change is wrong, they will search for arguments to prove its error. If experience shows that their arguments are mistaken, they will search for new ones to support their position. They will jettison their arguments but not their beliefs. Those who defended the ideal of womanhood used arguments from economics, comparative anatomy, physiology, and religion.

Throughout the nineteenth and the twentieth centuries the possibility of a revolution of relations between the sexes has generated arguments for and against it, which have varied with the intellectual fashion of the time. In our own day we have witnessed a surge of pressure towards equality of the sexes, countered by a reiteration, in a new form, of the counter-arguments presented for the first time during the nineteenth century.

Given the consistency of belief held by those who opposed higher education for women during the nineteenth century, we have to consider how a change in society on the issue was brought about. First, there was a formulation of ideas by a few people influential enough to experiment with new institutions for the education of women. The first colleges established in the late 1840s provided many women with a systematic, if not a university, education. These colleges initiated change. Some of the women educated in them established or taught in new girls' schools. It was pupils of these schools who became students at the women's colleges founded later in Oxford, Cambridge and London.

Meanwhile, the problems the first colleges had been designed to alleviate appeared to grow worse. As the middle classes increased in number and came to adopt the Victorian ideal of womanhood, more people felt it was a stigma for women to work, even temporarily. As described in chapter one, the types of jobs thought appropriate for women decreased, and the small percentage of women working was

held to be a sign of the maturity of English society. However, the decrease in the types of jobs available, combined with the stigma attached to working, presented an intolerable dilemma for women in families that could not support them financially. Men of the middle classes in the 1850s and 1860s were reluctant to face the dilemma because they had grown to maturity at a time when the ideal of womanhood was a challenge to be taken up by all men of ambition. Some might be unable to meet the challenge, and their families suffered as a result, but their failure was not allowed to divert the rest from trying to achieve the glory of the ideal.

For the next generation, the ideal was less appealing; it had not been formulated by them, and some of them saw that its demands were formidable. In an age of undulating prosperity and substantial insecurity respectable families could find themselves suddenly in financial difficulties. If young men at such times were encouraged to rely on their wits to retrieve their fortunes, there was no reason why equally intelligent young women should suffer the indignities of poverty. But they did suffer unless they had received sufficient education to fit them for remunerative work. The new generation abhorred this and, freed from some of the emotional investment their parents had made in the innocence and ignorance of women, they were prepared to accept the higher education for women which had been anathema to their parents. Insofar as they questioned the ideal of womanhood they did so because it appeared unattainable. Theirs was a need to find ways to provide for unmarried women and those who were widowed or abandoned by their spouses. Most reformers did not encourage women to step beyond their own sphere in searching for jobs, nor did they encourage them to work once they were married. In the last decades of the century, the ideal underwent a change; it contracted and was applied only to married women. Within women's sphere, unmarried women were encouraged to train for jobs of a status comparable to those of their brothers and fathers. They were able to do this because the economy expanded during the century, and new jobs evolved which were assigned to one sex or the other. In the years after 1860 middle-class women claimed for their own sphere a number of tasks which required skills that earlier in the century would have been considered inappropriate for women.

A few men and women, but only a few, claimed that the ideal was undesirable. Their arguments led logically, as opponents to higher education pointed out, to the suggestion that separate spheres were no longer functional. It was this position that opponents found most

threatening. They foresaw a time when chivalry would be abandoned, when women would claim equality with men in all walks of life including the most prestigious occupations, and when women would no longer be willing to marry and raise families. Given the Victorian convention that sex drives were felt only by men (and abnormal women), such a possibility threatened to leave men without sexual partners. Nor was the research at the end of the century which suggested that women shared sexual libido with men particularly reassuring. If that were the case, and if women continued their demands for work of equal status to men, how could their ambitions for careers be reconciled with their desire for sexual companionship? Without a complete reassessment of gender roles, women's two sets of desires were incompatible.

The claims of those who found the ideal wanting were summarily dismissed at the time we end our study. Not even those who supported higher education for women saw a way for most women to reconcile a career with marriage. Higher education insured that those women who chose not to marry could have satisfying careers, that those who wanted to work until they married could do the same, and that those who married immediately after university could become intelligent, well-trained wives and mothers. When higher education for women was grudgingly accepted at the end of the nineteenth century, it was because men were less strong, less capable of protecting women than they aimed to be, and because women's sphere had changed in response to the drive towards professionalism, not because the middle classes believed their ideal of womanhood had been mistaken.

Notes

1. See Brian Harrison, *Separate Spheres: The Opposition to Women's Suffrage in Britain* (London, 1978), part one.

2. The radical challenge of women's suffrage has been discussed in relation to the American movement by Ellen DuBois, 'The Radicalism of the Women Suffrage Movement: Notes Towards the Reconstruction of Nineteenth Century Feminism', *Feminist Studies* 1/2 (1975): 63-71.

3. See Zillah R. Eisenstein, 'Developing a Theory of Capitalist Patriarchy and Socialist Feminism,' (pp. 5-40) and Nancy Chodorow, 'Mothering, male dominance, and capitalism,' (pp. 83-106) in Zillah R. Eisenstein (ed.), *Capitalist Patriarchy and the Case for Socialist Feminism* (New York and London, 1979); Michelle Zimbalist Rosaldo, 'Woman, Culture, and Society: a Theoretical Overview', (pp. 17-42) in Michelle Zimbalist Rosaldo and Louise Lamphere (eds.), *Woman, Culture, and Society* (Stanford, CA, 1974).

Select Bibliography

The sources listed below are those which most clearly delineate the ideal of womanhood, argue against higher education for women, or interpret Victorian society. A more extensive list is to be found in the footnotes at the end of each chapter.

Periodical articles are listed alphabetically by author where known or by title where the author is unknown. This is except where a periodical has published a number of articles on the same topic, in which case the articles are listed chronologically under the periodical which is in turn listed alphabetically.

Primary Sources: Unpublished

Fawcett Library, London:
   autograph collection; miscellaneous letters; Josephine Butler collection; pamphlets and documents; minute books.
Girton College Library, Cambridge:
   correspondence of Barbara Leigh-Smith Bodichon and of Emily Davies.
Imperial College of Science and Technology, London:
   papers of Thomas H. Huxley.
University of London Archives:
   letters received and sent; memorials received; minutes of the Senate; reports of the Law Officers of the Crown to the University.
Westfield College Library, London:
   Constance L. Maynard, autobiography (ms. 1915); black book and green book diaries (mss.).
Dr Williams' Library, London:
   Elisabeth Jesser Sturch Reid, letters to Henry Crabb Robinson, 1841 – 56; Henry Crabb Robinson, diary (ms. Volume 21 (1846 – 50) contains entries about the founding of the Ladies' College, Bedford Square).

Primary Sources: Published

The Admission of Women to the University of Cambridge (Cambridge, n.d.)
Anthropological Review:
   George Harris, 'The Distinctions, Mental and Moral, occasioned by the Differences of Sex', 7 (1869), pp. 189 – 95, 215 – 19; J.

McGrigor Allan, 'On the Real Differences in the Minds of Men and Women', 7 (1869), pp. 195 – 215

Association for the Promotion of the Education of Women at Oxford, *Admission of Women to the B.A. Degree at Oxford: Report on Evidence Collected by Miss Rogers* (Oxford, 1895)

Barlow, Lady Nora (ed.), *The Autobiography of Charles Darwin 1809 – 1882* (New York, 1959)

Bloxam, George W., *Index to the Publications of the Anthropological Institute of Great Britain and Ireland* (London, 1893)

Bobbitt, Mary R., *With Dearest Love to All. The Life and Letters of [Caroline] Lady Jebb* (London, 1960)

Browne, George F., *The Recollections of a Bishop* (London, 1915)

Browning, Robert D. (ed.), *The Letters of Elizabeth Barrett and Robert Browning*, 2 Volumes (London, 1899)

Burgon, John W., *To Educate Young Women Like Young Men, and with Young Men — a Thing Inexpedient and Immodest. A Sermon* (Oxford, 1884)

Butler, Josephine, *Memoir of John Grey of Dilston* (Edinburgh, 1869)

Cambridge University Reporter

Case, Thomas, *Is it Proposed to Matriculate Women?* (Oxford, 1896)

—— *An Undelivered Speech Against Resolution (4)* (Oxford, 1896)

Chapone, Mrs Hester, *Letter to a New Married Lady* (London (1777), 1828)

Christian Observer:
  'The Education of Women', 64 (1865), pp. 542 – 56; 'A Lady on the Education of Women', 64 (1865), pp. 794 – 8; 'Further Remarks on the Education of Women', 64 (1865), pp. 870 – 5; 'On the Education of Girls', 65 (1866), pp. 89 – 94; 'Children in Religious Households', 68 (1869), pp. 111 – 19; 'Mill on the Condition of Women', 68 (1869), pp. 618 – 29; 'On Female Education', 68 (1869), pp. 655 – 66

Clarke, Edward H., *Sex in Education* (Boston, 1873)

Clough, Blanche A., *A Memoir of Anne Jemima Clough* (London, 1897)

Davenport Adams, W.H., *Woman's Work and Worth in Girlhood, Maidenhood, and Wifehood* (London, 1880)

Davies, James, 'Female Education', *Quarterly Review*, 119 (1866), pp. 499 – 515

Dawson, Sir John W., 'Thoughts on the Higher Education of Women', *Nature*, 4 (1871), pp. 515 – 16

Dee, Emme (pseud.), *Woman: Her Mission and Education* (London, 1876)

Distant, W.L., 'The Mental Differences between the Sexes', *Journal of the Anthropological Institute*, 4 (1875), pp. 78 – 87

Dodgson, Reverend Charles L., 'Resident Women-Students' (1896), *The Complete Works of Lewis Carroll* (New York, 1936)

'The Domestication of Science', *Intellectual Observer*, 1 (1862), pp. 474 – 5

Duffey, Eliza B., *No Sex in Education; or an Equal Chance for both*

Girls and Boys (Philadelphia, 1874)
Eclectic Review:
'Studious Women', 14 (1868), pp. 265 – 71; 'Lady Novelists', 15 (1868), pp. 300 – 15
Eddison, Annie T. and Eleanor Thompson, *Origin and History of the Yorkshire Ladies' Council of Education and of its Branches* (n.p., 1892)
Ellis, Sarah, *Daughters of England* (London, 1843)
—— *Education of the Heart: Woman's Best Work* (London, 1869)
Englishwoman's Journal:
'Watchwork versus Slopwork', 1 (1858), p. 282; 'The Dressmaker's Life', 1 (1858), p. 319; 'On the Adoption of Professional Life by Women', 2 (1858), pp. 1 – 10; 'Are Men Naturally Cleverer than Women?' 2 (1858), p. 336; 'What are Women Doing?' 7 (1861), letter from Caroline Cornwallis, 13 (1864), p. 238
Evangelical Magazine and Missionary Chronicle:
' "The Good Part" or Mary and Martha, a Word for Young Women', n.s. 39 (1861), pp. 223 – 8
Faithfull, Emily, *How Shall I Educate my Daughter?* (London, 1863)
Fortnightly Review:
Henry Maudsley, 'Sex in Mind and Education', n.s. 15 (1874), pp. 466 – 83; Elizabeth Garrett Anderson, 'Sex in Mind and Education: A Reply', n.s. 15 (1874), pp. 582 – 94
Gaskell, Peter, *Manufacturing Population of England* (London, 1833)
—— *Artisans and Machinery* (London, 1836)
Girton College Register (Cambridge, 1946)
Graduates of the University of London, *Memorial to the Rt. Hon. Robert Lowe, M.P., Home Secretary* (London, 1874)
Grant, Sir Alexander, *Happiness and Utility as Promoted by the Higher Education of Women. An Address* (Edinburgh, 1872)
Gregory, John, *A Father's Legacy to his Daughters* (London, 1774)
Grey, Maria G., *On the Education of Women* (London, 1871)
Grose, T.H., *Admission of Women to the B.A. Degree* (Oxford, 1895)
—— *Can the University Stop, if it Grants the B.A. Degree to Women?* (Oxford, 1896)
—— *Is it Proposed to Matriculate Women?* (Oxford, 1896)
Harrison, Frederic, *Realities and Ideals* (New York, 1908)
Hodgson, William B., *The Education of Girls: and the Employment of Women of the Upper Classes Educationally Considered,* 2nd edn (London, 1869)
Howe, Julia Ward (ed.), *Sex and Education: a Reply* (Boston, 1874)
The Humanitarian:
A.W. Verrall, 'University Degrees for Women: the Case for', 8 (1896), p. 250; Bertha J. Johnson, 'University Degrees for Women: the Case against', 8 (1896), p. 257
Huxley, Leonard (ed.), *Life and Letters of Thomas Henry Huxley, Volume 1* (London, 1916)

Justitia (pseud. of Mrs Henry Davis Pochin), *The Right of Women to Exercise the Elective Franchise* (London, 1855)

The Lancet:
  'Miss Becker on the Mental Characteristics of the Sexes', 2 (1868), pp. 320 – 1; 'Women and the Medical Profession', 2 (1869), p. 206; 'John Stuart Mill, "The Subjection of Women"', 2 (1869), p. 511; 'Report of Dr Robert Barnes' Lumleian Lectures on the Convulsive Diseases of Women', 1 (1875), p. 622; 'Report of Speech by Dr William Withers Moore, President, at the 54th Annual Meeting of the British Medical Association', 2 (1886), p. 315; 'The "Can" and "Shall" of Woman-Culture', 2 (1886), p. 688

Landels, William, *Woman: Her Position and Power* (London, n.d)

Leigh Smith, Barbara, *Women and Work* (London, 1856)

Lutyens, Lady Emily, *A Blessed Girl* (Philadelphia, 1954)

Maurice, Frederick (ed.), *Life of F.D. Maurice* (London, 1884)

Maynard, Constance L., *Ann Dudin Brown. Foundress of Westfield College* (Bridgwater, 1917)

Mill, John Stuart, *The Subjection of Women* (London, 1869)

Milne, John D., *Industrial and Social Position of Women, in the Middle and Lower Ranks* (London, 1857)

Mineka, Francis E. (ed.), *The Earlier Letters of John Stuart Mill*, 2 Volumes (Toronto, 1963)

M.L.G., 'Female Education', *Monthly Repository*, n.s. 9 (1835), p. 107

—— 'Men and Women', *Tait's Edinburgh Magazine*, n.s. 1 (1834), pp. 101 – 3

Murray, Margaret, *My First Hundred Years* (London, 1963)

Parker, Theodore, *The Public Function of Woman* (London, 1855)

Parkes, Bessie Rayner, *Remarks on the Education of Girls, with Reference to the Social, Legal and Industrial Position of Women in the Present Day*, 3rd edn (London, 1856)

—— *Essays on Woman's Work* (London, 1865)

Parsons, Benjamin, *The Mental and Moral Dignity of Women* (London, 1849)

Pfeiffer, Emily, *Women and Work* (London, 1888)

Philosophical Transactions of the Royal Society of London:
  J. Lockhart Clarke, 'Researches on the Intimate Structure of the Brain, Second Series', 158 (1868), pp. 263 – 331; Joseph B. Davis, 'Contributions towards Determining the Weight of the Brain in Different Races of Man', 158 (1868), pp. 505 – 27; John Cleland, 'An Inquiry into the Variations of the Human Skull, particularly in the Anteroposterior Direction', 160 (1870), pp. 117 – 74

'Report of the Council of the Ethnological Society of London. May 1867', *Transactions of the Ethnological Society of London*, n.s. 6 (1868), seven unnumbered pages at end of volume

'Report of the Council of the Ethnological Society of London. May 1869', *Journal of the Ethnological Society of London*, n.s. 1 (1869), pp. vii – xv

Report of the Degrees for Women Syndicate, March 1, 1897, and

Discussion of the Report, March 26, 1897, as Reprinted from the Cambridge University 'Reporter'

'Review of *Out of the Depths* (by H.G. Jebb)', *Westminster Review,* n.s. 16 (1859), p. 303

Rogers, Annie M.A.H., *Degrees by Degrees. The Story of the Admission of Oxford Women Students to Membership of the University* (Oxford, 1938)

Ruskin, John, *Sesame and Lilies* (London, 1865)

—— *Diaries,* 2 Volumes (Oxford, 1956)

Russell, Bertrand, *Portraits from Memory* (New York, 1956)

—— *The Autobiography of Bertrand Russell, Volume I* (Boston, 1967)

Saturday Review:
'Caius and Caia', 4 (1857), pp. 55 – 6; 'Industrial Occupations of Women', 4 (1857), pp. 63 – 4; 'Lady Morley', 4 (1857), p. 557; 'The Englishwoman's Journal', 5 (1858), p. 369; 'A Woman's Thoughts about Women', 5 (1858), pp. 376 – 7; 'Queen Bees or Working Bees?' 8 (1859), p. 576; 'Feminine Wranglers', 18 (1864), p. 112; 'Women's Friendships', 18 (1864), pp. 176 – 7; 'Husbands', 18 (1864), p. 416; 'Review of J.S. Mill, *The Subjection of Women*', 27 (1869), p. 813; 'The Probable Retrogression of Women', 32 (1871), pp. 10 – 11; 'The British Mother Taking Alarm', 32 (1871), pp. 334 – 5; 'Mr Lowe on Universities', 43 (1877), pp. 135 – 6; 'Women at the Universities', 43 (1877), pp. 660 – 1; 'The Modern Schoolmistress', 43 (1877), pp. 732 – 3

Spencer, Herbert, *Education: Intellectual, Moral and Physical* (New York, 1860)

—— *The Principles of Biology,* 2 Volumes (London, 1864 – 7)

—— *An Autobiography, Volume 2* (New York, 1904)

—— *Essays on Education* (London, 1911)

Stanley, Lady Henrietta M., of Alderley, 'Personal Recollections of Women's Education', *The Nineteenth Century,* 6 (1879), pp. 308 – 21

Tait, Robert Lawson, *Diseases of the Ovaries* (London, 1883)

Taylor, Mrs Ann and Jane Taylor, *Correspondence Between a Mother and her Daughter at School* (London, 1817)

Thorburn, John, *Female Education from a Physiological Point of View* (London, 1884)

Trollope, Anthony, *North America,* 2 Volumes (London, 1862)

—— *Higher Education of Women* (London, 1868)

Ure, Andrew, *The Philosophy of Manufactures,* 2 Volumes (London, 1835)

Wallington, Emma, 'The Physical and Intellectual Capacities of Woman Equal to Those of Man', *Anthropologia,* 1 (1874), pp. 552 – 65

'Women at Oxford and Cambridge', *Quarterly Review,* 186 (1897), pp. 538 – 9

'Women: Capabilities and Disabilities of', *Westminster Review,* 67 (1857), p. 42

'Women of Business', *Tait's Edinburgh Magazine,* n.s. 1 (1834), pp. 596 – 7

Wordsworth, Christopher, 'On Intellectual Display in Education', *Occasional Sermons,* 3rd series (London, 1852)

—— *Christian Womanhood and Christian Sovereignty* (London, 1884)

Wordsworth, Elizabeth, *Glimpses of the Past* (London, 1912)

'Work as a Necessity for Women', *Victoria Magazine,* 18 (1872), p. 221

Secondary Sources

Anthony, Sylvia, *Women's Place in Industry and Home* (London, 1932)

Bailey, Gemma (ed.), *Lady Margaret Hall. A Short History* (London, 1923)

Banks, J.A., *Prosperity and Parenthood* (London, 1954)

Banks, J.A. and Olive Banks, *Feminism and Family Planning in Victorian England* (Liverpool, 1964)

Bell, E. Moberly, *Josephine Butler. Flame of Fire* (London, 1962)

Bliss, Kathleen, *The Service and Status of Women in the Churches* (London, 1952)

Branca, Patricia, *Silent Sisterhood: Middle Class Women in the Victorian Home* (Pittsburgh and London, 1975)

Briggs, Asa, *Victorian Cities* (London, 1963)

—— *Victorian People* (Harmondsworth, 1965)

Brittain, Vera M., *The Women at Oxford; A Fragment of History* (New York, 1960)

Britton, Karl, *John Stuart Mill* (Harmondsworth, 1953)

Bullough, Vern and Martha Voght, 'Women, Menstruation, and Nineteenth Century Medicine', *Bulletin of the History of Medicine,* 47, 1 (1973), pp. 66 – 82

Burn, W.L., *The Age of Equipoise* (New York, 1965)

Clark, G. Kitson, *The Making of Victorian England* (Oxford, 1962)

Cominos, Peter T., 'Late Victorian Sexual Respectability and the Social System', *International Review of Social History,* 8 (1963), pp. 18 – 48, and 216 – 50

Crow, Duncan, *The Victorian Woman* (New York, 1972)

Degler, Carl, 'What Ought to Be and What Was: Women's Sexuality in the Nineteenth Century', *American Historical Review,* 79, 5 (1974), pp. 1469 – 90

Delamont, Sara and Lorna Duffin (eds.), *The Nineteenth-Century Woman: Her Cultural and Physical World* (London, 1978)

Dunbar, Janet, *The Early Victorian Woman: Some Aspects of Her Life, 1837 – 1857* (London, 1953)

Dunsheath, Percy and Margaret Miller, *Convocation in the University of London. The First Hundred Years* (London, 1958)

Dyos, Harold J., *Urbanity and Suburbanity* (Leicester, 1973)

Dyos, Harold J. and Michael Wolff (eds.), *The Victorian City: Images and Realities* (London, 1973)

Ellsworth, Edward W., *Liberators of the Female Mind: The Shirreff Sisters, Educational Reform, and the Women's Movement* (Westport, 1979)

Firth, C.B., *Constance Louisa Maynard* (London, 1949)

Fox, Greer Litton, ' "Nice Girl": Social Control of Women Through a Value Construct', *Signs: Journal of Women in Culture and Society* 2, 4 (1977) pp. 805 – 17

Gathorne-Hardy, Jonathan, *The Unnatural History of the Nanny* (New York and London, 1973)

Harrison, J.F.C., *Learning and Living 1790 – 1960* (Toronto, 1961)

Horn, Pamela, *The Rise and Fall of the Victorian Servant* (New York, 1975)

Houghton, Walter E., *The Victorian Frame of Mind, 1830 – 1870* (New Haven, 1957)

Ideas and Beliefs of the Victorians (London, 1958)

Irvine, William, *Apes, Angels, and Victorians* (New York, 1955)

Kamm, Josephine, *Hope Deferred. Girls' Education in English History* (London, 1965)

—— *Indicative Past: A Hundred Years of the Girls' Public Day School Trust* (London, 1971)

Kaye, Elaine, *A History of Queen's College, London, 1848 – 1972* (London, 1972)

Killham, John, *Tennyson and 'The Princess'. Reflections of an Age* (London, 1958)

McBride, Theresa, *The Domestic Revolution: Modernization of Household Service in England and France* (New York and London, 1976)

McCann, Phillip (ed.), *Popular Education and Socialization in the Nineteenth Century* (London, 1977)

McGregor, O.R., 'Bibliography on the Social and Political Position of Women: 1850 – 1914', *British Journal of Sociology*, 6 (1955), pp. 48 – 60

McWilliams-Tullberg, Rita, *Women at Cambridge: A Men's University — Though of a Mixed Type* (London, 1975)

Manton, Jo, *Elizabeth Garrett Anderson* (London, 1965)

Marcus, Steven, *The Other Victorians* (New York, 1967)

Millerson, Geoffrey, *The Qualifying Associations: A Study in Professionalization* (London, 1964)

Montgomery, Robert J., *Examinations* (London, 1965)

Musgrove, F., 'Middle-Class Education and Employment in the Nineteenth Century', *Economic History Review*, 2nd series, 12 (1959 – 60), pp. 99 – 111

Neff, Wanda F., *Victorian Working Women 1832 – 1850* (London, 1929)

Pedersen, Joyce Senders, 'The Reform of Women's Secondary and Higher Education: Institutional Change and Social Values in Mid- and Late-Victorian England', *History of Education Quarterly*, 19,

1 (1979), pp. 61 – 91

Percival, A.C., *The English Miss, Today and Yesterday* (London, 1939)

Perkin, Harold, *The Origins of Modern English Society, 1780 – 1880* (London, 1969)

Pinchbeck, Ivy, *Women Workers and the Industrial Revolution, 1750 – 1850* (London, 1930)

Praz, Mario, 'The Victorian Mood: A Reappraisal' in G. Metraux and F. Crouzet (eds.), *The Nineteenth-Century World* (New York, 1963)

Quinlan, Maurice J., *Victorian Prelude. A History of English Manners 1700 – 1830* (New York, 1941)

Raverat, Gwen, *Period Piece* (London, 1952)

Reynolds, Myra, *The Learned Lady in England, 1650 – 1760* (Boston, 1920)

Robbins, William, *The Newman Brothers. An Essay in Comparative Intellectual Biography* (London, 1966)

Rover, Constance, *Love, Morals and the Feminists* (London, 1970)

Scrimgeour, R.M., (ed.), *The North London Collegiate School 1850 – 1950* (London, 1950)

Stephen, Barbara, *Emily Davies and Girton College* (London, 1927)

—— *Girton College, 1869 – 1932* (Cambridge, 1933)

Streeter, Burnett H. and Edith Picton-Turbervill, *Women and the Church* (London, 1917)

Thomson, Patricia, *The Victorian Heroine, A Changing Ideal, 1837 – 73* (London, 1956)

Tilly, Louise A. and Joan W. Scott, *Women, Work, and Family* (New York, 1978)

Todd, Margaret G., *Life of Sophia Jex-Blake* (London, 1918)

Tuke, M.J., *A History of Bedford College for Women, 1849 – 1937* (London, 1939)

Vicinus, Martha (ed.), *Suffer and Be Still: Women in the Victorian Age* (Bloomington, 1972)

—— (ed.), *A Widening Sphere* (Bloomington, 1977)

Welch, Edwin, *The Peripatetic University: Cambridge Local Lectures, 1873 – 1973* (Cambridge, 1973)

White, Cynthia L., *Women's Magazines 1693 – 1968* (London, 1970)

Williams, Raymond, *Culture and Society, 1780 – 1950* (Harmondsworth, 1961)

—— *The Long Revolution* (New York and London, 1966)

Woodward, John and David Richards (eds.), *Health Care and Popular Medicine in Nineteenth Century England* (New York and London, 1977)

Young, G.M., *Victorian England. Portrait of an Age*, 2nd edn (London, 1953)

Index

Acland, Thomas Dyke 43
accommodation, Piagetian process of 21
Aldis, Dr Charles B. 97n11
Alexandra Magazine 142n27
Allen, Grant 117n36
anatomists, comparative: studies by 76 – 9
Anderson, Elizabeth Garrett: combines marriage and career 140, 147; elected to school board 164n1; Evangelical background 136; reply to Henry Maudsley 82n24, 86, 87; struggle for medical training 59, 68n24, 130, 154 – 7
Anthony, Sylvia 140n1
anthropologists: studies by 76 – 81
Arnold, Thomas 39
assimilation, Piagetian process of 21, 158
Association for Promoting Higher Education of Women in Cambridge 158
Association of Collegiate Alumnae: report of 150, 165n13
Austen, Jane 137

Barlow, Lady Nora 116n6
Barnes, Robert MD 92
Barrett, Elizabeth 71
Becker, Lydia 164n1
Bedford College 23 – 4, 127
Beeton, Mrs Isabella 38 – 9, 143n42
Bennett, John 68n35
Bliss, Kathleen 146
bluestockings 74
Boucherett, Jessie 127
brain: differences between men's and women's 77 – 80
Branca, Patricia 111
British Medical Association 86, 104
Brontë, Charlotte 61, 106, 137
Browne, George Forrest 162, 166n40
Browning, Robert 71
Bryce, James 152 – 3

Burgon, John W. 33, 100, 104
Buss, Frances 86
Butler, Josephine 113, 124, 129, 158

Cambridge University: admission of women to degrees and governance 101, 164, 166n46; poll degrees and women 159 – 60; special examination for women 158 – 9
Carlyle, Thomas 90
Carroll, Lewis: *see* Dodgson, Reverend Charles L.
chaperons 19, 21, 150
Chapone, Mrs Hester 33
charity work 57, 64
Charnock, R.S. 82n31
Cheltenham Ladies College 24, 156, 160
Christian Observer 108, 115n1
church schools 16; use of by middle classes 24, 29n18
civilisation: and women's work 58, 76 – 7
Clarke, Edward H. 85, 92, 94 – 5, 96n4, 98n31, 150
class mobility 16, 18, 128
Cleland, John 82n26, 82n29, 82n30
clergymen: support for the ideal woman 99
Clough, Anne Jemima 159
college women: and religion 148 – 9, 158 – 9; health of 87 – 8, 92, 150 – 1; marriage rate 148, 150; threat to clerical influence in universities 100 – 1, 161
Cominos, Peter T. 111, 117n36
competition: effects of on women 43, 58 – 63, 80, 107
competitive examinations 11, 17 – 18, 152 – 3, 165n16
Comte, Auguste 47n39
Contagious Diseases (Women) Act 129
Cox, Sergeant 82n25
craniometry 77 – 9
creativity: and women 73 – 4

181

Dall, Caroline 88
dame schools 16
Dampier, W.C. 97n29
Darwin, Charles 75, 83n37, 102, 116n6
Darwin, Erasmus 141n9
Davenport Adams, W.H. 81n12
Davies, Emily 25 – 6, 49, 86, 136; and poll degrees 160; and special examinations for women 152 – 3; and university local examinations 25, 43; elected to school board 164n1; opposition to Henry Sidgwick 159
Davies, James 47n38
Davis, J.B. 82n26, 82n27
definitions of class 12
demi-mondaines 112
depressions: effects of on women 120
Dillon, Henrietta Maria: *see* Stanley of Alderley, Lady
Distant, W.L. 81n16, 82n27, 82n28, 82n31, 83n37
Dodgson, Reverend Charles L. (Lewis Carroll) 162
Douie, Vera 164n1
Downe, Dr Langdon 97n11
Dudin Brown, Miss Ann 136
Duffey, E.B. 94
Duncan, Matthews 90
Dunsheath, Percy 157
Dyhouse, Carol 163

economy, structure of 53 – 8
Education Act 1870 16
education: and physiological differences between men and women 87, 89; as technical training 17; for the ideal woman 36 – 41, 107 – 10, changes in 40; of girls and women 16, 22 – 8, 107 – 10
Eliot, George 82n36
Ellis, Sarah S. 39, 49, 105 – 7, 116n17
Elwin, Reverend Whitwell 141n4
emigration of men: effect of on women 60
emigration of women 127, 142n28
Emme Dee (pseud.) 104
employment for women: opportunities broadened 127
energy, conservation of and women 91, 97n29
Englishwoman's Journal 65, 68n23, 142n27
Ethnological Society of London 125 – 6, 142n26

Evangelical beliefs and unmarried women 135 – 6
evolution: and sexual selection 79 – 80; effects of on men and women 76 – 80

Faithfull, Emily 141n6
family: effects of reduction in size of 134; fear of its destruction 50, 114 – 15
Fellenberg, Phillip Emanuel von 95
finishing schools 24
Fitch, Joshua G. 157
Freud, Sigmund 91

Gardner, Percy 88
Garrett, Elizabeth: *see* Anderson, Elizabeth Garrett
Garrett, Newson 154
Gathorne-Hardy, Jonathan 117n39
Geological Society 125 – 6
Girls' Public Day School Company 26, 71, 134, 143n46
Girls' Public Day School Trust (GPDST): *see* Girls' Public Day School Company
Girton College 26, 34, 87, 148, 159; pioneers 166n33; prayer meeting 148
governesses 50, 134; qualifications of 23 – 4
Graham, Patricia A. 51
Gray, Henry 82n28
Grazebrook, Mr 81n12
Gregory, Dr John 37, 81n15
Grey, Margaretta 69n43, 123
Grey, Maria 25, 53
Grote, George 154 – 5
Gurney, Emelia 122, 141n8
Gurney, Russell 122, 141n8, 156

Harris, Frank 98n31
Harris, George 81n13
Harrison, Frederic 31, 45, 46n3, 47n39, 124, 129
Harvard University 85 – 6
Health Statistics of Women College Graduates: see Association of Collegiate Alumnae
Health Statistics of Women Students at Cambridge and Oxford and their sisters: see Sidgwick report
Higginson, Thomas Wentworth 97n14
higher education 51 – 3; as occupational training 52; as trans-

mission of cultural heritage 52; for women: dangers at menstruation 91 – 5; direct influence of opponents on 151 – 63; effects feared on marriages 42, 95 – 6; effects feared on single women 42; effects feared on wages 54 – 5, 65; fear of their loss of faith 108 – 9; indirect influence of opponents on 146 – 51; threat to clerical power at universities 99 – 101; unsound investment 50

Hodgson, W.B. 67n7

home: as a retreat 31 – 2; changes in 132 – 5

home life: fear of its destruction 56, 58; *see also* family

Houghton, Walter E. 40

household goods, commercial production of 132 – 3

household management and the ideal woman 38 – 9, 134

Howe, Julia Ward 86

Hunt, James 78

Huxley, Mrs. T.H. 93

Huxley, T.H. 44, 125 – 6, 142n26, 163

ideal of womanhood: and God's will 101 – 10 *passim*; and social control 11; as reality 12, 132 – 40; Biblical evidence for 102 – 10 *passim*; contradiction in women's roles 112; criticised 12, 132 – 40, 171; effects on marriage 136 – 7; modified 131, 171; relationship to prostitution 112 – 15; support for claimed from New Testament 104 – 5; support for claimed from Old Testament 103 – 5; support from clergy 99; versus higher education 41 – 6

intellectual characteristics: of men 70 – 5; of women 70 – 5, 86

intuition and women 37, 72 – 3

Jebb, Lady Caroline 143n52

Jex-Blake, Sophia 136, 147

Justitia: *see* Pochin, Mrs Henry Davis

Kay-Shuttleworth, J.P. 68n21

King's College London 18

Ladies College, Bedford Square: *see* Bedford College

ladies' educational associations 25

Lady Margaret Hall 26, 100, 148, 160

Lancet, The 71, 86, 131

Landels, William 102, 105, 113, 131

Langham Place women reformers 127, 142n27

learned societies, women excluded 125 – 6

Leigh Smith, Barbara 61, 68n24, 68n32

leisure: and civilisation 58, 76 – 7; and status 30 – 1; for women of middle classes 30, 119

Leitner, Gottlieb W. von 82n22, 98n45

Liddon, Henry 100

Linton, Eliza Lynn 44, 126

London Anthropological Society 142n26

Lowe, Robert 53, 156 – 7

Lutyens, Lady Emily 112

Lyell, Charles 126

male control of Oxford and Cambridge 101, 161 – 2

Malthus, Robert 53

marriage: as women's duty 58 – 9, 120 – 1; effects of the ideal on 136 – 8

married women: paid employment in home 142n30

Married Women's Property Act 106, 120

Maudsley, Henry 85, 88, 90 – 1

Maurice, Reverend Frederick Denison 23

Maynard, Constance Louisa 33, 108 – 9, 136, 148

medical degrees for women 59, 85, 156 – 7

menstruation and education 91 – 5, 162 – 3

mental fatigue: effects of on women 80 – 1, 96, 162 – 3

Merrington, Miss 164n1

middle classes: annual income 13; attitude towards lower classes 63 – 4; distinctions of status among 18; downward mobility of employed women 68n23, 128, 142n31; effect of political reforms on women 19 – 20; financial support of women 35, 118 – 21; lifestyles 13 – 16; numbers 13, 54 – 5; rise in standard of living 35; servants 14, 134; unmarried women 14, 35, 42 – 3, 95, 128 – 30, 147; women's activities 14, 18,

30 – 5, 38 – 40, 122 – 8, 132 – 6; women to set example 57, 66
middle class social reformers and women 58 – 9, 66
Miller, Margaret 157
Mill, James 54
Mill, John Stuart 44, 53 – 4, 78 – 9, 89 – 90, 106, 130 – 1; on sons' attitude to mothers 133
Mitford, Nancy 141n7
moral principles and the ideal woman 39 – 40
Morley, Lady 33
Murray, Margaret 64, 68n41, 114, 136

National Association for the Promotion of Social Science (NAPSS) 25
Newnham College 26, 149, 165n32
Northcote, Sir Stafford 71
North London Collegiate School for Girls 24
North of England Council for Promoting the Higher Education of Women 25, 158

opposition to higher education for women: direct influence of, special examinations for women 151 – 61, women's university 161 – 4; indirect influence of, religious arguments 146 – 9, scientific and medical arguments 149 – 51, role of clergy 99 – 115 *passim*, 162; role of physicians 85, 157 – 8, 162
opposition to women in professions 154
Oxford University: admission of women to degrees and governance 101, 164, 166n46; special examinations for women 160

Paget, Sir James 157
Paris commune 139
Parkes, Bessie 127
patriarchy 167 – 8
Peacock, Dr Thomas B. 82n27
Pedersen, Joyce Senders 24
Pestalozzi, Heinrich 95
Pfeiffer, Emily 60, 97n11, 97n13
physicians: opposed to higher education for women 85 – 96, 157 – 8
Piaget, Jean: concepts of assimilation and accommodation 21, 158
Pochin, Mrs Henry Davis (Justitia, pseud.) 88, 134

Portsmouth, Eveline Countess of 93
prostitution 112 – 15, 128 – 9
public-and-private sphere 21, 158, 168
public schools, reform of 18, 39
Punch 38

Quarterly Review 31
Queen's College 23 – 4, 99, 127
Quetelet, Adolphe 77

Reade, Winwood 113
refinement of manners 15
Reid, Mrs Elisabeth 23
relations between the sexes: danger to 44 – 5, 65 – 6; fear of revolution in 27, 66, 114 – 15, 138 – 9, 168 – 9
religious journals: articles on women's education 115n1
Ricardo, David 53 – 4
Rossetti, Dante Gabriel 111
Royal Holloway College 163
Ruskin, John 48

St Hilda's College 160
St Hugh's College 160
Saint-Simonians and feminism 139, 144n59
Saturday Review 41, 44, 47n26, 68n32; and purpose of higher education 53; and threat of revolution in relations between the sexes 80, 139
Schools Inquiry Commission 67n2, 97n11
Scott, Joan W. 55, 118
self control 16, 21, 113 – 14
self denial as a virtue for women 105 – 7, 146 – 7
self improvement 11, 16 – 17; aspirations of women for 135 – 6, 139, 143n52
Senior, Nassau 54
separate spheres 18 – 22, 63, 119, 129 – 32; changes in men's sphere 19 – 20; changes in women's sphere 19 – 20, 27, 36, 167 – 9; effects of on intellect 76 – 8; effects of on men and women 55; segregation of labour 19, 53 – 67 *passim*, 167 – 8
sewing machine, effects of 132 – 3, 143n43
Sex Disqualification (Removal) Act 146
sexual morality 111 – 15
Shove, Edith 156
Siddal, Elizabeth 111

Sidgwick, Henry 152, 158 – 9
Sidgwick Report (Eleanor Sidgwick) 150, 165n11
Sigsworth, E.M. 117n38
social change: opposition to 169 – 70.
social control 11
Society for Promoting the Employment of Women 127, 142n27
Society of Apothecaries 59, 130
Somerville College 26, 160
special examinations for women: at Cambridge University 158; at Oxford University 160; at University of London 154 – 8, 165n23
Spencer, Herbert 91, 94, 98n45
stamina, women's lack of 74 – 5, 92 – 3
Stanley of Alderley, Lady 122, 141n7
Stephen, Leslie 163
Storrar, John MD 157

Tait, Robert Lawson FRCS, L1D 85 – 6
Taylor, Isaac 81n12
Thorburn, John MD, FRCP 85 – 6, 92, 94
Tilly, Louise A. 55, 118
Todd, Margaret G. 69n43
Trevelyan, G.M. 163
Trollope, Anthony 49

United States: medical evidence against higher education for women 87 – 8
University College London: courses for women 85 – 6; opened 1828 18
university extension programmes 25, 166n35
university local examinations 24 – 5, 41, 84, 151 – 4
University of Edinburgh 59
University of London 59, 163; admission of women to degrees and Convocation 26, 157 – 8; special examinations for women 154 – 8, 165n23; struggle between Convocation and Senate 155 – 8
University of St. Andrews 59
upper middle classes 12, 121 – 2, 131
upward mobility and education 50

Victorian prudery 15
Vogt, Carl 78, 82n31

Wallington, Emma 81n22, 82n24

Warren, Mrs Eliza 39
Wedgwood, Hensleigh 122, 141n9
Westfield College London 34, 59, 109
Westminster Review 128
White, Jessie Meriton 59, 68n24, 154
Williams, Dr Ivy 164n1
Williams, Raymond 46n1, 144n62
Withers Moore, William MRCS, FRCP, DCL 85 – 6, 90, 104
Wollstonecraft, Mary 36
woman: as helpmeet of man 103 – 4; as scientific class 149, 151; as wife and mother 52, 95, 133 – 4, 168
women: and admission to Oxford and Cambridge 101, 164, 166n46; and business 122, 130; and charity work 57, 64, 107; and creativity 73 – 4; and intuition 37, 72 – 3; and lack of stamina 74 – 5; and leisure 30, 119; and mental fatigue 80 – 1, 88, 150; and midwifery 123; and morality 72, 109 – 10, 113 – 14; and organised games 88, 97n15, 149; and personal property 105 – 6; and professions 49, 65, 85, 99, 130 – 2, 153 – 4; and purity 31, 33, 45, 110; and self-denial 105 – 7, 146 – 7; and university governance 158, 160; and virginity 111 – 14 *passim*; as amateurs 124 – 6; as cheap labour 58 – 63 *passim*; as skilled artisans 61, 122 – 4, 141n11; as typists 130; easily corruptible 113 – 14; economic and sexual exploitation of 61 – 2, 68n37, 128 – 9; effects of intellectual attainment on 74 – 5; employment of 55, 58 – 9, 127, 142n27; excess over men 34 – 5; from Evangelical families 135 – 6, 147; innately sinful 114; in primitive societies 76 – 80; intellectual characteristics of 70 – 5, 86, 'scientific proofs' 75 – 81; pharmaceutical books by 141n12; special examinations for 145, 151 – 61, failure of 156, 159
Women's Educational Association of Boston 86
women's: magazines 34; suffrage 167, 172n2; ultimate goals 48 – 51; university 145, 161 – 3, 166n38
Wyke, T.J. 117n38